DO OR DIE

In the twilight, tracer ammunition crisscrossed the sky. Before we made it over the LZ, Slick Three pulled up sharply and broke hard to the north, his gunner slumped half out the door in a lifeless heap.

"They're coming in for the kill," the one-zero hissed from the ground. "Heavy movement twenty meters to our northeast. Put the hurt on them!"

I listened to that pathetic whisper, and without thinking about what I was saying, I finally blurted out, "I can't take the responsibility for dropping stuff that close to your position. You'll have to move and give us some room to work."

The team leader's response felt like somebody had punched me in the stomach: "Son, forget your goddam rule book and get on with it. I'd rather take my chances with you killing me than let the VC get us."

I took another gulp from my water bottle before I answered. "Get your heads down. I'm in from the West!"

Da Nang

A Forward Air Controller's Year of Combat over Vietnam

Diary

COL. TOM YARBOROUGH

SMP

ST. MARTIN'S PAPERBACKS

"The Ballad of the Green Beret." Copyright 1963, 1965, 1966 Music, Music, Music Inc. Reprinted by permission.

DA NANG DIARY

Copyright © 1990 by Thomas R. Yarborough.

Plane photo on cover: Larry Burrows/© Time Inc.; Pilot photo on cover: © Philip Jones Griffiths/Magnum Photos.

Library of Congress Catalog Card Number: 90-36887

ISBN: 0-312-92616-2

Printed in the United States of America

St. Martin's Press hardcover edition/November 1990
St. Martin's Paperbacks edition/November 1991

10 9 8 7 6 5 4 3 2 1

This book is dedicated to the memory and fighting spirit of the 338 U. S. Air Force forward air controllers who were lost in battle in the skies over Southeast Asia.

"Give honour to our heroes fall'n, how ill soe'er the cause that bade them forth to die"

William Watson
"The English Dead"

Contents

PROLOGUE

April 9, 1973

Several other pilots had joined me for dinner at the well-appointed officers' club at Ubon Air Base, Thailand. It felt great to relax over a couple of beers and a good meal, especially since my day had started at 0430, some fourteen hours earlier. Even though the war in Southeast Asia was winding down, you would never know it from the intense combat missions being flown by a handful of forward air controllers (FACs) at Ubon. As one of those FACs, I had started my day by directing five hours of air strikes in Cambodia, landing my OV-10 at Phnom Penh to refuel and rearm, then logging another four-and-a-half-hour mission before landing back at Ubon.

At the table next to us, a group of newly assigned pilots talked somewhat boisterously among themselves. They had just reported to our squadron and had yet to fly their first combat mission. Like so many before them, the young lieutenants tried to mask their nervousness with bravado and macho talk. Though not meaning to eavesdrop, I couldn't help overhearing their conversation.

Their talk focused on the war and what it would be like to go up against the highly trained and experienced North Vietnamese antiaircraft gunners. They speculated on various tactics and maneuvers for avoiding the deadly flak. Predictably, the discussion turned to Lieutenant Joe Gambino, one of my close friends, who'd been shot down and killed just two days earlier, on his twenty-fourth birthday. They had heard that Joe was one of the best, and if it could happen to him, well. . . .

As I sat listening to the new pilots, my thoughts drifted back to when I had first arrived in South Vietnam as a new FAC, almost three years earlier to the day. Eager but green, just like the kids at the next table, I would have given anything to have one of the "old heads" sit down and tell me what an actual combat mission was like. I had wanted to know everything at once. At the time it seemed vitally important to me to know if the North Vietnamese gunners really used red and green tracers, if they truly hated FACs as we'd heard, if captured FACs were summarily executed or tortured to death. I wanted to hear firsthand from a veteran which type of fighter aircraft dropped the most accurate ordnance, how close to friendly troops you could really work an air strike, how low a FAC should fly to be really effective. Although I never would have considered asking anyone, I also wanted to know if there were tricks or gimmicks to control the fear, the emotions.

After my friends and I had finished dinner, I called over the young Thai waitress and ordered a Sing Ha beer. When it arrived, I took a long sip, then a deep breath, and walked over to the next table. The new guys looked up and immediately fell silent. I suspected word had gotten around that I was the instructor pilot who would train them. As an old head and the only two-tour FAC in the squadron, I had the dubious distinction of having seen lots of action. Evidently that status made me somewhat of a celebrity to some of the pilots—certifiably crazy to the others. Regardless of what the new troops thought of me, their upturned faces radiated a strange mixture of suspicion, awe, and anticipation. Looking down at them, I felt old—at twenty-nine!

"Anybody interested in hearing a few war stories?" I asked. The faces collectively broke into wide smiles; someone scooted up an extra chair, and a barrage of questions began.

Everybody talked at once. "Tell us about the SA-7." "Do the Cambodian ground commanders speak English?" "How much flying time will we get?" "What do you think is the best pattern to fly when you're working fighters?" "What happened to Joe Gambino?" "Are there restrictions on strafing with our machine guns?"

Over the din I gave the time-out sign. I chuckled to myself, recalling how I had asked similar questions but had never received a straight answer. When it quieted down, one of the lieutenants, looking a bit more reserved than the others, asked cautiously, "I'd like to know what you think it takes for new guys like us to become experienced FACs?"

Good question. To myself I thought, "Time—time and the knack to anticipate the unexpected," but from my own experiences I knew the young Air Force officers sitting around that table didn't want to hear double-talk or abstract philosophy on acquiring combat sense and judgment. They wanted practical answers in terms they could relate to, from a pilot who'd been there. The only way I knew how to answer the question was by telling them what it had been like for me, three years earlier, when I stepped off the airplane as a nervous young lieutenant, about to begin my combat tour as a forward air controller.

APRIL

Indoctrination of a Rookie

A gloved hand reached out and gently shook my right shoulder. When my eyes opened, I found myself staring into the boyish face of a young Air Force staff sergeant. "Sir," he said, his left hand cupped against my right ear, "the aircraft commander says we're getting ready to start our descent into Cam Ranh Bay. The jump seat's all yours if you want it."

"Thanks," I answered groggily. "Tell your boss I'll be right up as soon as I grab a cup of coffee." The young load master smiled and shuffled off in his faded green flight suit, trailing a long black cord connected to his headset and boom microphone, the other end attached somewhere inside the large C-141 jet transport aircraft.

I stood up, stretched, and took a look around the interior that had been our home for the three hours since the predawn takeoff from Clark Air Base in the Philippines. Fifty or so military men sprawled sleepily in the rear-facing airliner seats. Behind the seats, three large pallets of cargo filled the remaining available space. An intricate weave of canvas webbing held the contents of each pallet neatly in position. There seemed to be boxes and crates of every size and description, all of it priority cargo headed for the war effort in South Vietnam. The fifty of us on board constituted the priority human cargo.

As I stood there watching the other men sleep, I stole one last glance at the third pallet. Although it was partially obscured by the other pallets, there was no mistaking the distinctive shapes stacked three high—bright, shiny aluminum military caskets. I wanted to shift my gaze, but I couldn't. The metal boxes held my eyes captive. With no one watching me, I stared shamelessly at that third pallet. The caskets represented an abstract concept I wasn't prepared to confront, much less deal with. I was going to Vietnam to serve my country, as duty and honor demanded. Buying space in one of those caskets wasn't part of my dream, my big adventure, my rite of passage, my trial by fire. Death might snatch the other guy, but it wouldn't take me. It wasn't my destiny. With only the slightest hesitation, I snapped out of the momentary trance, turning away from the scene as easily as I might have switched channels on a television set.

As a young Air Force pilot anxious to get into combat before the war ended, I wasn't at all sure where reality and my destiny would cross. The next few days would clarify where I would fit in. In the meantime, one fact *was* perfectly clear: in April 1970 there was a lot of war raging all across Vietnam. In spite of President Nixon's announcement of the Vietnamization program for turning the fight back over to the South Vietnamese, there were still 429,000 U.S. troops in Southeast Asia. As a forward air controller about to be stationed right in the middle of the war, I felt certain I'd see my share of the fighting.

Walking toward the flight deck, my ears popped as the cabin altitude surged, probably because the pilot had reduced power to start the enroute descent into Cam Ranh Bay. As I climbed into the jump seat between and just behind the two pilot seats, the flight engineer handed me a headset. When I was wired for sound, the pilot pointed to the TACAN set and announced, "We're 180 miles out of Cam Ranh, descending through flight level three-one-zero. We should be on the deck in about thirty minutes. This your first time in-country?"

Without waiting for a reply, the aircraft commander continued, "Somebody on the crew told me you're gonna be a FAC. Sporty job. Let me be the first to welcome you to the war."

With that, the pilot turned back to the controls and began hand-flying the big silver Starlifter toward the approach and landing at Cam Ranh, one of the key aerial supply ports in Southeast Asia. As we pressed to within a few miles of the runway, the high-pitched whine of the hydraulic pumps told me the copilot must have activated the gear and flap levers. Slowing to 135 knots, the pilot picked up a two-and-a-half-degree visual glide slope and deftly planted us on the centerline of the big runway, a little over three hours after our "oh-dark-thirty" departure from Clark Air Base.

As I waited in the passenger terminal for my B-4 bag, I hid my nervousness and apprehension by watching the steady stream of "grunts" milling around. Most wore soiled, sweat-stained fatigues and "boonie" hats. A few were even covered with red clay, which had dried to dust. It was obvious they had just come in from the bush, the infantryman's pet name for the jungle. To me, they all looked mean and irritable. Ironically, they were leaving Vietnam and should have looked happy. In terms of numbers, the departing troops equaled the well-dressed, well-scrubbed new arrivals. If the scene in the passenger terminal represented the U.S. troop drawdown, the plan was already in trouble—I seemed to be part of a one-for-one swap.

Within a short time, my small group of pilots linked up with a passenger-service NCO, who loaded us onto a fifteen-passenger van for the short ride to our temporary barracks. From there the NCO hustled us across the street to a tin-and-sandbag hut for administrative processing and briefings.

In the small, stuffy briefing room, the young Air Force major standing before the group of new pilots made a lasting impression. Looking professional yet relaxed, he fit my mental image of a combat veteran—suntanned, short blond hair, a faded K-2B flight suit with subdued black rank insignia, pilot wings, and name tag. To me, the most striking visual cue of all was that he sported well-worn jungle combat boots with canvas inserts, not the plain black leather boots that marked the twenty or so of us in the briefing room as new guys and rookies. All of us felt a strange combination of envy and anxiety as we watched the major deliver his welcome briefing. In front of us stood a combat-ready forward air controller who knew what being shot at felt like, who had probably handled air strikes all over Vietnam against enemy positions just a few yards from friendly troops. Watching him stand beside the podium, I couldn't help wondering how I would react to actual combat. The bottom line was that he had been there; we hadn't. Our briefer's attitude suggested arrogance and superiority. The intimidation was unspoken but very real.

"Okay, gents," he said, hands on hips, looking supremely confident. "I know you're all tired from Jungle Survival School at Clark and from chasing women in Angeles City, but now you start earning your sixty-five dollars a month combat pay. While you're here at Cam Ranh, the 504th Tactical Air Support Group will be your home. The group owns all FACs in Southeast Asia, so after five days of indoctrination with us, we'll assign you to one of the FAC squadrons. Most of you will stay in-country with either the 19th, 20th, 21st, or 22nd Tactical Air Support Squadrons, TASS for short. A few of you lucky souls will be on your way to a hardship tour with the 23rd TASS at NKP, Thailand. But before we really get into the assignment thing, let's see what you guys know about the vocabulary of the trade here in South Vietnam. I just happen to have a short pop quiz for you—a real chance for you to excel."

The briefing room echoed with groans of disbelief and protest. Some major sitting near the front piped up with "You got to be shitting me!" The briefer flashed his best "Steve Canyon" smile and passed around mimeographed sheets. The questions, about ten of them, were actually terms for which we were to supply definitions or explanations. I knew a few of them and could guess at a few more, but on others I drew a complete blank. My ignorance made me laugh right out loud. If my future assignment in any way hinged on the results of the test, I was destined to spend a year at the grungiest hellhole in Vietnam. I had seen Morley Safer from CBS News broadcast from "War Zone C," but I couldn't remember exactly where it was. "VNAF" was easy—the South Vietnamese Air Force. I guessed "playmate" was a wingman and got it right. I knew "Panama" didn't refer to the country but had no idea what it was, and there was no telling what "QC" signified or what a "Dust-Off" was.

After the quiz we all breathed a collective sigh of relief when the major informed us that it wouldn't count; we didn't have to put our names on the test. Had he stopped right there, his point—we were green and ignorant—would have been made. Instead, he looked slowly around the room for dramatic effect, then announced in deliberate, clipped words, "This little exercise was meaningless as a test. Its real purpose is to bring you prima donnas back down to earth, to take the wind out of your sails, to prove to a bunch of cocky pilots that you really don't know as much about fighting this war as you think you do."

He lost me at that moment. Here we were, our first day in Vietnam, crammed into school desks designed for sixth graders. Our black boots were an embarrassment, our flight suits, covered with regulation TAC insignia and unit patches with every color of the rainbow, marked us as being right off the plane from the States. We all knew we were novices and just wanted to shed our new-guy image and blend in. The major was our bridge; he had the answers but wouldn't share them with us. As if we didn't already sense the gulf between the old heads and the rookies, he seemed to enjoy making us feel like FNGs.

The briefing droned on for another thirty minutes, but I tuned it out. All I could think about was getting over to Supply and drawing my jungle boots and subdued rank and wings. Then some irrational compulsion forced me to find the tailor shop and bribe someone to sew the insignia on while I waited. It was all very unsettling. How could I be so totally absorbed with something so trivial? All other explanations aside, it came down to one selfish notion: I may not have been a combat veteran, but I sure wanted to look like one.

Steve Canyon was only one of many briefers we endured that day—April 19, 1970. An assortment of colonels, intelligence specialists, administrative clerks, and finance wizards trooped across the stage in succession, each intent on convincing us that his particular bailywick was the real reason the war was being waged. But the grand prize for the day went to the medics. A kindly looking Air Force flight surgeon took the podium just before lunch. He had silver hair and wore gold wire-rimmed glasses. He projected a great fatherly image but seemed too old to be only a captain. While several of us commented under our breaths about how many times he'd been passed over for promotion, he turned on the 35mm projector and flashed the first slide on the screen. The room instantly fell silent. On the screen was a sickening photograph of what appeared to be a man's genitals, turned purple and literally rotting off. Slide after slide followed, each more graphic and grotesque than the one before. The flight surgeon rambled on about the social diseases rampant in Southeast Asia, but he needn't have: if ever a picture was worth a thousand words, there it was, in living color.

The doc wound up his presentation as all the other briefers had, with a slide of a gorgeous, naked, large-breasted young lady right out of the pages of *Playboy*. When the oohs and ahs died down, the doc smiled and said, "Gentlemen, this is what you're fighting for." Loud applause filled the briefing room. He continued, "If you're gonna fool around, do it with a round-eye like this. Don't get mixed up with the local Vietnamese women. When the horny factor starts to take over your intellect, try to remember the pictures I've shown you today, and then ask yourself if it's worth it. For those of you who will totally disregard everything I've said, don't wait too long to come see us. We'll probably say we told you so, fill your ass full of penicillin, then send you back to duty." Nervous laughter greeted his prediction. He ended with "Any questions? If not, let's break for lunch."

After the doc's show-and-tell, our appetites weren't very keen, but we gaggled over to the dining hall just to see where it was. After waiting in line for a few minutes, I was the first of the new pilots to reach the cashier table. An airman first class, obviously bored with the whole process, demanded sixty-five cents. When I handed him a crisp dollar bill, the world came crashing down. The airman turned red with anger and shouted, "Jesus Christ, what are you trying to do to me? I can't take green. Scrip! Don't you have any scrip, you know, MPC—military payment certificates?"

From the blank look on my face, the airman must have sensed my dilemma. In a calm but sarcastic tone, he continued the tongue lashing. "Jesus, don't tell me you're one of those new turkeys from the 504th. We've told them a hundred times to convert your money before you clowns come to the dining hall. Why can't they get it right?"

Just as I was about to stammer out some kind of explanation, a crusty old major named Mac, who'd been with us all through the pipeline training preparing us for duty in Southeast Asia, stepped forward. Mac scruffed his short-cropped red hair with his fist, wrinkled his forehead into a hundred deep furrows, then fixed the mouthy young airman with a glare that would have frightened Boris Karloff.

"Let us through this line right now, or I'll personally kill you where you sit. Then I'll court-martial your dead ass and send it home to your mother with a dishonorable discharge! So what's it gonna be? You gonna let us through the line, yes or no?"

The airman mumbled yes, and Mac replied, "Wise choice. Just put this on my tab." With that, we eased down the cafeteria line and loaded our trays, not out of hunger but out of spite for dining-hall bureaucracy.

My first night in Vietnam was made a lot easier than I deserved. My father-in-law, Lieutenant Colonel Ken Wood, was stationed at Cam Ranh as chief of maintenance for the 483d Tactical Airlift Wing, equipped with the C-7 Caribou. His job became a nightmare when the F-4-equipped 12th Tac Fighter Wing packed up and went home, leaving behind all the jet-trained maintenance troops to work on reciprocating engines. In spite of the obstacles, Ken Wood was one of the best; this was his third war, and he was able to work miracles on the Cam Ranh flight line.

That night we had a quiet dinner at a Navy club right on the water. After six months in Vietnam, Ken looked tired and skinny, but the old spark and constant work ethic were still there. I filled Ken in on the latest from home, and he gave me his insights into the war effort at Cam Ranh. It was the same old story—trying to keep enough airframes flying to haul the massive amounts of supplies and equipment necessary all over Vietnam. Scheduling was a guessing game because Ken never knew where a big supply push might be needed. The tactical situation drove the requirements, and all too often, the Viet Cong dictated the tactical situation. In a war without any defined fronts, a trouble spot could pop up anywhere in the country at any time. Ken's Caribous had to be ready to respond to the "trash haulers" motto: you call, we haul. In Vietnam tactical airlift was critical because it was the only reliable way to avoid the very real danger of enemy ambushes along the roads.

As Ken and I talked, the ocean breeze tempered the tropic heat, so all in all it was a very pleasant evening. We might have been sitting anywhere in the States having a few beers and talking over old times. But as night began to fall, the immediacy of the war crept back into my conscious thoughts. At frequent intervals security posts around the air base perimeter fired flares into the night sky. Each flare exploded with an audible pop and then drifted slowly to the ground, suspended under a small white parachute. The flares gave off a flickering sort of illumination, an eerie yellow, wavering cast. When the flare burned out, the area was plunged back into total darkness. At that instant it was easy for me to imagine VC sappers hiding from the light, then scurrying forward in the darkness. At any second I half-expected a firefight to erupt right in front of us. I felt almost disappointed the next morning when I realized that not a single shot had been fired overnight.

The following day, our combat indoctrination began in earnest. We were briefed on how FACs had worked with the famous 101st Airborne Division during the assault on Hamburger Hill, located in I Corps's infamous A Shau Valley. We learned about the heavy enemy infiltration and bloody fighting going on in the Central Highlands of II Corps. Next we found out about the frustrating battles raging in III Corps's War Zone C, where enemy troops retreated across the border at will to sanctuaries in Cambodia. Finally, we heard about the activities in IV Corps—known to everyone as "The Delta"—about the seesaw battles around such places as Can Tho, Ben Tre, and Vinh Long.

With so much to learn and so little time, our teachers at the 504th used the fire-hose approach: they stuck the nozzle down our throats and turned the flow up full blast, hoping we'd retain enough of the information to be effective—and to survive.

Four days later, resplendent in our new jungle boots and subdued insignia, twenty of us took our customary seats at the sixth-grade desks in the now familiar briefing room. Rumor had it that the powers that be had finally decided on our assignments. We weren't sure that the powers had given the subject much thought, but we mortals had kicked it around a great deal, especially over cold beers at the bar.

Our small group ranged in rank from second lieutenants to one lieutenant colonel, with a few first lieutenants, captains, and majors thrown in. We'd been in training together for a long time, in some cases over eight months. Most of us had started as fledgling fighter jocks in the 27th Tac Fighter Wing at Cannon Air Force Base, New Mexico. From there we moved on to Hurlburt Field, Florida, for FAC training in our assigned aircraft, the 0-1 Bird Dog, the 0-2 Skymaster, or the OV-10 Bronco. After completing Jungle Survival School at Clark Air Base in the Philippines, we were about to split up and go our separate ways. We each hoped a few of us would stay together, but we were ready to take whatever came—as long as we got our first choice!

Each of us had his own idea about the perfect FAC job. I desperately wanted to fly in III Corps with the famous Twenty-fifth Infantry Division, known throughout the Pacific as "Tropic Lightning." My second choice was to fly for the Americal, the Twenty-third Infantry Division at Chu Lai. In the FAC community, the Americal had a reputation for being hard-nosed, tough fighters, always in the thick of something—which meant lots of action for their FACs. Unfortunately, the tragedy at My Lai had tarnished the Americal's otherwise outstanding combat record, which stretched back to Guadalcanal during World War II.

In either case I would be assigned the classic FAC mission of directly supporting the Army. It would be a steady diet of visual reconnaissance, close air support, and troops in contact. My strong attachment to the Army probably stemmed from my own background as an Army brat. My father was a retired colonel and, in my estimation, one of the most dedicated officers in the U.S. Army. My younger brother was an active-duty grunt lieutenant with the Eighty-second Airborne Division at Fort Bragg, so my empathy for the troops on the ground was genuine if not obvious. Additionally, the rules specified that FACs supporting U.S. troops had to be fighter pilots, and as one of the few young fighter-qualified jocks available, I thought getting one of my choices was a shoo-in.

Virtually all of our group agreed on one thing. We didn't particularly aspire to jobs with the 20th TASS "Coveys" or the 23rd TASS "Nails." Those squadrons flew a special FAC mission called SCAR—strike control and reconnaissance. The mission was interesting, but where they flew it was unsettling. Coveys and Nails flew over the Ho Chi Minh Trail in Laos, interdicting supplies being shipped south along a twisting network of dirt roads and paths. The North Vietnamese and the Laotian Communist Pathet Lao virtually owned the Trail from North Vietnam south through Laos and into Cambodia. There were no "friendlies" on the Trail, no close air support, no troops in contact. It was a secret war over one of the most remote areas of the world. The ground fire in South Vietnam, where pilots flew through a hail of small-arms and automatic-weapons fire, was plenty dangerous, as loss rates showed. But in Laos, low-flying, slow-moving FACs flew against the same big guns that defended Hanoi, murderously accurate 23mm, 37mm, and 57mm anti-aircraft artillery—"triple A" for short. A single round from any of them could blow an aircraft to bits. The Trail just wasn't my idea of a good time. On top of that, the Coveys at Da Nang lived on a virtual ground zero, with the VC lobbing rockets indiscriminately into the base at regular intervals. Da Nang came by its nickname honestly—Rocket City.

The rumor mill had been correct—our assignments were firm. Our old friend Steve Canyon did the honors, dutifully reading off each man's assignment in rank order. When he got to me, I heard no sound at all but simply stared in abject disappointment as his lips formed the words "20th TASS, Covey Da Nang."

That afternoon I hurriedly packed, all the while trying to convince myself to make the best of a situation I considered patently unfair. I managed a quick call to my father-in-law and a brief good-bye to my buddies who were scattering to every corner of South Vietnam. By late afternoon six of us had thrown our B-4 bags into the back of a C-130 transport and were airborne on the two-hundred-mile flight north to Da Nang, the second-largest city in South Vietnam, situated just seventy air miles south of the demilitarized zone—the infamous DMZ.

The name Da Nang really applied only to the old Vietnamese city of Tourane, but the name was commonly used for everything in the surrounding area. Starting with the big U.S. buildup in 1965, Da Nang had mushroomed into a sprawling series of military installations clustered around the port facilities and the two long north–south runways. The Marines and the Military Airlift Command's aerial port occupied the west side of the airfield. A conglomeration of ARVN, Special Forces, and Navy units were packed onto the two-mile-wide spit of land between China Beach and the I Corps bridges. Air Force units operated from the area immediately adjacent to the east runway. The largest outfit, the F-4 Gunfighters of the 366th Tac Fighter Wing, owned most of the real estate, but 20th TASS had carved out a nice chunk of land occupying the northern section along the east runway.

The Coveys lived in an old French area of the base known as the main compound. Surrounded by high walls, the buildings were right out of *Beau Geste,* with tile roofs and thick white stucco walls. The Covey FACs occupied the second floor of the large H-shaped building just inside the compound gate. The "Jolly Green" rescue helicopter pilots shared the ground floor with a detachment of A-1 pilots from the 56th Special Operations Wing. The main compound also housed a dining hall, small theater, post office, officers' club, nurses' quarters, and a number of trailers that housed the senior officers. Such was the setup that greeted me on April 23, 1970.

My accommodations in the Covey hooch were nothing to write home about: a small ten-by-twelve bare room with one desk, two metal wall lockers, and a set of bunk beds, all painted gray. As a first lieutenant about to make captain, I technically outranked my second lieutenant roommate, but since he had arrived two weeks earlier, according to the "new bean" pecking order and the law of the jungle, I inherited the top bunk.

My roomie turned out to be an interesting character who talked constantly and came across as a bit of a blowhard. He had already flown two or three combat training missions, which, at least in his mind, entitled him to link himself with the in crowd of old heads, throwing around insider terms and saying things like "we do this on a mission" or "we've found it's best to do that." He seemed just a little too sure of himself, and within two days it was obvious the veterans had no use for either of us until we could pull our own weight as combat-ready FACs.

It took me only a few more days to decide I didn't want to spend my entire tour with this guy. Besides the incessant talking, two other things about Roomie bothered me. First, when sitting around the barracks, most of us wore our flight suits or just our underwear. Not my roomie. He always wore faded Levis and a white T-shirt with a pack of cigarettes rolled up in the sleeve. He was harmless enough but looked for all the world like a hood out of *West Side Story*.

My second gripe involved noise. Roomie had just bought himself a brand-new Akai tape deck, which he played at full volume. And he played only one song, Creedence Clearwater Revival's "Proud Mary." Now I was a devoted CCR fan and had spent many happy hours at the Eglin Beach Club rocking the night away with my wife while a local band valiantly tried to imitate John Fogerty and the real CCR, so Roomie's choice of music was no problem. The kicker was that he insisted on running the volume up to the point where the eardrums bled, then he'd back it off a decibel to show how considerate he was. I'd come strolling into the room, only to be flattened by the sound ricocheting off all four walls. When I complained, Roomie couldn't hear me. Polite requests and irrefutable logic had no effect, so I was forced to take drastic action. Using my best Major Mac glare, I yelled, "Turn that goddamn thing down right now, or I'll kill you where you sit. If you think I'm bluffing, just try me!" The shocked look on Roomie's face quickly turned into a pout, his lower lip poking out like a small child's. I had to turn away to keep from laughing, but Roomie obediently cranked the volume down and left it down.

Things settled into an all too familiar routine of in-processing and administrative briefings. Each day I'd watch the other Coveys go out to fly combat missions while I remained behind, filling out one administrative form after another. When I tried to draw the old heads out a little on what it felt like to fly against the big guns on the Ho Chi Minh Trail, they'd respond with an amazingly similar refrain: "Oh, you'll get all that during your checkout. Right now, just enjoy the time off while you can."

The Covey intel officer was a little more talkative. Since he wasn't a pilot, he couldn't supply the stick-and-rudder perspective; he was, however, very helpful with background information. One afternoon, following an aircrew briefing, the intel officer sat down with me and launched into a thumbnail sketch of the operation. He explained that the very unconventional air war over Southeast Asia had produced some strange but very effective hybrids. One of the many innovative ideas used in the Vietnam War was the introduction of the FAC into the politically sensitive command-and-control system in Laos. Because of the murky political-military situation there, the restrictions on U.S. bombing seemed to outnumber the people. Known as rules of engagement (ROE), these dos and don'ts were so convoluted that nobody could understand them, much less apply them. The bureaucrats had devised some real doozies: you could drop bombs only within two hundred meters of a major line of communication—a road, trail, or river; you could not fire unless the enemy fired first; pagodas couldn't be bombed, even though the North Vietnamese Army's 316th Division had its headquarters in one. Frustrated Air Force and Navy fighter pilots rightfully felt hamstrung as a result of all the restrictions promulgated by all the verbalized jitters and "what ifs" some nervous strap hanger had dutifully recorded as ROE. Enter the FAC.

To regain control of an admittedly tough situation, USAF commanders inaugurated a program in which FACs flew daily missions over designated sectors of the Ho Chi Minh Trail. The FAC became the on-scene strike controller and referee. With firsthand insights into the situation, the FAC, orbiting above the target in his slow-moving aircraft, could work out the political kinks of the air strike through direct radio contact with Laotian ground commanders and with the U.S. Embassy in Vientiane. The program worked so well that, beginning in November 1968, planners devised Commando Hunt Operations, an air campaign designed to place a constant air umbrella over the roughly two-thousand-square-mile sector of the Trail contiguous to South Vietnam. That section of roads running down the southern Laotian panhandle was codenamed "Steel Tiger." The Da Nang Coveys were one of the FAC units assigned to work Steel Tiger around the clock, with the OV-10 Broncos handling the day duty and Cessna O-2s fighting the battle at night.

After hearing the intel officer's story, I was ready to go. I was itching to get back into the OV-10 after a six-week layoff. Finally, on April 28, I flew the first of four local refresher rides with squadron instructor pilots (IP).

Until then I had compiled a grand total of forty-three hours in the OV-10, so I wasn't a pro by any stretch of the imagination. All of the new local rules and procedures, coupled with my own rustiness from lack of stick time, made the need for going up with an IP to work out the kinks painfully clear. Fortunately, my instructor for the day, Captain John Tait, was a patient soul with lots of empathy for new beans like me.

As John and I walked up to the sandbag-and-metal revetment sheltering our assigned aircraft, number 654, he gave me some advice on the plane's aerodynamics: "Take a good look at this little beauty in the clean configuration. You won't see her that way often, much less fly her that way. The bird is sleek looking today, just like you flew in training back at Hurlburt. But within a week you'll be flying her loaded down with a 230-gallon centerline fuel tank and all kinds of rocket pods. With all that stuff hanging, the frontal drag is tremendous. It'll be like switching from a sports car to a truck."

I was hanging on John's every word while drinking in the view of the machine I was about to spend the next year flying and fighting in. Being able to fly the OV-10 was like a dream come true. The Bronco was a relatively new aircraft, first flown in 1967. That made it all the more appealing to me. Originally designed as a counterinsurgency aircraft, the OV-10 entered the Air Force inventory in the forward air controller mode in April 1969.

The Bronco was deceptively large, measuring forty-one feet long, fifteen feet high, and sporting a forty-foot wingspan. Sitting on the ramp in its gray war paint, the OV-10 conjured up two vivid images for me. First, it looked mean, like a praying mantis about to spring. Second, with the fuselage and cockpit suspended between twin booms and twin tails, it reminded me of the legendary P-38 Lightning of World War II fame. As a kid, I had devoured every airplane book in the libraries, and some of my favorite stories were about the exploits of the P-38 pilots of the Southwest Pacific, such as Dick Bong, Tom Lynch, Tom McGuire, and Tom Lanphier's incredible interception and shoot-down of Admiral Yamamoto. I used to fantacize that it was more than mere coincidence that I shared the same first name with most of them, that there was a direct link flowing from past to present. But the tangible link lay in the physical similarity between the two airplanes. I may have been born too late to fly the P-38, but the OV-10 was all mine, and it was a love affair from the beginning.

John introduced me to the line chief and to several of the Covey crew chiefs. He didn't make a big deal about doing it, but the gesture told me a lot about John and his respect for the hard-working maintenance troops. I made a mental note to copy John's style of talking to the crew chiefs often, of sharing a few details about the missions.

The moment had finally arrived. Following a lengthy preflight, I strapped into the front ejection seat while John did the same in back. Fumbling around with the maze of switches and controls, I silently chided myself for being so nervous. Sweat poured off me in buckets. I wanted to get off on the right foot with John, to make a good impression on him. My future reputation in the squadron might well hinge on whether John Tait thought I was a good prospect or a dufus klutz.

After running through the rest of the checklist, I signaled the crew chief by extending my right index finger in a twirling motion. He repeated the signal, so in sequence I cranked the right, then the left, Garrett turboprop engines. We taxied out of the revetment area and within minutes were airborne.

Using my new call sign, Covey 221, I checked in with "Panama," Da Nang's tactical radar control center. We started a climbing turn to the east, which carried us across the narrow strip of land between the runway and the beach. There wasn't much opportunity for sight-seeing, though: My head was on a swivel because the air was filled with every conceivable size and shape of aircraft. I counted at least a dozen helicopters in the immediate area, all milling around like bees at a hive. A flight of F-4 Phantoms arched gracefully in front of me, leaving an exhaust trail of black smoke visible from ten miles away. The MiG pilots up north didn't need good eyes—the Phantom's black smoke was a dead giveaway. Sandwiched in among all those war birds, a C-7 Caribou at my altitude droned slowly south along the coastline, and an O-2 slightly below me cruised in directly over the twin spans of the I Corps bridges. I asked John over the intercom, "Is it always this crowded?" As he keyed his intercom button, I watched in the mirror as he nodded yes.

"That's one thing you'll have to get used to about Da Nang. You've really got to stay alert with all this traffic. But it's not always this bad. Check your clock." Puzzled, I glanced at the instrument panel. It was about 12:10. John smiled and continued, "Lunch time. Everybody comes back into the pattern at once. We must be having something good at the dining hall today. Hell of a way to fight a war, isn't it?"

Climbing through fifteen hundred feet, we crossed the coast and went "feet wet," the radio term used to signify that we were flying over the warm waters of the South China Sea. In one of our intel briefings, the briefer had solemnly advised us that, if we had the choice, a feet-wet bail out was preferable to one over dry land, because there were "no bad guys to speak of, and no ground fire. It makes for an easy helicopter rescue." As I thought about his advice and looked down into that incredibly blue water, I wondered about sharks.

It was a perfect day for flying. Visibility was clear and a million miles in bright, dazzling sunshine. In our sector there wasn't a cloud in the sky. Far to the east I could see a squall line moving toward shore. By late afternoon a few of those cells would top fifty thousand feet, but at the moment they were no threat to us. All I could think about was how great it was going to be to go upside down again and pull Gs. When we were about ten miles off the coast, John seemed to read my mind. "Okay, Tom, I know it's been a while. Go ahead and wring her out. Just don't break anything." He didn't have to say it twice. I rolled the aircraft inverted into a split-S and off we went. Coming out at the bottom of the maneuver, heading in the opposite direction and doing well over 250 knots, I sucked in four Gs and pulled us up into a loop. As we zoomed straight up through the vertical, I tipped my head back to pick up the horizon, then eased the OV-10 over the top on her back, using the inverted horizon as a reference to keep the wings level. Coming down the back side, I fed in the back pressure with just a little too much "ham fist," causing a mild bucking action called a buffet or burble, the airplane's aerodynamic way of telling me to ease off the Gs or we'd go into an accelerated stall. At the bottom of the loop, it felt too good to stop. I pulled us right back up into a Cuban-eight, followed by all four leaves of a cloverleaf, and finished off the series with an Immelman. Reluctantly, I had to give in when John insisted we get on with the profile. I demonstrated a traffic pattern stall series and some slow flight, then we headed back to Da Nang for some practice instrument work.

As we coasted back toward Da Nang Bay, I spotted a lone O-2 about a mile to my left on a parallel course but slightly lower. It was the perfect setup for an old-fashioned bounce. Briefly, I considered the wisdom of showing my fanny on my very first ride, but on the other hand, the IP might think less of me for not being aggressive. Mind made up, I dropped behind the O-2 and closed in from his six o'clock position. I couldn't be sure if my "victim" had ever "rat-raced" before—he might embarrass the hell out of me. But at Hurlburt, I'd hassled with a few O-2s, and although they could be a handful with the right pilot at the controls, they were generally no match for the OV-10. Known as the "Oscar Deuce," the O-2 was essentially the military version of the Cessna Skymaster, a light aircraft with one 210-horsepower recip engine in front and another at the rear. Among some O-2 jocks, the unique engine placement spawned another nickname, "Suck and Blow."

As I pulled up beside my target, I could see it wasn't a FAC-configured O-2 but rather the psychological warfare version, equipped with a loudspeaker and a vent for dumping propaganda leaflets over the enemy. Throughout Southeast Asia everybody referred to them as "bullshit bombers."

John must have known what I had in mind, but he never said a word. He simply watched intently as we slipped into a wide-route position beside the O-2. I waggled my wings to get his attention, and when the pilot looked at me, I started the rat race by executing a barrel roll over the top of him. Watching from the inverted position out the top of my canopy, I knew he'd played the game before when he pitched out into a hard left bank and dived for the deck. I dished out the bottom of the barrel roll at full power and closed the distance between us in no time.

The O-2 jock responded by performing a series of abrupt clearing turns, first to the right, then back to the left. Rather than match him move for move, I hung back several hundred feet and just below him, safely tucked into his natural blind spot. Each turn finally became less severe until the O-2 gradually settled into wings-level flight. Dumb. The guy didn't deserve to be let off the hook, so I moved directly in trail with my gunsight pipper superimposed on his rear engine. Switching my radio to Guard emergency transmit, I blasted him with a loud "tac-tac-tac-tac-tac," simulating machine-gun fire. Everyone listening to Guard frequency instantly recognized the sound and probably chuckled at the humiliation they knew the bounced pilot must be feeling. When I moved back into a route position off his left wing, we had a clear view of the pilot staring at us, but I couldn't see his eyes because his dark visor was down. A boom microphone attached to his helmet partially hid his moving lips, but it didn't take a genius to figure out what he must have been muttering. As confirmation of his bad mood, the O-2 jock pressed his gloved left hand, middle finger extended, against the window, then rolled into a gentle right bank for his unceremonious departure from the scene.

With the fun and games over, it seemed prudent to press on with the rest of the training mission. For starters, Da Nang Approach Control cleared me for a straight-in TACAN approach to Runway 18 Left. I was supposed to fly strictly on instruments while John kept a sharp eye out for other traffic. It was harder to do than it sounds. Sitting in the front cockpit, focusing on instruments and concentrating on my cross-check, I could still see everything going on around us through my peripheral vision. I couldn't resist peeking as two helicopters crossed my final approach course. Then John warned me about a VNAF A-37 turning final in front of me; just when the distractions were about to drive me into a fit of frustration, Approach Control sent us around for two F-4s behind us who had declared emergency fuel.

The same sort of thing happened on a radar approach. The controller finally broke me off at two miles from touchdown. As the controller radar vectored us away from the field, John explained to me that Da Nang was the busiest airport in the world, with more takeoffs and landings each year than Chicago's O'Hare. We decided to give it one last try. Finally, we got clearance back to the beacon for an ADF approach. I screwed up the holding pattern entry royally, but eventually we managed to shoot the published approach all the way to a touch-and-go landing. Rather than press our luck, we stayed in the closed pattern for six more touch-and-goes. After the novelty of the first few wore off, I mentioned to John that the takeoff roll seemed a little too long and the plane felt sluggish at lift-off. With just the slightest edge in his voice, John explained, "You're not back in that balmy weather at Hurlburt. Runway temperature here is over one hundred degrees, so the engines aren't cranking out as much shaft horsepower. Accept the longer takeoff roll, and let her get a few more knots before you lift off. Just wait till you fly this baby at max gross weight. The roll is so long you've got time to sing all four verses of the Air Force song." Embarrassed at not having thought about the effects of high temperature, I let the subject drop. John took the full-stop landing, and we taxied back to the Covey revetments.

When we climbed out of the cockpit, I was soaking wet and really tired. John looked fresh; his hair wasn't even messed up. He must have seen the expression on my face because as we walked back to operations to debrief the ride, John told me, "You should carry some water with you. I use a baby bottle, but anything unbreakable will do. This heat will really dehydrate you fast, so take a few big gulps now and then and you won't get so worn out." I never flew another mission without a baby bottle full of water.

MAY

Flying Over the Ho Chi Minh Trail

O n the first of May I flew a morning training mission with John Tait. We had concentrated on the basics, yet for some reason, my flying had been sloppier than on our ride three days earlier. After the flight, as I sat listening to John recite the litany of my mistakes and foul-ups, another IP came crashing into the room.

In an excited voice, he asked, "Hey, did you guys hear the news? Armed Forces Radio just announced we've invaded Cambodia. It's about damn time. Now we start kicking ass and taking names!"

The IP's enthusiasm wasn't because of the invasion itself, or the associated fighting and dying. It had more to do with a feeling of relief, a sense of fair play. Finally, old nagging frustrations would give way to a surge of optimism. No longer would U.S. troops in War Zone C be forced to fight with one hand tied behind their backs. The political wall protecting the enemy in his Cambodian sanctuary had been shattered. For the first time in the war, American ground forces had been allowed to attack in strength across an international border in order to destroy NVA base camps and supply caches. For the first time, there was no place for the bad guys to hide. Units from the First Air Cavalry Division, the Fourth, Ninth, and Twenty-fifth Infantry Divisions, along with the 101st Airborne Division, could take the fight to the enemy right in his own private game preserve.

President Nixon's decision to cross the border was a bold one and a radical departure from the previous administration's hands-off policy on sanctuaries. Of course, the political climate had shifted dramatically in mid-March when General Lon Nol had ousted neutralist Prince Sihanouk, opening the way for the U.S. incursion. Militarily, the decision gave a big boost to the morale of U.S. troops and gave fair warning to Hanoi that the new president meant to give his Vietnamization program every chance of working.

For the Coveys at Da Nang, the Cambodian incursion was welcome news. As the man said, it was about time our side could kick ass. Of more immediate concern, the invasion of the Cambodian sanctuary meant that Laos became the only route the North Vietnamese could use to infiltrate troops and supplies south. Business on the Trail was bound to pick up.

That same afternoon, armed with a new sense of urgency, I flew an ordnance training mission with Major Norm Edgar. For the afternoon go, Norm and I headed for a deserted rock in the ocean about fifteen miles east of Da Nang. We were armed with four LAU-68 rocket pods, each containing seven white phosphorous rockets. Called "willie pete" for short, these rockets were the stock and trade of the FAC. When a willie pete detonated on the ground, the white-hot lethal explosion produced a large snow-white cloud of smoke easily visible to fighter aircraft circling the target area. If a FAC sang out, "Hit my smoke," the orbiting fighters knew exactly where to put their bombs. If the rocket was a little off, the FAC gave a correction, such as, "Hit fifty meters west of my smoke." In such a case, frame of reference became the toughest variable. To the FAC flying at two thousand feet, fifty meters was a clear and definite measurement. Besides, it was his yard stick. For the fighter pilots circling the target at twelve thousand feet, however, fifty meters was an indistinguishable blur, at best a "wag"—a wild ass guess. If the FAC really wanted to get good bombs from the fighters, he'd pick some ground object, regardless of its actual size, and make that his base reference. "Okay, Gunfighter flight, see that straight stretch of north–south road just east of the target? I'm calling that road ten meters wide. Put your bombs fifty meters west of my smoke." From the cockpit of Gunfighter Lead's F-4, the road might look like a pencil line on the ground, but he could now imagine five pencil lines west of the willie pete, and he'd be right on the FAC's target.

As we approached the island, I carefully set my switches on the armament panel and turned on the gunsight. In the mirror I could see Norm looking around the back of my ejection seat to make sure I had the switches in the correct position. In plenty of cases, an eager student had set the toggle switch to "drop" instead of "fire." Any IP would feel sick when the stud in the front seat had a good run on the target and squeezed off that first rocket, only to have the whole pod drop off the bottom of the plane.

The switches were good, so I rolled in on the first pass. Once established in a forty-five-degree dive angle, I placed the gunsight pipper below the target and let it track up to the outcropping. When the pipper was superimposed on the target, I fired the rocket and pulled the stick back into my lap in a healthy four-G pull-off. Everything felt right on the pass, so I was pleased but not surprised when the willie pete hit the target dead center. Norm grunted a little under the G forces but came on the intercom with, "Not bad. Can you do it again without a long setup? Keep pulling her up through the vertical, then whifferdill right back down for a second shot while the bad guys are reloading."

After coming over the top inverted, I rudder-rolled her right side up and made a couple of coarse stick-and-rudder corrections to put the pipper back where I wanted it. I fired number two and pulled off. Beautiful! Another direct hit. Laughing, I asked Norm, "Any other questions?" He laughed too, seeming to enjoy my success as much as I did.

We attacked the rock repeatedly, trying different tactics and dive angles on each pass. Norm seemed to know a hundred different tricks and techniques. Finally, he took the aircraft and announced, "Now we get serious. Loser buys the beer tonight." In the OV-10 the back-seater couldn't fire ordnance, so we went over the procedures. Norm would do the flying and when he gave me the signal, I'd fire the rocket for him. As I watched intently from the front seat, Norm set up the pass. We were tracking nicely when he came on the intercom: "Ready, ready, fire!" I squeezed the pickle button on my stick, and the rocket roared away, impacting on target just a few feet left of center. It was a remarkable shot, especially since Norm had no forward visibility to speak of and no gunsight. He was using the old "TLAR" method—that looks about right. Then it was my turn. The way my blind luck had been running, I just knew I had him. Sure enough, my rocket went right down the stovepipe. It was a great feeling, particularly after my less-than-sterling performance earlier in the day. As we cruised back to Da Nang, I could already taste that ice-cold beer.

I completed the phase I refresher checkout with a night sortie the following evening. The flight consisted of flare drops and night rocket firings followed by some touch-and-go landings. The mission was uneventful until we returned to the Da Nang traffic pattern, where I saw my first ground fire. For some reason, Da Nang tower had us enter downwind on the west side of the field, about a mile in trail behind an O-2. All I could see were his position lights and his red rotating beacon. Suddenly, two distinct streams of tracers arched up out of the darkness at the unsuspecting Oscar Deuce. The sight of the bullets made my pulse shift into high gear. I thought to myself, "This is the real thing. This is a shooting war, and I'm actually in it!" At that moment I experienced strong feelings of excitement and dread, but the sensation had a mystical, detached quality about it, not at all unpleasant or unnerving. Then the sound of my IP's voice brought me back to the present.

"Did you hear what I said? Turn off the goddamn lights!" Barely stopping for breath, he screamed over the radio, "O-2 on right downwind, you're taking ground fire. Break hard left." Without having to be told again, I immediately turned off all our outside lights. For some unknown reason, the O-2 continued to drone on straight and level, drawing several more long bursts from his assailants on the ground. My instructor was livid. "That stupid SOB must have his head up and locked. Look at him just fly through the stuff like he was on a picnic." I was about to chime in with an agreement when the IP clicked the mike button. "Tower, that O-2 getting ready to turn final just got hosed by about a hundred rounds of M-16 fire from the marine compound. You better get on the horn and tell those morons to knock it off."

After a short pause, the tower responded, "Roger. We'll notify Gunfighter Ops. They'll have to relay the protest, not us."

I couldn't believe what I was hearing. Over the intercom I asked the instructor, "You mean those are our own people firing at us? What the hell kind of games are they playing?"

His voice heavy with disgust, he answered, "What makes me so mad is that this isn't the first time it's happened. Periodically those dudes get all liquored up and try their hand at night target practice against aircraft in the pattern. It's a good thing they're probably drunk, or we'd really be in a world of hurt."

With nothing to prove by staying in the shooting gallery, I told the tower we were breaking out and reentering the traffic pattern for the other runway. We completed our touch-and-goes on the east runway without incident. Initially, I considered the episode my baptism under fire. It was my first time under the gun, and I hadn't panicked or become flustered. But it wouldn't sell—they weren't really firing at me. And besides, I didn't want my initiation to come from my own troops shooting at me.

Since I had over 750 hours total flying time, the squadron considered me to be a high-time pilot. For that reason, my phase II checkout was the short version, consisting of two back-seat rides watching old heads work the Trail and four front-seat rides under the watchful eye of an IP. If all went well, I'd get a final check ride and be certified as combat ready. My first chance to fly an actual mission over the infamous Ho Chi Minh Trail came on May 5, when I jumped into the back seat of First Lieutenant Homer Pressley's OV-10.

Homer was from Georgia and had an easygoing approach to almost everything. He was a super pilot and one of the most experienced Coveys. I couldn't have teamed up with a better role model. Unfortunately, Homer's best efforts couldn't make up for the miserable time I had in his back seat.

First there was the constant "jinking" to throw off any North Vietnamese gunners who might have been trying to aim at us. Homer abruptly changed directions and altitude more times than I care to remember. Most pilots pride themselves on maintaining perfectly coordinated flight, but on the Trail, that kind of predictable flying could get you killed in a hurry. So we went through an endless succession of skidding or slipping turns, climbs, and dives. We must have exceeded the wildest expectations of any gunners watching, because they didn't fire a shot.

The jinking was bad enough, but when coupled with constantly looking at the ground through high-powered binoculars, the effect was almost nauseating. As I intently watched the road below, Homer caught me off guard more than once with an unexpected reversal of direction. In all its magnified glory, the lush Laotian jungle rushed past my field of vision, producing uncontrollable waves of dizziness. Up until then, I'd never been airsick in my life, but Homer's jinking was about to do me in. The sensation was totally miserable, and I would have been just as happy to cruise straight and level and let the gunners have at us.

Just when I thought I couldn't stand another second of the roller-coaster ride, something on the ground caught Homer's attention. "Tom, I think we got something. See that football-shaped clump of trees just south of where the road forks? We just may have ourselves a couple of trucks." Using Homer's directions, I focused on the target. The trucks weren't clearly visible to me at first, but then I made out the straight lines of the bed and the unmistakable shape of the cab—two camouflaged trucks deep in the shadows along the tree line. The lingering dizziness was gone in an instant. As Homer checked the map coordinates, I picked out two more shapes, two more trucks. Trying to cover my excitement, I nonchalantly announced my discovery. Homer shot back, "Good peepers.

With eyes like that, you're gonna be a natural in this business.''

Within minutes, two flights of F-4s carrying five-hundred-pound MK-82 bombs rendezvoused with us. Homer gave them the standard briefing, and before I could digest it all, the strike was on. With the fighters covering us, Homer rolled in and put a willie pete right into the tree line. Flight Lead called in from the north, but I never saw him until he pulled off. The next instant all eight MK-82s went off around Homer's mark. The explosions and concussion waves were tremendous. I was totally enthralled, having never seen live ordnance dropped that close. Back at Red Rio Range in New Mexico and at Range 73 at Hurlburt, we had dropped only BDU-33 practice bombs. And my experience from the States explained why I couldn't pick up the fighters visually as they rolled in to drop their bombs. The dive to the target was known as "coming down the chute," and I was conditioned to looking just above the horizon for propeller-driven A-1 Skyraiders or for other OV-10s.

On the next pass, I watched Homer's head tilt back and look out the top of the canopy. I followed his gaze and there, almost vertically above us, I saw the wingman coming down the chute. No wonder I couldn't find Lead on the first pass. Two's bombs exploded about where his leader's had, but the smoke and dust were so thick that I couldn't make out anything on the ground. Quickly, Homer worked the second set of fighters and had them orbit the target "high and dry" while we took a close look at the results. Because the bombs had been right on the mark, I fully expected to see four smashed trucks or what was left of them. When the dust finally cleared, every tree in the target area had been completely blown away or splintered. Yet miraculously, all four trucks, as well as two trailers we hadn't seen before, were still sitting there, looking no worse for the ordeal. We knew they had to be badly damaged, but I couldn't imagine how they had survived that pounding intact.

We loitered in the area for another thirty minutes, hoping for more fighters, but no flights were available. In that part of

Laos, an airborne battlefield command-and-control center inside an Air Force C-130 parceled out the limited fighters to the sector FACs along the Trail. Operating under the tactical call sign of "Hillsboro," the command center evidently felt that Homer had received his quota for the day. It was a classic case of supply and demand. Hillsboro promised to keep us in mind if any stray fighters showed up, but my front-seater was less than optimistic about the prospects. It seemed such a waste to leave those trucks sitting there. I couldn't help thinking that the other targets on the Trail that day must really be doozies for Hillsboro to pass us by in favor of someone else. Since it was my first true combat mission, it seemed compellingly important to me that we bag those trucks. The bitter disappointment sapped the interest right out of me. Homer felt it too as he reluctantly broke off the vigil and headed north to continue the visual reconnaissance.

At that point we were more than two hours into the mission, the longest single stretch I'd ever spent in the OV-10. With the excitement of the trucks and air strikes behind us, I found myself once again dwelling on creature comforts—or lack of them. The rock-hard ejection seat was giving my butt rough sledding. No matter how I squirmed around trying to get comfortable, it still felt like I was sitting on a bed of nails. The midmorning sun didn't help either. Blazing through the canopy into the cockpit, the sun rays gave a good imitation of being the high-temperature setting on a very efficient convection oven. Finally, my armor-plated helmet seemed incredibly heavy. In reality it only weighed an ounce or two more than a regular helmet, but I could swear it weighed at least fifty pounds. The fit wasn't exactly right either, resulting in a "hot spot" on the back of my head that was killing me.

It seemed my whole thought process was negative and self-defeating. Angrily, I told myself to stop bellyaching and get on with the job. My circumstances weren't perfect, but they were a hell of a lot better than the mud and slime those army and marine grunts crawled around in. I concentrated on map reading and on asking Homer about tactics and visual reconnaissance (VR) techniques. Gradually, I forgot my discomfort and even managed to pick up some good tips from my very capable teacher. Exactly 4.8 hours after takeoff, Homer set us down for a perfect landing back at Da Nang. It was only 10:50 in the morning, but it had already been a long, exciting day.

Back in Covey Operations, Homer debriefed the flight with me, describing sights, sounds, and nuances that I hadn't even noticed. At one point, as he talked about the bombs missing the trucks but probably blowing the drivers away, a strange feeling came over me. Until that moment I hadn't really thought about the people in the target area, only about the inanimate trucks. I had no hang-ups or moral aversion to killing those drivers—they were the bad guys and would have iced us if given the opportunity. Still, the notion of actually killing another human being bothered me, made me feel uncomfortable with myself and with the impersonal nature of the air war over Laos. Today's bombing mission had been my first exposure to inflicted death. It affected me in another way too. I couldn't stop thinking about the grunts slugging it out in the jungle with their bad guys.

The next day, after an uneventful second back-seat ride, I was delighted to see from the yellow grease penciled names on the scheduling board that Captain Albert D. Jensen was going to be my IP for my first front-seat ride over the Trail. Any organization informally rates its own people, and while all the Covey IPs were capable pros, Don had the best reputation among the young pilots. He was about average size with slightly thinning sandy-colored hair. Don was outgoing and good-natured, but there was an intensity about him that convinced you he knew his stuff.

On the morning of May 7, we discussed the mechanics of the flight, then walked out the back door of Ops and across the Covey barbeque area to the intel shop for our formal briefing on targets, threats, and weather. Inside, a large floor-to-ceiling map showed every geographic detail of the southern panhandle of Laos, code-named Steel Tiger. Every segment of the Ho Chi Minh Trail had been carefully drawn in over clear acetate. As elaborate as it was, one feature on the map was more eye-catching than any of the others. A series of red circles covered the Trail, each representing a triple-A gun that had recently fired at one of our FACs. The effect was immediate: the whole damn map was nothing but red circles! For comic relief, and in the best traditions of war and gallows humor, some wit had playfully written in grease pen across the top of the map: "Send your favorite zip gunner on an all-expense-paid vacation to visit Buddha. Donate a MK-82 to a worthy cause."

The briefer gave all the latest data, including extensive warnings about every gun up and down the Trail. He cautioned us, "Be very careful flying around Delta 87. There are two active 23mm guns in that area; they seem to have an unlimited supply of ammo. The gun right here on the east side of the road is real bad news—a nine-level gunner if ever there was one. From other pilot debriefs, we've been able to determine that this joker knows how to lead a target, especially from right to left. His buddy on the other side of the road is probably a trainee. He's wild in his shooting, but he could always get lucky."

After painting the threat picture, the briefer moved on to specific duties. As part of the mission, we drew two "preplanned strikes"—dedicated fighters assigned to targets picked by the planners down at 7th Air Force Headquarters in Saigon. Other targets, generated by the FACs, were called "immediate requests" or "targets of opportunity." After our mission data cards were filled with all the essentials, the briefer sent us out the door with a cheerful "Have a good mission." Don and I strolled across the street and picked up our survival vests, helmets, and .38 revolvers from the personal equipment shop, then headed out to aircraft 799.

John Tait had been right. With four rocket pods, two pilots, and that monster centerline tank, the takeoff roll of the OV-10 seemed to take half a day. At a gross weight near fourteen thousand pounds, the plane's climb rate was not impressive either. To compensate, the initial turnout of traffic was to the east, rather than west toward the Trail. After gain-ing a few thousand feet of altitude over Da Nang Bay, we circled back over the airfield and headed for the Laotian border, eighty-five air miles away. At the border I gave Panama the traditional "across the fence" call, the code phrase that let them know we were leaving South Vietnam and crossing into the secret political-military world of Laos. Next stop, Ho Chi Minh Trail.

After we checked in with Hillsboro, we learned the fighters for our first preplanned strike had arrived an hour early; Hillsboro wanted to know if we could hack it. The race to the target would be tight, and my overall lack of familiarity with the region and procedures would slow things down even more. Rather than let some other FAC have our fighters, Don relayed an optimistic "Can do." We were still ten minutes away when the fighters checked in on our discrete UHF radio frequency. Much to my relief, Don decided to "demonstrate" the first strike. I knew he was just being kind so I wouldn't embarrass myself. Everything had happened so fast—my mind was still back in the arming area at Da Nang. But the quick turn of events had little effect on Don. Because he knew the area like the back of his hand, he briefed the fighters as all of us converged on the assigned visual reconnaissance area. The target was a suspected truck park just off a main segment of the Trail. With the four ship of F-100s orbiting impatiently overhead, Don quickly circled the scene, navigating around scattered clouds hanging over the target. He located his objective and rolled in for the mark. We were using the same system Norm Edgar and I had used a few days earlier: while Don flew, I would fire the rocket for him. While we were still at the top of the chute, the radio crackled.

"Covey, Litter 31. You're taking ground fire from your nine o'clock. Keep it moving."

Don answered, "I copy, Lead. See if you can pinpoint the gun." Switching to the intercom, he told me, "This is great. You get to duel with a gun on your first mission. Some people are just born lucky. Okay, get ready. Ready, fire!" The rocket swished out the tube and was on its way. Don sucked in about six Gs and racked us hard right, then back to the left. He came back on the intercom in an excited tone: "Tom, look out to our left, just a little above our level. See them? See those gray-colored puffs? That's 37mm, about two clips worth or ten rounds." I searched the horizon and picked out a couple of small clouds drifting by, but I wasn't at all convinced they were man-made.

Litter flight had a visual on our smoke, so Don cleared them in on target. As each camouflaged Super Saber rolled in and dropped his ordnance, we kept our eyes peeled for ground fire but, strangely, saw none. Through it all, I kept wondering if any of the pilots might be former squadron mates from back at Cannon Air Force Base. I was also fascinated by the way Don probed the triple-canopy jungle, trying to find and hit trucks that could not be seen from the air. After Lead dropped, Don directed: "Two, put your bombs on the west edge of Lead's bombs"; "Three, give me a pass one hundred meters south of Two's bombs."

In spite of the methodical probing, the strike turned up nothing. We spent the next few minutes looking at the destruction through our binoculars but saw only clouds of red dust and busted trees. Don sent Litter flight home with a less-than-spectacular bomb damage assessment, (BDA): "100 percent of the ordnance on target, but no visual results due to smoke and foliage." I watched in the mirror as Don used his grease pen to write all the strike data on the side of his canopy. Homer Pressley had done the same thing; I had incorrectly assumed it was a technique unique to him. When I asked about it, Don laughed, then explained, "If a FAC loses his grease pen, he declares an emergency and calls it a day. Besides, writing on the canopy keeps your head out of the cockpit, makes you concentrate on what's happening outside."

As we moved north along the Trail, Don pointed out some of the landmarks that would help me navigate in VR-6, the Covey portion of the route structure. Paralleling the main Trail, the Xe Kong River meandered along, twisting and turning to form some strange figures with its bends and cutbacks.

With a little imagination it was easy to visualize the most prominent ones: Snoopy's Nose, the Man's Head, the Twin Boobs, and the Dog's Head. On a clear day, high-flying fighters could see those features from miles away, so the river sculptures made great spots for FAC and fighters to rendezvous.

Our second preplanned strike involved a road cut where Highway 96 crossed a fairly large stream. The idea was to crater the road approaches to the ford, making it impossible, or at least difficult, for enemy trucks to cross the stream. Don told me the strike was all mine. He'd back me up with suggestions and ultimate safety of flight authority, but the basic decisions and fighter control were up to me. Armed with that guidance, I headed for the target twenty minutes before the scheduled rendezvous with the fighters. I figured it would be easy enough to find the spot where the road crossed the stream. When we arrived in the general area, I was shocked to see at least four roads or trails crossing the stream! Three of the four weren't even on the 1:50,000 scale map I had spread out all over the cockpit like I intended to wall paper the place. Through an agonizing backtracking process that took every second of the twenty minutes, I finally identified the correct ford. While I was still folding maps and trying to get organized, a two-ship of Navy A-4 Skyhawks checked in, low on fuel and ready for an immediate strike. I took a deep breath and gave the A-4s my best briefing, desperately trying not to sound as nervous as I felt. Any mistake of omission or commission on my part might cost one of those pilots his life; I definitely felt the pressure. My fighters seemed to absorb my briefing without difficulty, so I continued my orbit until in position to roll in from the south, parallel to the road four thousand feet below. Lining up the road in the gunsight, I fired the rocket and announced, "Mark's away." Pulling off target, there was no apparent ground fire, but I kept jinking, just in case. Looking back over my shoulder, I saw the white smoke from my rocket drifting up from the north bank of the stream, just on the edge of the road. Not bad for my first try in actual combat. I flew in a loose orbit directly over the target, then advised my fighters, "Okay, Lead, hit from my smoke to fifty meters south anywhere along the road. You're cleared for random headings, just call the direction you're in from." In a high-threat area, Don had told me that random headings gave the fighters the option to attack from any point on the compass, making it tougher for the gunners to know where to aim. I assumed that because of the orientation of the road the Skyhawks would use a north or south run-in. It was a major confidence builder when Lead rolled in from the north and put his bombs right on my smoke. To get the biggest craters, I had directed the fighter jocks to arm up their bombs for delayed fusing. As a result the whole area was obscured by red dust from the detonations. Lead pulled off to the east, directly into the late morning sun, making detection even harder for any ambitious gunners who were hoping to pop off a few rounds at these very professional Navy pilots. Because of the dust, the wingman continued around and came in from the south and put a beautiful string of bombs on the south ford, blowing away a large chunk of the road. Preoccupied with watching the dust clear over the target, I was somewhat surprised to glance up and see Two pull off to the west instead of into the sun as his leader had. Almost on cue the white puffs of 23mm exploded just below and several hundred feet off Two's right wing tip. Before I could react, Don came up on the radio and shouted, "Two, break hard left. You're taking ground fire!" Without acknowledging, Two executed a crisp left turn and within seconds was out of danger, continuing his climbing turn around the circle to rejoin his leader.

When we landed back at Da Nang, Don talked to me at length about the fine points of controlling air strikes. He complimented me on my handling of the strike, noting that the mechanics had been just fine. He went on to remind me that my responsibility included the fighters' safety as well as their effectiveness. When the Navy wingman had taken the ground fire, Don pointed out that I should have been monitoring him instead of worrying about where the bombs hit. Being a good FAC involved a lot more than marking targets and having guts. The key was in developing situation awareness, a sort of sixth sense for evaluating everything going on around you.

The next day we tried it again. Without a lot of prompting, I managed to get us to the target and to run a reasonably smooth strike against a suspected storage area and transshipment point. For the remainder of the mission, Don put me through some tough navigation problems. He'd find some obscure point on the map, read off the coordinates, then tell me to take him to it. We were en route to the third practice target when Don let out a yelp from the back seat. "Tom, bring her back around to the right. Now look at that straight stretch of road cut into the face of that bright red-colored cliff. Got it? Now tell me what you see." I immediately saw the shape he was talking about but couldn't believe my eyes, so I took out the binoculars and looked closer. Sure enough, it was a large truck right out in the open. Don couldn't believe it either. Day-shift Coveys rarely saw trucks at all, since virtually all movement on the Trail occurred at night to take advantage of the darkness. And since trucks almost never ventured out in daylight, OV-10 jocks relied on sharp eyes or blind luck to find vehicles parked and hidden under the dense, green triple canopy jungle.

We asked Hillsboro for help, and twenty minutes later I contacted Wolfpack 41, a flight of four F-4s from the 8th TAC Fighter Wing at Ubon, Thailand. "Wolfpack, Covey 221," I announced proudly. "Say your mission number and type ordnance, over."

I was mildly shocked by their response: "Roger, Covey. We're mission number 632. Lead, Three, and Four are each carrying one 'Pave Way.' Two is the designator ship. We can give you ten minutes of play time."

Pave Way was the code name for a highly accurate weapon, a laser-guided two-thousand-pound bomb. Because the system was so new, most FACs and fighters had never used Pave Way, and as a rookie I was certainly no exception. Under the right conditions, the process was relatively simple, although it required a lot of choreography. The early concept called for the designator ship to circle the area, with the back-seater employing a Buck Rogers hand-held device used to illuminate the target with an invisible laser beam. The other strike pilots maneuvered their aircraft so as to roll in and come down the chute directly over the top of the designator. If all went well, the free-falling bomb would intercept the laser beam and track all the way to impact. Accuracy of Pave Way was reported to be uncanny, but because of the rigid parameters the pilots had to fly, they were all sitting ducks for any proficient gunner who felt lucky and had a lot of ammunition stored up.

As I marked the target for Wolfpack 41, a strange thing happened. When my rocket fired, evidently one of its four folding fins failed to open, sending it careening off at a ninety-degree angle to our flight path. I quickly pulled up into a vertical climb in order to reposition for a second shot. Hanging at the top of the whifferdill, slow and very unmaneuverable, the vulnerable Bronco was evidently more temptation than the gunners could stand. Two guns opened up from the top of the next ridge to our east. Within seconds, we were bracketed by 23mm airbursts, all very close and very ugly looking. Instinctively I kicked hard bottom rudder to get the nose below the horizon. With the help of gravity and both engines screaming at 100 percent power, we gained flying airspeed quickly. In short order I reengaged the target and had the pipper back on the truck. Just before I fired, the guns hosed us a second time. I happened to glance directly at the southernmost gun when he fired, so I got a good fix on his position. I pulled off the pass with some inspired jinking and climbed back to altitude. My mark wasn't great, but the F-4s picked out the truck with no difficulty.

As was customary on a Pave Way strike, I was about to turn control over to flight lead when I had second thoughts. The idea of attacking the truck while the bad guys used us for target practice didn't sit well. Instead, I found myself saying, "Hey, Lead. I just got a good tally on that south gun. I'm game to go after him if you are." I thought I heard a small groan from Don in the back seat, but he choked off any comment and just gave me a "thumbs up" signal.

Lead came back with the answer I had hoped for: "Covey 221, I didn't get a fix on either one of the guns, but if you mark 'em, we'll blow 'em away."

"Roger that, Lead. FAC's in to mark. Keep me covered." Rolling in from the east almost directly out of the sun, I roared down the chute for a quick attack. As we pressed in, it seemed oddly unreal to be going head to head with a gunner who was intent on killing me, yet there was a strange excitement, an exhilarating feeling about it. Up till now the gunner had had his way, but with any luck, I was determined to change that.

Easier said than done. A couple of flak bursts off our left wing shattered my concentration, and I fired before I had the sight picture nailed. Right away I knew the rocket would be short, so I squeezed off a second one and pulled off to the south in a gut-wrenching high-G turn that tunneled my vision.

Don came on the intercom instantly. "Keep it turning to the left. That other gun is tail-shooting us. That's it, keep it turning. Now, break back hard to the right!" Stick full against my right leg, we were in ninety degrees of right bank in a heartbeat. Out the top of the canopy, I could see a line of nasty-looking little puffs. Surprisingly, they were quite a distance away. I unloaded the G forces so we could accelerate and then eased back toward the ridge where the guns were waiting. Neither of my rockets scored a direct hit, but they formed a nice bracket around the suspected position. There was nothing left to do but turn control over to Lead and move out of the way.

"It's your show, Lead. Go get him."

"Rog, I got control. Nice work, Covey."

With Lead's verbal pat on the back, my spirits soared. It wasn't a gushing tribute; still, I sensed the bond between aviators, I sensed Lead's admiration for us slow-movers who ran the gauntlet of fire to get the job done, I sensed some things about myself that had worried me but would no longer. At that moment, any self-doubts about my ability to handle the stress of combat evaporated.

The designator ship was doing his job at about twelve

thousand feet when Lead called in from the southeast. The gunners must have known their stuff was weak because neither opened up. Lead called off, and ten seconds later a huge explosion ripped the jungle wide open exactly where the gun pit had been. Since nobody had pinpointed the northern gun, Lead moved his traveling laser show back to the red cliff where the truck still sat. A few seconds later, Three dropped his bomb into the imaginary basket to score a direct hit on the large truck. When the smoke cleared, Don and I couldn't believe it. There was absolutely nothing left—not a wheel, fender, or a single scrap of metal—just a large, smoking hole. After a short discussion with my IP, I passed the BDA to the fighters. We settled on one truck destroyed and one 23mm gun silenced and probably destroyed. Wolfpack 41 went home happy, and I felt like I had learned a lot about the war and about myself.

A few minutes later, just before we started back to Da Nang, the bubble burst. I heard Don talking to another FAC on our Covey FM frequency, and I turned up the volume to listen. The voice asked, "Hey, Jensen, did your stud just put a strike in on a truck at the red cliffs?"

Don answered, "Roger that. A direct hit. We put a Papa Whiskey on it, and there was nothing left of the mother."

There was a long pause before the other FAC responded. "There was nothing left because it wasn't a real truck. It was a fake, just a flak trap, and you dumb shits fell for it! It's been sitting there for a week. Where have you been? Boy, this is rich. Just wait till the guys get wind of this. You'll be buying the bar for a month."

It was like someone slapped me in the face. I felt myself flush as the anger and embarrassment welled up inside me. It wasn't so much that I had been suckered in by the fake truck. My IP had fallen for it too. The sting and bitterness came from hanging it out for no good reason. For the life of me, I couldn't figure out how the fake truck had gone unreported, how it could have been passed off as a joke, just waiting for some fool to stumble across it—especially when I was the fool. The truck on the red cliffs sure as hell was a flak trap, and a bunch of us had just put our butts out in the breeze so somebody could have a good laugh at our expense. I shuttered to think what the price could have been. As we headed for home, all I could think about was punching out the imbecile who had masterminded the prank.

On May 11 Norm Edgar gave me my combat-ready check ride. We were scheduled for one preplanned air strike against a suspected truck park out in the middle of nowhere. The mission was totally uneventful, but my handling of the air strike generated a mild controversy.

When I finally located the target coordinates, they turned out to be in the middle of the jungle, far from any roads, trails, or dry streambeds capable of supporting truck traffic. Norm and I spent thirty minutes staring through our binoculars from every conceivable angle, trying to find any clue that a truck might be hidden under those thick trees. It had to be a mistake, so I widened my search pattern and finally came across another clump of trees almost a thousand meters west of the preplanned target. A small, dusty trail ran along the tree line and then ducked into the woods near a small stream. It looked a lot more plausible for a truck park than the other spot. I thought about playing it straight, just hitting the original coordinates and letting 7th Air Force do the explaining. I also considered talking the situation over with Norm, but that would have been the easy way out—it was my decision, and he wouldn't be in the back seat for my whole tour. When the fighters showed up, I directed their bombs against the point where the trail entered the trees. We probed all around the area but came up empty-handed. As the fighters left the scene, I gave them the BDA and evidently left them with the impression that they had hit the preplanned target.

On the way home, Norm quizzed me about my decision. "Tom, you know you put that strike in west of where you were supposed to. How come?" Somewhat defensively, I outlined my reasoning, to which Norm responded, "I agree. If I'd been in your shoes, I'd have probably done the same thing." Norm thought I'd done everything else well, so I figured the episode was closed.

That night an impromptu party developed in the hallway of the Covey barracks. One of the old heads had finished up his tour, and the celebration included generous portions of French 75s, a killer concoction of cheap champagne and brandy. In a fairly short period, nobody was feeling any pain. In celebration of my own new combat-ready status, I managed to do a good job of keeping up with the most ardent of the revelers. To my surprise, few if any of the Coveys showed the slightest interest in my accomplishment. To them, I was still just one of the new guys.

At some point in the evening, a captain named Mike pulled me off to the side. He was the same pilot who had called on the radio about the fake truck, so I wasn't kindly disposed toward him at the outset.

We were standing just outside the community shower room, and Mike had one foot resting on a bench as he started talking. "I was out in the area today when you put in that air strike. You weren't even close to the coordinates you should have hit. I don't know what your problem is. Maybe you can't read a map, maybe you're just sloppy. Either way, that kind of behavior won't hack it in this outfit."

I felt the same flush I had experienced a few days earlier. Angrily, I shot back, "Let me get this straight. You were sneaking around out there watching my strike without checking in with me like you were supposed to? How about explaining that little breach of flying safety?"

Mike then said exactly the wrong thing. In an arrogant tone, he hissed, "I just wanted to see how Jensen's star pupil handled himself without Daddy Don there to bail him out."

I literally saw red. I shouted back, "You asshole!" Then my right fist slammed into his left cheekbone, sending him sprawling onto the shower room floor. He landed like a sack of potatoes, then groggily shook his head. He propped himself up on both elbows but made no other effort to get up. I knew this round of the fight was over.

Mike looked at me for a couple of seconds, trying to get his eyes to focus, probably more from the effects of the

French 75s than from my less-than-ferocious right lead. He said, "What the hell did you do that for?"

I walked over to the shower and turned the cold water on him full blast. As he tried to squirm out of the way, I yelled, "You're a creep. If you ever play games with me out in the area again, the next time I'll take your whole head off."

I was more shocked by the episode than Mike. It had been years since I'd been in a fistfight. The whole incident was so out of character. Somewhat guiltily, I wondered if flying against the big guns on the Trail could have triggered some sort of macho aggressive reaction in me.

As far as I could tell, Mike never said a word about the fight, but the news spread through the Coveys like wildfire. The next day I figured it was all over when the Covey commander, Lieutenant Colonel Ed Cullivan, called me over to his table in the officers' club. He had a sly smile on his face as he started talking. "Don't you get enough combat out over the Trail?" He grabbed my right hand and inspected my bruised knuckles, then motioned me a little closer. "Just between you and me, that SOB's had it coming for a long time. Don't do it again, though."

In spite of the unpleasantness with Mike, I felt I'd reached a milestone. I was extremely proud of becoming a combat-ready FAC. I certainly didn't feel disturbed about flying combat missions—no nightmares, no chills, no guilt-ridden anxiety attacks. Yet somewhere in the back of my mind, amid the jumble of new emotions, I wondered if I ought to be feeling something negative. After all, *Stars and Stripes* ran daily articles on the antiwar outcry over the assault in Cambodia. Could it be that I was out of step in approving of the incursion? By approving, did that mean I felt no sense of loss or shame over the terrible shooting tragedy at Kent State? It might have been a cop out, but I slid through the process without answering my own questions. I decided to leave morality to the folks back home, who had the time and luxury to consider it. My waking moments seemed to have room for only one reality—the trucks and the guns on the Ho Chi Minh Trail.

I enjoyed the flying more than I ever could have hoped. Being alone in the front seat of the Bronco provided me with an incredible sense of freedom, an enormous feeling of satisfaction. Yet there was a price to pay. Time and missions became open ended and consequently a heavy physical drain. The grind came from having no sense of calendar. Even as a new guy, I rapidly found myself losing all track of time. I could always count on logging four hours of combat time over the Trail, but the missions started running together, just like the days of the week. I had hoped to improve as a FAC by analyzing every mission. It didn't work. I could vividly recall some events but had blurred recollections of others. Some anonymous sage captured part of the feeling with some latrine-wall graffiti when he observed, "A Covey mission is four hours of boredom punctuated by a few minutes of stark terror." I wasn't sure about the stark terror, but the rest struck a familiar note. I could vouch for one thing: after a hot gun battle out in Steel Tiger, the letdown following that adrenalin surge was exhausting. And we went out and did it again the next day and the next and the next.

Except for brief notes scribbled in my journal, memory-jogging events replaced days of the week as a means of tracking time. "Those were fresh eggs at breakfast this morning." "That gunner by Snoopy's Nose is really getting good." "Did you see the set on that new nurse?" "*M*A*S*H* is playing at the flick tomorrow." Unfortunately, some of the events were traumatic, not necessarily the sort of things you shared with family and friends back in the States. Toward the end of May, several memory joggers shook me out of my rut.

About four o'clock on the afternoon of May 22, I strolled into Covey Operations to pick up my mail. Uncharacteristically, the place was packed. Half the people were scurrying around, while the other half just stood there dazed. Usually a few people were always hanging around playing darts, but it was obvious that nobody was in the mood for games today. At that moment the duty officer sprinted in the back door and began nudging his way through the crowd. I tapped him on the shoulder and asked, "Bill, I just got here. What's going on?"

Bill's eyes met mine briefly, then his stare dropped down to his boots. "Rick Meacham's been shot down. He bought the farm."

I didn't know what to say. It was an awkward moment. I heard myself ask, "How? Where?" My voice echoed as if I were talking in a barrel.

Bill answered, "We don't know any of the details, but he went down in the triborder area near Khe Sanh." Bill looked back up at me, then continued to elbow his way through the crowded room.

My mind raced, confused. I had barely known Rick; we had talked only a couple of times. Still, it was a shock to be told he was dead. Then a thought struck me. What the hell was he doing up at the triborder? That wasn't even part of the assigned Covey area. Then I remembered Rick was part of a "sneaky-pete" flight within Covey, a small group of six pilots who flew some super-secret mission about which the rest of us knew nothing. The six of them kept pretty much to themselves and took a lot of good-natured kidding from us because they were always off in some corner whispering. Everyone knew them as "Prairie Fire" pilots.

I'd heard the Prairie Fire pilots on the radio with Hillsboro once or twice. They talked about "playing some ball game" or about a certain area being "hot," obvious code words with no meaning to an outsider. In our preflight briefings before each mission, the intel officer always went to great lengths to point out a series of square boxes on the map called "no bomb lines" or NBLs. The NBLs were located in some nasty areas just inside the Laotian and North Vietnamese borders, with the largest concentration located in the DMZ, the no-man's-land dividing North and South Vietnam. Rumor had it that the NBLs had something to do with Prairie Fire pilots.

Although none of us knew the Prairie Fire pilots that well, Rick's shoot-down and death had a sobering effect on all the Coveys. Initially, it made most of us stop a minute to reflect on our own mortality. But the scope was wider than that; the impact on the unit as a whole was more profound. Rick's death was the first Covey combat loss in nineteen months. Statistically, we were long overdue, and everyone had been expecting it. Now the unspoken question was, would we go another nineteen months, or were the floodgates open? Somewhat guiltily, I figured I was the only one thinking along those lines until I heard one Covey tell another, "We're really in for it now. Bad things always happen in threes."

As a measurement of roster strength, Rick's death represented only a small decrease in the percentage of available manpower. But the deep emotion everyone felt at losing a gifted pilot, one of our own, hit much harder and in ways not quantifiable on a morning strength report. Rick's death proved beyond any shadow of a doubt that in a close-knit flying unit, a synergistic effect was at work: the total amounted to more than the sum of the individual parts. The missing man diminished us but at the same time made us stronger.

Rick was gone, but life went on. A few mornings later, I had the day off. Just like in the popular fighter pilots' song, I was "not on the schedule, not earning a dime." Blissfully tucked into my top bunk, I was attempting to sleep late on the taxpayers' time. At some point I heard someone rattling around the room. No blaring "Proud Mary," so it wasn't my roomie. Through bleary eyes I saw our Vietnamese maid squatting in the middle of the room, polishing my boots. She already had my dirty laundry piled in the floor beside her. Even in the flattering soft morning light, Mamma San had to be one of the ugliest women I'd ever seen. Somebody had her in mind when they coined the old saying, "Beauty may be only skin deep, but ugly goes all the way to the bone." She was short and pudgy, with long, black hair combed back into a tight bun. The effect emphasized her very square face covered with unsightly zits. Her perpetual smile revealed teeth stained black by years of chewing betel nut. Mamma San wore a white blouse and classic black pajama bottoms, standard garb for civilians—and the Viet Cong. Watching her, I couldn't help staring at her bare feet. Her toes looked like a man's gnarled fingers, spread wide apart. She'd probably never worn real shoes in her life. On the plus side, Mamma San was cheerful and tried her best to take good care of us.

I jumped out of bed and ambled down the hall toward the community shower, with Mamma San right behind me carrying an armload of sweat-stained flight suits. Standing under the steady stream of cool water from the shower nozzle, I began to revive. The brownish water sprayed all over me and felt great. Everyone from the flight surgeon on down swore that Da Nang's rusty-colored water was fit for human use, so I numbly accepted their oaths as gospel. I accepted the water, but even after a month at Da Nang, I was still somewhat self-conscious about taking a shower while all the maids watched.

Mamma San and two other maids squatted directly outside the shower room, stacking laundry into piles and chattering away to each other in Vietnamese. As they gossiped and sorted clothes, all three kept their eyes glued on whoever happened to be in the shower. If I made eye contact with one of them, she would smile and all three would break into uncontrollable giggles. I wasn't sure whether to be flattered or embarrassed by the unwanted attention. Fortunately, one of the night-shift O-2 Coveys staggered into the shower room and was greeted by the same giggles. I convinced myself that Mamma San and her buddies were watching the other guy.

A few days earlier, I'd heard a couple of pilots complain that their flight suits never seemed clean. Coming out of the shower, I found out why. Mamma San gathered up about twenty-five flight suits and laboriously stuffed them into one automatic washing machine designed for less than one-third that load. Fascinated, I watched as she produced a giant box of Tide from the Covey supply locker and then measured out one tiny cupful into the overstuffed tub. She pushed the right buttons, and the machine rapidly filled with brown water. When the wash cycle finally kicked in, the agitator in the overloaded machine only moved about an inch in either direction. I started to say something to her, but she looked so pleased with herself that I didn't have the heart. Late that afternoon Mamma San neatly stacked my less-than-clean but beautifully ironed flight suits on the corner of my desk, then proudly walked out of the building with an almost full box of Tide.

On May 28, as I preflighted aircraft 693, I understood why nobody liked to fly late-afternoon sorties. The hot afternoon sun reflecting off the concrete ramp transformed the whole place into an inferno. My sympathies went out to the crew chiefs, who were forced to endure the searing heat over eight-hour shifts. Stripped to the waist, climbing all over the scalding hot metal surfaces of the OV-10s and O-2s, the young airmen did their jobs efficiently and still managed to be fairly cheerful as they helped me strap in.

The other reason nobody cared for the afternoon go also stemmed from the weather, but for a different reason. With the temperature, humidity, and convection building throughout the tropical day, a line of hefty thunderstorms would likely be in their usual spots along the mountain range separating Vietnam and Laos. Picking your way through the bottoms of those monsters in a light aircraft with no radar was definitely sporty.

Dripping wet from sweat but glad finally to be airborne, I headed for the "fence." From my cruising altitude of eighty-five hundred feet, I could clearly see a solid wall of thunderstorms waiting to test my skill and nerve. The tops of the largest cells, already towering above forty grand, appeared to be building faster than even a jet fighter could climb, so I knew my choices in the Bronco were limited: go home, go under, go through, or go around. Forget the first choice. Going under might be an option over flat terrain, but in the mountains strong down drafts could slam an aircraft into a peak without warning. Punching through a storm was risky and dumb, so I struck off to the south, hoping to end-run the ominous-looking cells.

After about fifteen minutes on a southwesterly heading, I stumbled across the most awesome sight I'd seen in years. Seemingly out of nowhere, a five-mile-wide corridor opened up in the solid line of thunder bumpers. Through it I saw beautiful, dazzling sunshine. The sun hung there like a huge orange-red ball, shimmering thirty degrees above the western horizon. I hesitated a second, wondering if the corridor might be a temporary sucker hole, but as if drawn by some uncontrollable force, I pushed both power levers up and plunged into the breach.

Flying between the huge, boiling walls of clouds, I kept thinking about the scene in *The Ten Commandments* when Charlton Heston parted the Red Sea. At any moment I half-expected the spell to break and the whole shooting match to come tumbling in on top of me. Pressing on through the canyon, I was fascinated by the light show flickering about on either side of me. Lightning strikes deep inside the cells produced a continuous pulsating series of glowing discharges of static electricity. In spite of their eerie beauty, I knew that in a matter of seconds the awesome power inside any one of those babies could transform my airplane into a pile of junk.

And suddenly I was out of it. The storm was behind me, and before me was nothing but sunshine and deep afternoon shadows. My attention turned to the Trail, but in the back of my mind I knew I'd have to face the thunderstorms again on the return trip—only then it would be pitch black.

On each of the last few missions, the intel types had been asking us to watch a suspected enemy headquarters complex and truck park along a particularly hot section of the Trail. All the indicators of enemy activity were there: a nearby water supply, plenty of cover, and lots of dust on the trees lining the road, strong evidence that trucks were in the immediate area. In an earlier probing strike, one of the Coveys had encountered stiff ground fire, another indication that the bad guys were hiding something worth protecting.

As I flew over the suspect area, all seemed quiet. I circled for about fifteen minutes, but if there was anything down there, I couldn't see it. The long shadows made it especially difficult to pick out detail. Just as I was about to leave, a mirrorlike reflection from the ground caught my eye. It disappeared in a split second, but it had been there long enough to convince me it was a reflection off a glass surface—maybe a truck windshield. I concentrated my search on the small valley where I'd seen the flash. My excitement faded, however, with the passing minutes because all I could see was an endless sea of green trees. I thought about requesting an air strike from Hillsboro, but the chances of my target making the priority list seemed slim at best. I decided not to bother.

Flying north along the Trail, I was lost in my own thoughts when the radio startled me. "Covey 221, Hillsboro. We've got a divert flight of F-105s. You got a target for them?"

"Funny you should ask, Hillsboro. There's a suspected truck park I'd like to probe. Send them to the Dog's Head for a rendezvous."

"Roger on the Dog's Head. You'll be getting Bear flight. They're on the tank right now topping off with gas and should be with you in about twenty minutes."

While waiting for my fighters, I scoped out the area one last time, then moved several miles north so as not to telegraph my intentions to bomb the place.

I set up an orbit over a wide spot in the road called Chavane. The place was short on looks but long on history. Our maps showed Chavane to be an active airfield, but it was actually nothing more than a large, relatively flat meadow. During World War II, the Japanese had a fighter outfit stationed at Chavane. As I looked down on the abandoned grass runway, I could visualize a flight of Zeros bouncing across the rough ground on a formation takeoff, scrambling to intercept a gaggle of Allied bombers intruding into the Chavane sector. I wondered if those young Japanese pilots of my imagination were successful in their intercept. Did they die? Was it just another mission? Ultimately, the answers seemed unimportant, and the questions, timeless. Thirty years later, a backwater known as Chavane was still caught up in war.

"Covey 221, Bear flight checking in over the Dog's Head with four of the world's finest. Everybody's got four Mark-117s and twenty mike-mike. Over."

"I copy your lineup, Lead. Take up a heading of due east

for ten miles. I'm orbiting directly over the first stretch of dirt road you come to. I've got a suspected truck park for you. Target elevation 2,150 feet. Highest terrain in the area goes up to 4,750, about twenty klicks to the northeast. We've got two known 23mm guns in the area, and you can also expect small-arms and automatic-weapons fire. Nobody's shot at me so far, but they're probably saving it for the world's finest. How copy so far?''

Lead answered, "Real funny, Covey. Keep going—we're all ears.''

"Okay, gents, if you get in trouble, your best emergency bail out is heading 045 into the high mountains. This close to sunset, you can count on spending the night if you go down. Your closest emergency airfield is Da Nang, 125 miles due east. There are no, repeat, no friendlies in this area. Once I mark, I'll hold over the target. You'll be cleared for random headings. If anybody pinpoints a gun, you're automatically cleared in on him. Unless you've got questions, let's do it.''

To start the rocket pass, I rolled the Bronco almost inverted into 135 degrees of left bank, then applied back pressure to the control stick to pull the nose below the horizon and down toward my target in the center of the small valley thirty-five hundred feet below me. Before I could roll back to wings-level, a stream of tracers raced toward me from a saddleback-shaped ridge just to the east. The tracers looked different from those I'd seen on earlier missions. These seemed to be moving much faster and glowed with a deep red, almost burgundy, color. The first half of the stream passed well in front of me, left to right, but the last few rounds streaked directly over the top of my canopy at a tremendous rate.

Whoever that gunner was, he caught my attention; I kept one eye in his direction and the other on the target as I lined up and fired. The rocket evidently penetrated to the jungle floor before exploding, so that only small whiffs of white smoke seeped up through the foliage and trees. Bear Lead rolled in to give it a try, but halfway down the chute, he came up on the radio. "Covey, I'm taking it through dry.

Lost your smoke in the shadows. How 'bout putting down another mark?''

As Lead pulled off to the south, I kept my eyes glued on the general area where I'd received the ground fire. Not so much as a whimper came from that gun, but when I glanced back to check on the lead F-105, half a dozen airbursts strung out behind the rapidly climbing Thud. I had no idea where the new stuff came from.

"Any of you Bears get a fix on that second gun?" I asked.

"Covey, this is Three. He's over to the west of us somewhere. I saw the tracers but no muzzle flashes."

"Thanks, Three. Okay, gents, I'm back in to mark. Keep your eyes open."

I pressed in out of the west at a fairly low dive angle, hoping to keep the sun directly behind me. The guy on the saddleback wasn't fooled a bit. Looking into the dark shadows, I could see his muzzle flashes for a split second. I had the sensation of flying right down his gun barrel. The tracers, reddish brown this time, floated directly at me, then speeded up as they zipped by the right side of the cockpit.

I really sucked in the Gs pulling off the run. To keep the blood from pooling in my legs, I pushed out as hard as I could with my stomach muscles and grunted loudly. Flight surgeons called it the "M-1 Maneuver," a technique used to fight against blacking out under heavy G forces. The M-1 wasn't for use in polite company, but it definitely came in handy in combat.

It was a relief to see a thick white cloud of smoke billow out of the small valley. Before I could give any verbal instructions, Lead cut off my radio call. "Lead's in from the north. I'm going after your gun. Covey, move a little to the west. You're right in my flight path." I racked it around hard to the west as Lead barreled down the chute, just missing a collision by less than two hundred feet. Muzzle flashes once again lit up the tree line just as Lead pickled off four 750-pounders. The bombs fell in perfect formation toward the trees, then exploded in a giant fireball on a slope just above the gun. The blast probably hadn't killed the gunner, but he obviously had one hell of a headache, not to mention two busted eardrums.

Before anyone could interrupt me, I keyed the mike button. "Two, go for the tree line one hundred meters north of Lead's bombs. You're cleared in hot. Go get him!"

The tree line offered no resistance as Two dived on his target. I watched through my binoculars searching for a gun pit, but the overhangs and trees cast such dark shadows that it was impossible to make out any detail along the ridge. As Two climbed away, the ground just north of where I thought the gun was erupted in a wall of dirt and flames. Close but no cigar. I thought about having Three split the difference, but the gun appeared to be out of commission, and I needed some bombs to probe the original target. The smoke from my second willie pete had completely dissipated, so for the third time I rolled in to mark the target for the orbiting Thuds.

Nobody fired a shot as I lined up west to east and squeezed off three rockets into the little valley. Three evenly spaced white puffs filtered up through the jungle, providing all the reference my fighters needed. Bear Three's bombs hit dead center, and Four's overlapped to the west, blowing gaping holes in the stand of trees. Circling the area, I strained to see into the craters. Finally, on the very edge of Four's last bomb hit, I made out some sort of structure. The thatch building was rectangular, with the long axis oriented north to south. The west wall had blown in, causing the roof to collapse. A well-used trail, easily capable of supporting vehicles, led to the south.

Bear flight still had five more minutes of play time, so Lead asked permission for one strafing pass each before heading home. I wasn't keen about the request because, to be effective on a strafe pass, the fighters had to press in to a fairly low altitude. The target didn't seem worth it, but I was still too green to have the good sense to tell them no. Lead had made the suggestion, so what the hell.

With reservations, I cleared them in. The big F-105s

sprayed the Trail with withering 20mm cannon fire, the impact of which created thousands of bright sparkles as the rounds exploded on the target.

After Bear flight departed for their base in Thailand, I eased out over the Xe Kong River to relax for a few minutes before continuing with my reconnaissance. With the sun teetering just above the horizon, I would have to move quickly to get a look at one more possible target before darkness set in. As I glanced out at the right engine, something unusual caught my eye. Three feet outboard of the engine in the leading edge of the wing, I saw what appeared to be a black spot about the size of a silver dollar. I banked around to the west to get a little sunlight on the wing, and sure enough, the black spot turned out to be a very real bullet hole. Funny, I had never heard it or felt anything when it hit. Then, in a panic, I thought about the fuel tanks in the wing. A quick check of the gauge showed no fuel loss. Thankfully, I remembered that the tanks were self-sealing. As I stared helplessly out at the wing, it occurred to me that if there was one hole, there could be another.

Being strapped into an ejection seat definitely limits a pilot's options for checking over the exterior of his aircraft. I twisted and turned in my seat as much as possible, then manipulated the mirror in an attempt to search back along the booms and tail. Something didn't look right on the top of the wing. Using the electric motor to run the seat up to its full height, I ended up pinning myself against the top of the canopy. From that contorted position I had a clear view, and it wasn't pretty. In the center of the wing, I could make out a jagged hole about three feet in diameter. Sharp metal pieces stuck up into the wind stream, indicating the skin had been blown out rather than pushed in. Since the fuel tanks seemed okay, my major concern was damage to the main wing spar, the long piece of beam that held the wing to the fuselage. If that baby buckled, the only choice was a long step over the side.

My first instinct drew me toward home plate at Da Nang, but one look at the line of thunderstorms blocking my flight path convinced me that a divert to Thailand was the smart decision. In the rapidly approaching darkness, my chances of finding another miracle corridor through the storms were slim. Then there was the small matter of bouncing my way through severe turbulence with a structurally unsound wing. I called Hillsboro and told them of my decision to divert.

I then tuned in channel 93 on my TACAN and received a good azimuth and a distance of ninety miles to Ubon Air Base. At sixty miles I called Ubon's GCI site. "Lion, Covey 221 on primary uniform, over."

"Covey 221, Lion. Squawk two-one-zero-zero ident and say your altitude." Without having to look, I reached to my right and momentarily hit the toggle switch on the transponder, a black box of electronic magic that sent encoded signals to the radar controller's screen at Ubon. "Lion, I'm at six point five requesting radar vectors to a straight-in approach to Runway 23. Be advised I've got battle damage and am declaring an emergency. Just to be on the safe side, I'd like to keep any maneuvering to an absolute minimum."

"Copy your emergency, Covey 221. Radar contact on the zero-nine-five degree radial for fifty-two miles. Say your fuel, souls on board, and nature of your difficulty."

"I've got nine hundred pounds of fuel, one soul on board. I've got battle damage and possible severe structural damage to the right wing."

Actually, I didn't want to panic myself into believing the situation was all that threatening. After all, the wing had held up even after some fancy high-G maneuvering. Still, by declaring the emergency, I'd get priority handling over other traffic. I just wanted to get myself and aircraft 693 on the ground in one piece. Lion asked a few more questions and at thirty miles turned me over to Ubon Approach Control. The night weather was good but hazy, so I didn't pick up the runway lights until five or six miles out on final. In spite of approach control's offer of a GCA, I opted for a visual straight-in. I was tired and didn't feel up to flying precise instruments.

At two miles out, I knew the landing would be a piece of

cake. The only distraction was that every fire engine and crash wagon on the base seemed to be positioned along the edge of the runway. They were there to assist if I had trouble and for that I was grateful, but to look down into the darkness at all those flashing red lights was unnerving as hell. I almost wished the crash crews didn't seem quite so eager.

I touched down on centerline five hundred feet down the runway and rolled out to the midfield taxiway—with all the fire trucks chasing along beside me. I felt almost guilty about disappointing them. After clearing the runway, I sat patiently through the drill while the de-arming crew put large safety pins attached to red streamers into each rocket pod, a precaution intended to prevent an inadvertent firing into the heavily populated base. Then a truck with a flashing yellow "Follow Me" sign led me to a parking spot in front of the control tower.

I felt stiff and exhausted sitting in the cockpit, and it was great to stretch and move around once I climbed out. Before I had time to collect my thoughts, a colonel, a lieutenant colonel, and two majors, all dressed in 1505 tan uniforms, tried to hustle me over to the TOC, the tactical operations center. Pulling away from them, I grabbed a big flashlight from one crew chief and jumped up on the ladder with the line chief, who was already up on the aircraft sticking his head and shoulders into the ugly rip in the top of my wing. He gave a low, mournful whistle as he backed gingerly out of the hole. Shaking his head and pointing at the jagged mess, he drawled, "Lieutenant, I sure as hell hope they don't make you pay for this. Your wallet could be light for the next twenty years." As I sat there on the wing wondering if the line chief knew something that I didn't, someone from flying safety climbed up the ladder with a caliper and began measuring the hole in the leading edge. I wasn't at all surprised when it turned out to be a perfect fit for a 23mm round.

Reluctantly, I climbed down from the wing and followed the four impatient officers into the TOC, where everyone on base had some form or another for me to fill out—intel report, battle damage report, incident report, air traffic control report, maintenance report. It was a glorious day for the bureaucracy. Just when there seemed to be a light at the end of the administrative tunnel, a lieutenant colonel with knife-edge creases in his 1505s lowered the boom on me. Leaning forward with both hands on the table where I sat, he started lecturing: "You know, the only way you could have taken a hit like that was to be down in the weeds trolling. I don't know what kind of rules exist in your squadron, but around here we observe certain minimum altitudes which, incidently, go a long way toward preventing what I've seen here tonight."

Deja vu. Could this guy be related to Mike, my antagonist back at Da Nang? He sure had the same arrogant, self-righteous, confrontational style. I frowned, trying to make some sense out of his ridiculous accusation. My first response was rage. Then I glanced up at a couple of F-4 jocks leaning against the far wall. They just smiled and rolled their eyes. With their unspoken support, I mellowed. Lieutenant Colonel Knife-Crease was probably just a harmless "wing weenie" who had forgotten or had no idea that a 23mm's maximum effective range was over fifteen thousand feet. To hide my disgust, I laughed and asked the colonel to call Bear Lead over at Korat for confirmation that I had simply been doing my job. On that note I got up, grabbed his hand, and shook it like he was an old buddy, then stomped out the door to shouts of "Wait a minute, I'm not finished yet."

My troubles weren't over. I dropped into the officers' club to grab a hamburger only to encounter the reverse of the money situation I'd run up against at Cam Ranh. My MPC scrip wasn't negotiable at Ubon—only good old American "green" was acceptable. I had about had it with administrative hassle when I literally ran into an old friend of mine from Hurlburt. Vern loaned me some real money and even found me an empty bunk to sleep in. One cheeseburger and two beers later, the world seemed a lot brighter. Vern and I were at the bar on our second scotch when the assistant club manager walked up. "There's a phone call for you. Some colonel over at the TOC needs to talk to you about some battle damage.''

We chugged our drinks and stood up. I asked Vern, "Is there a place I can hide out?" He nodded yes as we bolted for the side entrance. I yelled back to the manager, "Tell him I said to get screwed." Howling with laughter, we stumbled out the door and headed for the "Night Owl" Squadron party hooch to continue the festivities.

Late the next afternoon, a Covey O-2 flew in to take me back to Da Nang. The crew kindly brought along a spare parachute, buckled me into it, and crammed me into a back seat not meant to be occupied by man or beast. Once we were airborne, the ride east wasn't too bad, even though my knees were directly under my chin. My cordial pilot appeared unconcerned as he punched through the heavy line of afternoon thunderstorms near the fence. The turbulence slammed us around but only lasted a few minutes. Watching him maneuver between the cells, I wondered how my wounded OV-10 would have stood up under a similar pounding.

On short final approach at Da Nang, the pilot turned the controls over to his navigator, who did a decent job landing from the right seat. The nav flared just a little high and dropped us in with a thunk, but it was good to be back home in anybody's airplane with any kind of landing. As we taxied into the revetments, I stared at the empty spot where 693 normally parked. The regular crew chief, a young airman named Bennie, stood forlornly in the vacant revetment, arms folded across his chest. As I climbed out of my cramped seat in the O-2, he loped across the ramp with easy athletic strides. Bennie had been a star basketball player at McClymonds High School in Oakland with aspirations for a college scholarship. Unfortunately, everybody thought Bennie was too short for even the collegiate ranks.

Eyes squinting in the sunlight, he asked, "Lieutenant, are you okay? We got worried when you didn't show up last night."

"I'm fine, Bennie. Sorry about messing up your airplane." Bennie's face tightened with concern.

"How bad was it?" I told him about the dud 23mm round cracking the spar in half then ricocheting out the top of the wing. Bennie looked away for a second, his mind's eye contemplating every detail of the damage. He looked back at me, then his expression eased into a broad smile. He shook my hand and said, "How that wing stayed on I'll never know. You must be one lucky dude! And we'll get my bird back in no time." He was right that I was lucky, wrong about the plane. Neither of us could know it would be another eight months before 693 was repaired and back in the war.

JUNE

X-Ray Mission: Laos

In a war with no front lines, American soldiers, sailors, and airmen had no place to hide. Even the rear-echelon troops might come under sniper fire or rocket attack at any moment. Ever since the Tet offensive two-and-one-half years earlier, everybody serving in South Vietnam knew the score. Although the government boasted about secure areas, we knew differently. "Charlie" had the capability to swing into small-unit action at will. Since we couldn't hide, the next best thing was to forget. And one way to forget involved a change of scenery. Thanks to the foresight of some anonymous morale and recreation officer, Vietnam offered the American soldier in-country R and R, and one of the favorite R-and-R spots turned out to be Da Nang's own China Beach.

On June 3 I flew the early go and returned to the Covey hooch by 11:30. One of the advantages of flying a dawn patrol mission was having the rest of the day off. It was a beautiful day, so rather than sit around, four of us struck out for an afternoon at China Beach. The logistics of getting there became half the fun. Since all the Covey M-151 Jeeps were in use, we decided to hitchhike.

The main road between the air base and the beach bustled with the heavy traffic normally found in a large city. The difference was that virtually every vehicle here was U.S. military. A bewildering assortment of trucks, buses, jeeps, and carryalls bounced along at a steady clip from sunrise to sunset; with darkness came curfew, effectively eliminating all movement except for military police jeeps or an occasional truck convoy. Sharing the road during the day with the heavier motorized traffic, a steady stream of pedestrians and motor-bike riders snaked along in the oppressive heat. Many of the hikers were GIs hoping to hitch a ride with a buddy or some member of their outfit. As the four of us trekked along beside the busy road, almost all the troops immediately in front of us and behind us got rides in a matter of minutes. Evidently four pilots in flight suits with towels and swim trunks under their arms didn't evoke sympathy from the drivers of the passing vehicles. Finally a three-quarter-ton carryall with a young marine lance corporal at the wheel pulled up. In a loud, confident voice, he shouted, "Good afternoon, Sir. May I interest you in a ride, Sir?"

As we walked up to the front door, our marine's stiff manner gave way to a slightly more casual attitude. His right hand was on the wheel, his left arm draped comfortably out the open window. Something in the expression on his old-young face left no doubt that everything was negotiable. We eyed each other cautiously for a few seconds; then I asked, "What's the deal?" His face took on a pained look, then he broke into a wide smile.

"That depends on where you're going. If I had to guess, I'd say China Beach. Me, I got no time to go swimming, but something to drink would hit the spot. Sure is hot out here, isn't it, Sir? Only I'm not old enough to buy myself what I had in mind."

With that revelation, we knew where the conversation was going. Everything in Vietnam was rationed—booze, cigarettes, stereo equipment. Each of us had a ration card entitling the bearer to limited purchases in each category, the whole exercise designed to curb the thriving black market. The kicker was that underage enlisted troops weren't allowed to buy booze anyway.

The lance corporal sensed we understood his dilemma. "Here's the deal," he said in a low voice, his eyes darting around like those of a con artist making a back-room deal in a scene from a B movie. "We stop at the Class Six store. One of you gentlemen gets me a bottle of Southern Comfort with your ration card. Then I'll take you all the way to China Beach. Okay?"

Thirty minutes later, we piled out of the carryall at the front door of the beach snack bar. We sent our happy driver on his way with a promise not to open the bottle until he was back in his company area.

China Beach was no Waikiki, but it had possibilities. The beach itself was relatively narrow, with lots of small-grained white sand. On that particular day, overcrowding was no problem: there were only about twenty of us as far as the eye could see. The height of the surf surprised me, although the big waves didn't break until almost at water's edge. The only reminders of the war zone were the multiple strands of concertina wire blocking either end of the designated swimming area and the steady procession of low-flying Huey helicopters scoping out the beach for Air Force and Army nurses who might be sunbathing. When the Hueys came in on their low-level reconnaissance runs, the rotor wash whipped the sand around like a Sahara duststorm. Still, the beach was a great place to relax, a reminder of calmer, simpler times.

Even though my morning mission over the Trail had been relatively quiet, I felt tired and drained. It was a relief to sprawl in the warm sand, put my mind on hold, and soak up the rays. I wasn't the only one who was dragging. All of us had been shortchanged on sleep the night before. At about 2:30 in the morning, the VC had treated me to my first rocket attack.

I sat bolt upright as soon as the first piercing siren wail sounded over the compound speaker system. Within five seconds I heard the dull but loud "kah-woomp, kah-woomp" as the first of two 122mm rockets exploded somewhere on the west side of the airfield. It probably would have been a good idea to take cover, but climbing out of my top bunk seemed like too much trouble. I'd never experienced a rocket attack before, and my idea of how to react wasn't firmly established. When the rockets hit, a few guys swaggered around for the macho effect. A few others went to the opposite extreme, grabbing flak vest and helmet and diving under the nearest bunk. Both types were genuinely frightened; they just showed it in different ways. The majority of the Coveys acted indifferent or curious. The story going around was that the bad guys firing from the hills west of Da Nang couldn't aim at specific targets, they just pointed their rockets and hoped for the best. Their chances of scoring a direct hit on me seemed pitifully small, so I lay back in my top bunk and wondered why I was hearing two distinct sounds when each rocket exploded. In the midst of the noise and confusion, the security police came on the PA system and announced, "Condition Red. Da Nang is under attack." The voice repeated the warning over and over, long after the last rocket blew up.

Judging from the number of people running around in the hallway, few others had taken cover either. Finally I jumped out of bed and looked down the hall. At a small open stairwell at the far end, a crowd of wide-awake Coveys filled the doorway, half of them with cameras taking pictures of the fires burning across the runway. The scene reminded me more of a circus than a war. The animated group finally dispersed when the PA system announced the all-clear. By then it was after 3 A.M., and since I had to get up at 4:30 anyway, I pulled out a trashy novel to kill the time before my mission.

Stretched out on the hot sand of China Beach, I forced myself to block out any more thoughts of rocket attacks and missions over the Ho Chi Minh Trail. Before we started back to the barracks late that afternoon, I managed to finish the trashy novel, take a couple of refreshing dips in the ocean, and down a few beers with my fellow pilots.

There was a price to pay for the few hours of relaxation at China Beach. The next morning, as I flew down the Trail searching for trucks, the harness and straps holding me tightly in the ejection seat cut painfully into my sunburned shoulders. The Air Force nurses had been kind enough to donate some Noxzema to the cause, but it really didn't help, even though I'd smeared on a whole jar of the stuff. The body heat from my sunburn matched the heat in the cockpit, making me doubly miserable. During the past month, I had just about acclimated myself to the steam-bath flight conditions in my OV-10. It reminded me of sitting inside a hot car with all the windows rolled up, or worse yet, sitting inside a greenhouse—with the canopy rail at hip level and Plexiglas everywhere above that. The design was intended to provide the FAC with great visibility, and North American, the OV-10 manufacturer, had done a super job in that department. But they had forgotten an air-conditioning system. The aeronautical engineers were thoughtful enough to install an air scoop, which allowed outside air to flow into the cockpit, but when the temperature routinely exceeded one hundred degrees, the ram air blowing in felt like it came from a blast furnace. During the hottest months of the year, the flight surgeons claimed that on a four-hour mission OV-10 pilots lost between three and four pounds, mostly due to dehydration. There were plenty of days I thought that estimate was too conservative.

I couldn't allow myself to get distracted by my discomfort and by the hot air blowing into the cockpit, because the Trail below demanded all the concentration I could give it. At first glance the roads and paths always looked the same. The twists and turns in the road network, the lush vegetation, the jungle-covered mountains and ridges—they never changed. The area over which we flew covered hundreds of square miles filled with detail that boggled the mind. Learning all that detail was an ongoing process, based on experience and exposure. It was like studying a snapshot, day after day. And that routine sameness, the very quality the bad guys had hoped would hide them from our twenty-four-hour-a-day search, eventually became an advantage. Constantly flying over the same terrain, we came to memorize every detail so that when even the smallest particular appeared out of place, mental alarm bells sounded. Clues jumped out like neon signs: a different shade of dust on the foliage beside the Trail; freshly cut trees; a set of tracks that wasn't there yesterday; a muddy spot in a pool of water—anything that didn't exactly match the mental snapshot. The hard part came in figuring out where to start, how to let the mind's eye drink in the whole scene and then pick up the changes. The process wasn't unlike looking for the proverbial needle in the haystack. Rarely was anything out of place. Sometimes we'd fly for days without ever seeing so much as a twig pushed aside. On other days the targets we'd turn up were so blatant and bold it would roll your socks down.

Binoculars welded into my eye sockets, I continued flying down the Trail at a leisurely pace, power levers positioned to give nine hundred foot-pounds of torque per engine, producing 130 knots of airspeed. Glancing out the front windscreen, I could see Chavane up in front of me. For a few seconds, my thoughts drifted back to the late afternoon gunfight of a week earlier. That battle still seemed unreal, like it had happened to someone else. My right hand on the stick and feet on the rudder pedals both received the signal from my brain before I consciously noticed that my aircraft was tracking directly for the saddleback ridge where I'd let that gunner get the best of me. Whether professional interest or morbid curiosity, I had to take another look at the scene. If the gunner was still there, I was determined to put a rocket down his scrawny throat and blow his guts all over the ridge.

At the northern edge of Chavane's large meadow, a well-used dirt road branched off the main Trail and wound its way southeast toward the Vietnamese border. I had seen that particular segment of road a few times before, never giving it much attention since there was no cover on either side for several kilometers. As I passed overhead, my mental alarm bells went off. At first I could make out only what appeared to be a moving dust cloud. A closer look with the binoculars revealed four dudes dressed in khaki chugging along on black motorcycles. I'd never seen movement on the Trail before, much less people. Whatever they were up to, it had to be important to risk a run in broad daylight.

My heart pounding with excitement, I reefed the Bronco around in a high-G turn, the heavy burble letting me know we were right on the edge of an accelerated stall. When I rolled out, the line-up didn't look right, so I eased off the back pressure and continued with an aileron roll to the left to get the nose below the horizon and the wings relatively level. I still ended up tracking at a forty-five-degree angle to the road instead of flying directly down it as I wanted. By coming in at an angle, I introduced the lateral dimensions of right and left to the aiming solution. Had I taken a few more seconds to line up on the same axis as the road, I would have worried only about firing long or short.

As I continued the dive, my motorcycles realized I was after them and poured on the coals, making it tough to keep them in my gunsight. With what I hoped was the correct amount of lead, I popped off two willie petes and pulled up to reposition for a quick second shot. It's a good thing no one could hear me because I howled in genuine pain as the heavy G forces changed my weight from 165 pounds to something just over 675 pounds, stretching and pulling my sunburned skin in ways only a Spanish Inquisition torturer could appreciate. Nursing myself and the aircraft over the top of a loop, I watched as the two rockets exploded ten meters short of the road and abeam the last cycle. Everyone kept right on going, but the explosions must have shaken number four's concentration. As he sped after the serpentine procession in front of him, he took the only curve in the road a little too fast and skidded out in a magnificent cloud of red dust. Instead of stopping to help, his buddies raced around the curve and disappeared into the first tree line they came to. I broke off my pass and pulled around in a level turn to get the perfect line on the fallen cyclist. As I started the roll in, my target got up and pushed his machine about fifteen meters to a large, solitary tree just off the road at the very top of the curve.

From there the episode deteriorated into a scene from a Laurel and Hardy movie. Regardless of the direction I came in from, my quick-thinking target deftly put himself and his cycle on the opposite side of the large tree trunk. It was like playing a grown-up version of peek-a-boo. I actually began to respect that faceless, khaki-clad little man, scurrying ridiculously around the tree trunk. But after three aborted passes, I'd had enough. I climbed to five thousand feet and rolled into a vertical dive with the pipper superimposed on the top of the tree. I fired three rockets, then sucked in the Gs, all the while yelping in agony and wondering if this guy was worth it and why I was doing this to my sunburned body.

The first rocket hit short while the other two slammed into the top branches, creating a shower of searing, white-hot phosphorous. I circled slowly as the smoke cleared, half-hoping to see the NVA version of Evil Knievil running for the trees. Nothing. There was no discernible movement. The motorcycle lay at the base of the tree, but there was no sign of Evil. I suspected he might have climbed in the tree, and if that were the case, he was either hiding or fried to a crisp. Either way, it really torqued my jaws that the other three bad guys ran out on their buddy; to express my disgust at their cowardice, I blasted the tree line where they were hiding with a whole pod of willie petes. The results were questionable, but the sight of the explosions made me feel better.

From the large curve, I worked my way west, my interest piqued by the four motorcycles and where they might have been coming from and going to. Any thoughts of continuing south to revisit the saddleback had long since vanished. The open segment of trail below me obviously deserved more detailed scrutiny than I had given it. I combed every inch of it, but nothing out of the ordinary struck me until I returned to the fork on the main trail. Precisely at the V where the roads split, I spotted the most curious glass structure imaginable, so out of place it had to be a joke. What I saw made me start laughing, until I remembered the flak trap from an earlier training mission. Cautiously, but still smiling broadly, I made one low pass, then asked Hillsboro to send a fast-mover my way to confirm my strange target.

About an hour later, an F-100 fast FAC checked in with me. "Covey 221, this is Misty. Understand you've got a mystery target for me to look at. What's the form?"

A Misty FAC was the perfect guy to help me. They were famous throughout Southeast Asia as the crazy fighter jocks who flew modified FAC missions at low altitudes in high-threat areas.

Somewhat tentatively, I keyed the mike button. "Misty, Covey 221. I'm gonna talk you into this structure because I don't want to prejudice the case by telling you what I think it is. Right now I'm orbiting directly over Chavane. Have you got a tally on me?"

Misty replied, "I'm approaching the area now. Rock your wings or give me some smoke if you've got it."

My sunburn made it too painful to jerk the airplane around more than necessary. Reaching up above my head, I hit the smoke generator toggle switch, a handy little gadget that pumped oil into the left engine exhaust, creating a trail of white smoke just like the Thunderbirds used. Within seconds Misty had a visual on me.

"Okay, Misty. See that stretch of road on the north edge of Chavane? Follow it west about three klicks to where it intersects the main north–south trail. That intersection forms a V pointing roughly west. Look right into the V, not more than ten feet off the road, and tell me what you see. I'll stay at fifty-five hundred over Chavane."

Misty arced around to the east, then rolled in to begin his low-level run along the road. As the F-100 streaked by the target, the swept-wing fighter appeared to be low enough to drop the landing gear for a touch-and-go. The pilot gave new meaning to the concept of flying down in the weeds.

Misty executed a hard pull up to the north without saying a word. Since I knew he'd seen the target, it was impossible to keep my curiosity in check. "Misty, Covey 221. You saw it, didn't you? I saw the same thing, so just blurt it right out."

A long pause filled the air before Misty answered me. "Covey, nobody's gonna believe this except you and me. I got a real good look at your target. Either I'm stone blind or that thing is an honest-to-god Bell telephone booth. The door was wide open, and I'll bet there was change in the coin return. Is that what you thought it was?"

"That's affirmative. You don't suppose the truck drivers call back home to Hanoi to talk to their wives on it, do you?"

Misty mulled my question over for a few seconds, then

answered, "If they do, I hope a strange man answers or else the bastards get a busy signal."

Back at Da Nang during my debriefing, the intel officer was beside himself with glee. Never mind trucks, motorcycles, or guns—he wanted to know about the phone booth. He quizzed me for thirty minutes about size, markings, colors, visible wires, and exact map coordinates. As the debriefing wore on, I started to get a little impatient, but it was hard to get upset with the intel types for being as curious as I had been. The phone booth caper proved to be a good change of pace for all of us.

Two days and three VC rockets attacks later, the head Covey left word that he wanted to see me. Standing in the open door, I could see Lieutenant Colonel Ed Cullivan sitting at his desk, poring over a stack of paperwork. A fighter jock from way back, the good colonel had a ready smile and a gleam in his eye that told the world he had a genuine zest for living. Ed was of medium height with a slender build and had a head of black hair laced with gray, giving him a classic Cary Grant salt-and-pepper look. Much to the chagrin of all us young studs, the Da Nang nurses considered Ed the ultimate heartthrob. But more important, Ed Cullivan was a first-rate combat leader who knew how to get the most out of his young pilots without smothering them with too much supervision and needless bureaucratic rules.

Colonel Cullivan looked up from his work and motioned me into the small office, which he shared with his operations officer. "Tom," he asked, "have you ever heard of the X-Ray mission?" Before I could answer, he continued. "I want you to take a crack at it. You're still a little green, but you seem to have a knack for flying yourself out of tight spots, and that's what this mission calls for. I want you to get together with Mike McGerty. He'll be in charge of your checkout."

A few hours later, Mike filled me in on the X-Ray mission. Roughly once a month, each of the four Coveys involved took turns staging out of Ubon, Thailand, for three days. The drill involved picking up a Laotian back-seater known as the X-Ray. These back-seaters were villagers who had been recruited and trained by the American intelligence community. When one of the X-Rays got wind of or personally saw a lucrative Pathet Lao or NVA target in his area, he'd pass the word and arrange for a clandestine pickup by Air America, the CIA's private airline. The Coveys were never privy to the details, but just before our launch, the X-Ray showed up, ready to fly and eager to point out enemy troop concentrations, hidden supplies, and communication centers.

On my checkout ride, McGerty and I flew to Ubon to touch base with the intelligence officers who knew about the X-Ray program. After an hour of double-talk from them, we jumped back in the airplane for a leisurely look at our assigned area.

The area of operations, or AO, included the southern third of the Laotian panhandle, called Military Region IV. Laos was divided into four military regions: regions I and II were in the north, and III and IV were located in the panhandle. MR-IV was dominated geographically by the Bolovens Plateau, a huge piece of real estate sloping up from the Mekong River and east some seventy-five miles to the rugged cliffs overlooking the Xe Kong River near the Ho Chi Minh Trail. In between, the poorly led Royal Laotian Army responded sporadically to NVA and Pathet Lao efforts to infiltrate and occupy the entire plateau. Scattered throughout the Bolovens were a series of strongholds and dirt airstrips known as PS sites, which Americans had helped set up. As focal points for Air America and army activities, the PS sites acted as magnets, drawing repeated enemy attacks. As it turned out, most of our X-Ray missions were flown in support of Royal Lao troops deployed around various airstrips.

After Mike and I crossed the Mekong, we set up a lazy orbit over Pakse, the largest town in MR-IV. Pakse possessed a rich history and was absolutely vital to the defense of the region. The town's fascination for me had nothing to do with its native charm or location. Pakse served as regional headquarters for the Raven FACs, a small, elite group of U.S. Air

Force pilots stationed in Laos who posed as civilian employees for various government agencies associated with the State Department. Stories about the wild exploits of the Ravens had been leaking out for several years, so much so that their "cover" was certainly not a well-kept secret. According to rumors and word of mouth, they flew in anything but military uniforms. My less-than-authoritative sources told me standard garb consisted of Levis, cowboy boots, T-shirts, and dark sunglasses—spurs were optional. I had heard that Ravens did their FACing in the venerable O-1 Bird Dog but also checked out in the T-28 fighter bomber operated by the Royal Laotian Air Force. Supposedly Ravens took only volunteers who had at least six months of combat FAC experience, and then they took only the best of the lot. It was said that a history of family insanity helped, since the Ravens sustained an extremely high casualty rate—about 50 percent. In spite of the risk, the most appealing aspect was that Ravens could call their own shots, without any hassle from higher up. Just get the job done, whatever it took. To me that sounded too good to be true, and as I banked around Pakse, I made up my mind to set my sights on becoming a Raven.

From Pakse we headed east along Highway 23, circling occasionally so Mike could point out specific landmarks and trouble spots. We made a special effort to overfly each of the PS sites so I would become familiar with their location and general layout. Through breaks in the clouds, we caught glimpses of PS-39, with its partially paved runway and distinctive half-moon-shaped perimeter defense trench. Nearer the edge of the plateau, we had a good view of the desolate-looking PS-21, as well as PS-71, a triangular-shaped special forces 'A' camp with a small dirt airstrip alongside. The busiest strip by far appeared to be PS-38, a three-thousand-foot-long runway carved out of red dirt. At least a dozen buildings cluttered each side of the runway near midfield. While we circled, two short-takeoff-and-landing (STOL) Air America Pilatus Porters landed.

Finally we turned north for a short flight up to Saravane, the second-largest town in MR-IV. Saravane was on the western edge of the normal Covey AO, so I had seen it several other times. The situation there was particularly hot because NVA regulars virtually surrounded the town. Most people expected it to fall to the enemy at any moment. The airfield had already changed hands several times in as many days. One of our FACs reported seeing a 37mm gun sitting right in front of the flight operations building.

As we circled over the besieged town, Mike took the controls of the OV-10. He lowered the gear and flaps and turned on a base leg to the beat-up red-dirt runway. Until just before we touched, I figured Mike would do a low approach, but to my disbelief, he flared nicely and plunked us down onto the rough surface. Immediately he cobbed the power, and after a few bounces, we were airborne again. As we accelerated, I grabbed the landing gear handle and raised it, since the lever in the back seat could be used only to lower the gear. I recall looking out the left side at small clusters of people standing beside the runway. They just stood there, as if frozen in time, almost oblivious to one of the greatest daredevil stunts since Bernie Fischer landed his A-1 in the A Shau Valley to rescue a downed pilot. I couldn't believe it. We'd just executed a touch-and-go landing deep in Laos on a dirt airstrip about to be overrun by the whole North Vietnamese Army! I'm not sure what I expected from our unconcerned audience on either side of the runway, but a few cheers or a standing ovation would have been nice.

What I'd just sat through was probably one of the most stupid, show-your-fanny acts imaginable, but up to that point, it was the most exhilarating event of my short combat career. My aimless chatter to my back-seater reflected my feelings. "Mike, you crazy doofus! That was great! It was wild. I can't believe you did that. Just look at those lumps of coal standing down there. They don't even appreciate what you just pulled off!"

Mike responded in measured tones. "It wasn't that big a deal. Nobody's impressed except you 'cause they've seen it a hundred times. Hell, half the Coveys have shot a touch-and-go at Saravane and the other half will. Just don't blab this around when we get home.''

My euphoria began wearing off quickly at being told the stunt at Saravane was old hat. Still, the episode made for an interesting war story.

Cruising back over the Bolovens, I felt no sense of apprehension or foreboding as I did over the Ho Chi Minh Trail. The area was crawling with bad guys, but the scene below looked peaceful—just mile after mile of rolling hills covered with lush green rain forests. We'd occasionally come across a sleepy village or a road leading off to nowhere, but for the most part the countryside seemed untouched. Without the threat of the triple-A guns that harassed us out on the Trail, we could enjoy the luxury of flying low enough to see detail without using binoculars.

After our day of exploring, Mike and I landed back at Da Nang late in the afternoon. We'd covered a lot of ground and seen all the PS sitcs, including that closeup look at the airfield at Saravane. As Mike debriefed the ride, I couldn't help feeling dissatisfied. The checkout had generated more serious questions than answers. I was genuinely excited about the prospect of working with troops in contact, yet everything about the X-Ray mission seemed so slipshod and piecemeal. Nobody bothered to describe the tactical situation, unit locations, troop dispositions, ground-fire threat, enemy order of battle, or any of the other details that seemed essential to understanding the "big picture." It seemed like the intel types and "spooks" over at Ubon wanted us to know only the barest details, and woe be to anybody who was unpatriotic enough to ask a question. After thinking about X-Ray for a while, I concluded that the operation was more of a diversionary adventure for the pilots than a bona fide mission. Although the program had the potential for great fun, it was really a FUBAR (fouled up beyond all recognition) affair with lots of room for unpredictable results. Later that same evening, a bunch of us were given a dramatic lesson in how FUBAR our own Covey mission could be.

The night started innocently enough. Six of us were sitting in the officers' club bar, playing "hi-lo" for drinks. The game was ridiculously simple. The instigator produced an MPC or dollar bill and silently picked two consecutive numbers from the bill's serial number. In turn each player guessed a number, the instigator advising whether the choice was above (high) or below (low) his secret number. Each guess generated a new high-low, quickly narrowing the range to just a few numbers. At some point an unlucky soul inadvertently "guessed" the secret number and had to buy a round of drinks for everyone at the table.

While we sat there playing, one of our new young lieutenants took off with an IP on his phase I night training mission. The IP flew his student to a strip on the beach called Marble Mountain for some touch-and-go landings. For some reason the control tower cleared the OV-10 for the landing, but never mentioned a trench that had been dug across the runway. The eager student touched down on the dark strip and pushed up the power for takeoff. At the last second, he saw the three-foot-high dirt mound and reacted by jerking the Bronco into the air, avoiding what could have been a fiery crash. Unfortunately, the right main landing gear clipped the mound, bending back into a contorted position.

With the right main hanging limply, there was no way to retract the landing gear. The IP had two choices: eject or try for a crash landing back at Da Nang. It was a tough choice. Ejection might have been easier, but the plane would be lost, and there were no absolute guarantees on the "nylon elevator." Landing required a precise maneuver involving touching down on the left wheel and holding that position for as long as possible, while hoping like hell the aircraft didn't ground-loop or cartwheel into a giant fireball. Pulling off such a feat in broad daylight was tough enough. To do it at night was risky and enough to water a grown man's eyes—not to mention stain the seat of his shorts brown.

After talking it over, the rookie flyer and the IP elected to land at Da Nang. With a beautiful bit of flying, they put the bird down on the left side of the runway and held the right wing up until just before it lost all lift. Then they gently lowered the right main onto the concrete. Predictably, the gear collapsed, causing the OV-10 to veer sharply to the right and off the runway. The aircraft finally came to a halt some six hundred feet into the grassy surface between the left and right runways. Both pilots hopped out unhurt, obviously ecstatic that the ordeal was over. Unknown to the two Coveys, the episode had a tragic ending.

When he heard about a pending emergency landing, an airman on the approach end barrier crew walked out to the edge of the runway to watch the drama firsthand. As the OV-10 left the runway and skidded through the darkness, the right wing hit the unsuspecting airman, killing him instantly. The pilots' momentary jubilation at surviving the crash turned to instant horror and grief. That he was totally blameless did not console the new Covey pilot. A good man had died needlessly, the victim of an incredible series of flukes and screwups. Ironically, damage to the aircraft was minimal.

In the week following my initial X-Ray ride, flying time grew scarce. The southwest monsoon, so-called because of the prevailing winds, generated the first sustained stretch of nasty weather over the Trail. With all the rain and low clouds, picking out trucks became virtually impossible. Most of the Covey missions were canceled because of the weather before they could even launch. The situation was particularly frustrating because the weather was great on the Vietnamese side of the mountains. In a cycle probably as old as time itself, the weather pattern would continue until October, when the wind shifted to the northeast, bringing rain to Vietnam and drying sunshine to Laos.

The weather-inflicted inactivity made for some interesting studies in human nature. The officers' club bar seemed to do a better business than normal, and tempers grew short. Watching the grounded Coveys was like watching a group of highly trained athletes poised to play the big game, only to be told of another rain delay. It was tough to stay psyched up. When we did get airborne, there were either no targets or no fighters available. Our intel officer told us that the NVA used the weather to their advantage, moving heavy concentrations of men and supplies down the Ho Chi Minh Trail under the protective cloud cover. Within weeks the Trail would become a quagmire of mud, slowing the flow dramatically. In the meantime the North Vietnamese logistics network would continue to operate, in spite of our sophisticated technology. Over multiple scotch-and-waters, we concluded that the NVA bastards were thumbing their noses at us.

Finally, on June 18, the weather broke. I packed some underwear and a clean flight suit and launched to Ubon to fly my first X-Ray mission. En route, I was pleasantly surprised by the relatively good weather over the Bolovens—lots of holes in the clouds, big enough to work fighters through.

After landing at Ubon and bedding down my aircraft for the night, I wandered over to the officers' club bar, stopping long enough to cash a check. Armed with a handful of U.S. dollars and a cold beer, I studied the layout. Physically the building wasn't much larger than the Da Nang club, but the similarity ended there. Even in midafternoon the place seemed busy, with about half the dining tables filled and a good-size crowd at the bar. The dining room looked bright and cheerful, just like any nice club back in the States, and the little Thai waitresses were cute as buttons and quite friendly. By comparison, the Da Nang club resembled a big old barn, usually deserted unless a USO show blew into town. Our Vietnamese waitresses were as surly as they were ugly and seemed to take great delight in waiting until we selected something from the limited menu before cackling, "No hab."

Looking around the bar, I felt conspicuous in my faded green flight suit. Virtually all the other pilots in the place wore custom-made work suits, resembling flight suits but neatly tailored in assorted colors—dark green, gray, black, and several shades of blue. Evidently each squadron had its own version. I felt like a hillbilly in the big city.

Eventually, several friends drifted in, introduced me to their friends, and we ended up passing a pleasant evening sipping Sing Ha beer and trading war stories about our experiences in Thailand and Vietnam. Most of the people gathered around the table were young fighter jocks assigned to the 8th Tac Fighter Wing, known throughout the Air Force as the "Wolfpack." To a man they all sang the same tune, bemoaning their fate as F-4 GIBs, "guys in back." Because of a shortage of navigators, the young pilots found themselves flying in the back seat as copilots and weapons system operators behind more experienced front-seaters. Much to my surprise, many of them seemed genuinely envious of my adventures and responsibilities as a FAC.

At fifteen minutes before midnight, I ordered a half a dozen bottles of Champagne, made everybody swear not to drink them until I returned, then skipped out the side door to a nearby hooch where I was bunking. At precisely midnight I returned to the noisy table, only this time I was wearing my clean flight suit—with brand new captain bars. When I announced that the lieutenants at the table had better show a little more respect, they unceremoniously hosed me with my own Champagne.

By half past nine the next morning, I had completed the preflight and was killing time waiting for my X-Ray. At ten o'clock a white Toyota pickup glided to a stop beside me and deposited a small Oriental man carrying a helmet and a brown paper bag.

The little man walked up to me, carefully set his helmet and bag on the ground, then put both hands together as if to pray. He bowed slightly at the waist, placing his hands directly in front of his face in the traditional Thai greeting known as the *wai*. Somewhat awkwardly I returned the greeting. He smiled broadly at my bungling effort, then grabbed my hand and shook it. With a heavy, lilting accent he addressed me: "Sah wah dee, Kup. My Thai name Prasert. Today you be pilot, I be X-Ray. How you say your name?" We went through several tortuous attempts at Yarborough before he settled on "Captain Tom." It had a nice ring to it.

Prasert stood about five feet six inches tall, typically slender with jet black hair and deep brown eyes with no discernible pupils. He wore gray slacks, a white open-collar short-sleeve shirt, and jungle boots. He had a pair of Air

Force flying gloves stuffed in his back pocket. Prasert told me he was Thai by birth but had lived around Paksong, in Laos, for most of his adult life. I kept hoping he'd get around to discussing our mission because I had no clear idea of what we were supposed to do. Instead, we just stood there eyeing each other warily, wondering if the other was competent and what this day would bring.

Trying not to seem completely ignorant, I said lightheartedly, "Nice weather today. Hope you've got some good targets for us."

As if to signal he was ready to go, Prasert picked up his helmet and brown bag, then answered, "Plenty targets. I show you supplies we bomb. Maybe first we go talk to PS sites." It wasn't much of a clue, but at least it was something.

Clutching his brown bag tightly, Prasert deftly climbed into the back seat while I helped him strap in. I reviewed the radio wafer switch and a few emergency procedures, then climbed into the front seat. As I ran through the checklist, it occurred to me that only God, Buddha, and Prasert had any idea what was going on—and none of them was talking to me.

After engine start we taxied out toward the arming area. My curiosity finally getting the best of me, I asked Prasert what was in the brown bag. He answered innocently, "*Kin cow*—rice, my lunch." I smiled to myself at his simple explanation. What a letdown. I had been convinced he had something weird in that bag, maybe a shrunken head or some other exotic charm.

After the arming crew pulled the last of the safety pins, the tower cleared me onto Runway 05. With a quick peek at final to make sure the coast was clear, I pulled into position on the upwind side of the runway. Through the windscreen I surveyed the full nine thousand feet of concrete in front of me, focusing on a spot about three thousand feet away where we should theoretically break ground and become airborne. In the few seconds before takeoff clearance, I took a close look at the runway around me. Heavy black skid marks from hundreds of F-4 landings coated the surface. Although I couldn't see it from my position, the other end of the runway shared the same black color. By contrast the seven thousand feet of runway in between appeared at least three shades lighter.

Even before the tower controller could finish saying my call sign, I pumped the brakes and pushed both power levers forward. As the Bronco strained at full power, I quickly checked the engine instruments to confirm they were in the green. Through my earphones I heard, "Covey 221, squawk zero-three-zero-zero normal. Contact Ubon Departure when airborne. Wind calm, cleared for takeoff."

"Covey 221, rolling."

At brake release we lurched forward and accelerated slowly. The OV-10's counterrotating props virtually eliminated the torque that normally pulled an aircraft one way or another, and the two large rudders made directional control easy even at very low speeds. At just over one hundred knots, I eased in aft stick and we were airborne with a thunk, as the main gear struts bottomed out at lift-off.

Climbing eastbound out of Ubon, Prasert and I headed for the Mekong River, the border between Thailand and Laos. Peace on one side, war on the other. Passing overhead at Pakse, we looked down into the half-mile-wide river, floating debris clearly visible in the churning reddish brown water. Some of those floating logs and branches probably started their journey at the Mekong's origin, high in the mountains of China.

From Pakse Prasert asked me to fly over each of the PS sites, beginning with PS-39. En route, the weather turned reasonably good with scattered to broken low scud hanging over most of the Bolovens Plateau. Through breaks in the clouds, we could see large patches of green jungle.

At PS-39 Prasert took charge of the FM radio and contacted the small secret airfield. A friendly American voice answered, and within seconds the conversation deteriorated into an old-home-week chat. Prasert addressed the voice on the ground as "Dunc," whom I assumed to be either an Air America pilot or some sort of intelligence operative. Dunc and Prasert exchanged greetings and asked about each other's family, friends, and health for at least five minutes. At the first lull in the conversation, I butted in. "Dunc, this is Covey 221. Sorry to interrupt, but what's your tactical situation? Is there anything we can do to help you out?"

Responding in a somewhat icy tone, Dunc answered, "Negative, Covey. Prasert and I have everything under control here. There's a Raven in the area looking after us. You might try the boys over at PS-38. Things are pretty active down there. Now can you put Prasert back on?"

Miffed by the snub, I replied, "Sorry, Dunc. We're on a tight schedule. We'll swing by later to see how you're doing." Rather than answer directly, Dunc simply clicked his mike button twice, and that was the end of it. Or so I thought.

As we continued to cruise east, Prasert had little to say, obviously pouting over the episode at PS-39. I felt bad about spoiling the party; he and Dunc were clearly old friends and had probably been through a lot together. On the other hand, I felt like wringing his neck for using me as his personal limo driver. The airborne social call was new to me and seemed particularly out of place in view of the war raging around us, but the visits evidently meant a lot to Prasert, so I cautiously offered him a compromise. We agreed to check each site to determine the situation, then press on if they didn't need our help. In return I promised to fly back over the sites and, gas permitting, let Prasert shoot the bull to his heart's content.

After brief conversations with Art and Bill at PS-21 and PS-71 respectively, we checked in with Dev at PS-38. For the first time that day, I gained a little insight into the ground situation. Dev told us that their "Sierra was weak." Pathet Lao troops had dug in roughly four klicks east of the field and an 82mm mortar position directly off the end of the runway was really getting on their nerves. Whenever a Porter or a Huey tried to land, the mortar usually opened up. The incoming rounds rarely hit the buildings or the people, but more than a few explosions cratered the runway, the lifeline for the whole setup. Dev expected a full-scale assault in the next few days and didn't sound optimistic about the Royal Laotian Army's ability to repulse the attack. On that happy note Dev signed off, asking us to swing by in an hour when a Porter was due to land. He hoped having a FAC overhead would make the mortar crew think twice before firing.

I hated to leave the area. If Dev was right, a good fight was brewing, and selfish as it seemed, I wanted to be part of it. After a month of flying over the Trail, I felt confident in my ability to handle air strikes. But troops on the ground raised the stakes considerably. It's what I'd dreamed about and been trained for. As Prasert and I flew off to the west, a tinge of guilt colored my thoughts. I badly wanted to work troops in contact, a classic TIC. I wanted it bad. I couldn't exactly bring myself to wish a fight on Dev or the defending troops, but if a firefight came, I desperately wanted to be there to help—and perhaps to make a difference.

Just west of Paksong, my back-seater guided me to a small village several miles south of Route 23. When we first flew over the cluster of about thirty hooches, we saw a number of people milling around. On our second orbit, the place looked deserted. I could only guess that they knew what was coming.

Approximately a thousand meters south of the village, a narrow tree line formed the boundary between two large, open fields. Prasert told me that Pathet Lao troops had stacked a cache of supplies at the T intersection where the tree line joined a section of jungle. Although I saw nothing suspicious through the binoculars, there was no reason to doubt Prasert's claim. After all, it was his home turf, and pointing out the bad guys was what he was paid to do. After plotting out the coordinates on my map, I got on the horn to Hillsboro, using the code words on which I'd been briefed.

"Hillsboro, Covey 221. I've got a Statehouse-nominated, X-Ray-validated target for you, over." The normal scarcity of fighters had conditioned me not to expect a positive response to short-notice requests for air, so it came as a surprise when the code words apparently set some high-level wheels in motion. Within seconds Hillsboro offered to help.

The controller answered, "Copy your X-Ray-validated target. Statehouse confirms. Can you use some fast-movers? I've got a set of Fox Fours in Cherry Anchor about to come off the tanker. Gimme a rendezvous and they're yours."

I passed on a rendezvous off channel 72, the secret TACAN station located on the Bolovens Plateau, then began figuring out run-in headings, pull-offs, and the dozens of other details that are part of an air strike when civilians or friendlies are a factor. With Prasert's help I picked out a rugged-looking ridge line in case of an emergency bail out and then settled back to wait for the fighters. As we droned around, I agonized about the broken cloud deck at three thousand feet. There were plenty of holes for the F-4s to work through—it would simply be a matter of luck. One minute the tree line was clearly visible, the next a gray puffy obscured it. I couldn't decide whether to duck underneath the stuff or to stay on top so all of us could see each other.

A few minutes later my fighters checked in with lots of gas and wall-to-wall MK-82s. They picked up the highway and the village with no problem but couldn't get a clear view of the target. Several wide orbits later, a sucker hole opened up, so I rolled in to mark the target. Diving through the hole, I pressed in fairly low and got off a good rocket. Unfortunately, by the time Lead maneuvered around for an east-to-west restricted run-in to keep from overflying the village, the hole closed. We settled into a game of cloud tag. There was nothing we could do except fly the pattern a few more times and wait for the next opening. When it finally came, the fighters had "no joy" on the smoke from my first willie pete, so I rolled in a second time.

A split second before I fired, with the T intersection lined up perfectly in my gunsight, the tree line erupted in a huge explosion and fireball. At only two thousand feet slant range from the target and closing fast, the only course of action available to me was to honk back on the stick and try to pull clear of the blast pattern in front of me. The heavy G forces immediately tunneled my vision and blurred my eyesight as the blood drained from my head into the lower extremities.

My mind raced. What the hell had caused that explosion? Had my fighters dropped their bombs without clearance? Did my rocket ignite whatever was hidden in the trees?

Although momentarily blind, I could still hear and feel the aircraft struggling. We were about to stall. Concentrate! Get control of the airplane, then worry about the target.

As I eased off the back pressure, my visual cues returned almost instantaneously. We were in a near vertical climb directly over the billowing smoke of the blast. Before she stalled, I let the nose fall through the horizon and carefully banked us away from the immediate area. A quick glance at the instrument panel confirmed two good engines. When I looked back outside, my heart jumped into my mouth as the windscreen filled with the bottom of another aircraft, only about fifty feet away.

We barely had flying airspeed, so fancy maneuvering was out of the question. With more of a survival reaction than a conscious thought, I slammed the control stick full forward. This time the negative Gs forced me violently up against the seat belt, and without having to look back, I heard Prasert's helmet bounce off the rear canopy. Along with some of my maps and a couple of long-lost grease pens, a surprisingly large cloud of dust and debris from the cockpit floor floated up in front of my face. While simultaneously straining to see through the dust and pull myself back down into the seat, I watched helplessly as we covered the remaining few feet to the other airplane.

There was no sense of panic, no paralyzing fear, only the realization that Prasert and I were milliseconds away from dying in a fiery midair collision. There wasn't even time to flinch. In a split second, we flashed under the belly of the other bird and into the clear—without a scratch!

With the control stick back to neutral and using the airspeed we'd gained in the unloading maneuver, I pulled us hard to the right, hoping to catch a glimpse of the intruder. Ninety degrees through the tight turn, we spotted him—a lone Royal Laotian Air Force T-28 climbing back to altitude. Slipping to the inside of the T-28's turn in order to cut him off, I finally had a chance to say something to my back-seater.

"Prasert, are you okay?"

In a bit of philosophical understatement accentuated by a somewhat shaky voice he replied, "Okay, okay. We come too close." The man definitely had a lyrical way of cutting to the heart of the matter.

No sooner had Prasert answered me when we both jumped as a second string of bombs detonated off our left wing tip. The second T-28 climbed straight ahead to our altitude, then started a lazy turn to join up with his leader, who plugged along about a mile in front of us.

Leaning forward slightly, I switched to the emergency Guard transmitter and attempted to contact the Laotian pilots. "Laotian T-28s operating just south of Highway 23, this is Covey 221 on Guard. If you read me, come up on UHF frequency 282.0." Nothing. Not a peep out of them.

Prasert's voice, considerably calmer this time, came in over the intercom with a suggestion: "Maybe they hear better if I talk in Lao." Before I could digest the illogic of his suggestion, he rattled off a long string of strange-sounding words, all totally unintelligible to me, somewhat musical with a distinct pattern of rising and falling tones. Almost immediately a high-pitched voice answered in another long stream of tonal words and phrases. After several more exchanges, Prasert translated for me.

"T-28 pilot say he fly low along the highway when he see your rocket. When you fly back above clouds and nothing happen, he drop bombs on your smoke. Pilot say he think maybe kill beaucoup NVA."

As the translation sank in, I still couldn't believe it. A FUBAR situation if ever there was one. Without thinking, I mumbled into the intercom, "Irrefutable logic in a complete vacuum."

Innocently, Prasert asked, "What you say?" He had no idea what I was talking about, yet it wasn't his fault he couldn't handle a few abstract English words. I didn't know three words in Lao, much less the subtleties of a foreign language. Consumed with equal shares of guilt, embarrassment, and frustration, I mentally kicked myself for getting boxed in, for not knowing the language, for not being able to handle a simple air strike.

Whatever had been hidden in the trees, the uninvited T-28s had done a good job of blowing away the hiding place. Prasert and I saw a number of small boxes and lots of shredded straw and paper strewn around several of the bomb craters—not exactly the find of the century but provocative enough to warrant calling in the orbiting fast-movers. Carefully, I worked each F-4 in multiple passes on the target, always mindful of the possibility that the free-spirited Laotian Air Force might show up without warning. My fighters blasted the jungle cache with devastating precision, but we only turned up more boxes and straw. There wasn't a fire or secondary explosion to be had.

It was time to head back toward PS-38, so we turned eastward, leaving the village and the bomb craters and the boxes and the T-28s behind, physically and mentally. To ease the tension, I leveled off just above a ragged cloud deck that stretched for miles and looked like a sea of spun cotton. Because of the steadily rising heat, small whiffs had begun to build into columns. We darted in and out like a slalom skier running the gates at Squaw Valley. On a good downhill slope a skier might hit 60 miles an hour, no comparison to our three-dimensional slalom at 240 miles per hour.

Next, I aimed the OV-10 at the very top of a growing cloud column, the object being to slice through the top two or three feet of the swirling mass. A few of the larger columns boiled up at a rate of climb in excess of several hundred feet a minute, so looking out through the lighted reticle of the gunsight offered an interesting exercise in stick and rudder coordination. As we closed in on our cloud target, there was a momentary sensation of speed followed by a reflex tightening of the stomach muscles just before "impact." It was great fun trying to pull off a perfectly timed collision, with just the slightest tickle as we flashed through the cloud top. After several more demonstrations, I even let Prasert try his hand at it. His basic eye-to-hand coordination was good, though I suspected he really didn't understand or appreciate the game. He never seemed to get the hang of it.

Once at PS-38, with Dev's concurrence, I set up an orbit off the south end of the airstrip in the general vicinity of the worrisome mortar position. We gave the area a good going over and identified several likely spots, but there was no way to be sure unless the guy loaded the tube and fired.

I heard the Air America Porter call on Dev's frequency, indicating he was about five minutes out. To be on the safe side, I armed up the right outboard rocket pod, ready to roll in should the mortar crew give away their position by opening fire.

Prasert saw the Porter first, then we both watched as the strange-looking single-engine silver-and-blue aircraft set up on a modified straight-in from the north, holding an incredibly slow sixty-knot final-approach speed. While still about a hundred feet in the air, the pilot yelled into the radio, "Somebody cover us! We're taking heavy fire!"

Obviously "somebody" was me, and my first thought focused on the 82mm mortar. As I scanned the ground below in a furious search, I had absolutely no indication our boy had fired. It had to be a different threat. In the confusion, everybody tried talking at once. Dev and I keyed our mikes simultaneously to ask where—at precisely the same instant the Porter pilot tried to tell us. In the resulting garbled transmission, we cut each other out. Before anybody could retransmit, the little Air America bird touched down on the red-dirt strip no worse for the experience.

A long silence followed. We watched as the Porter taxied to midfield and shut down; the pilot and one passenger nonchalantly climbed out. Finally, Dev's easygoing voice filled the earphones in my helmet. He passed on the pilot's estimate of where the ground fire had come from. He cautioned me, however, that friendly troops were also in that immediate area. Dev must have sensed my frustration, because he signed off with a somewhat hollow pep talk.

"Thanks for your help, Covey. We really appreciate you

keeping that 82 off our backs. Swing by tomorrow and maybe we can have a go at the guys who shot at our Porter."

In my mind the day had been a complete wipeout, at best one of those days when everything you touch turns to dog do-do. Disgusted and disappointed, I pointed the Bronco westward, climbed back to altitude, trimmed her up for hands-off flight, and then rested both my arms on the canopy rails. From my actions Prasert probably guessed we were heading home, but he asked the question anyway.

Without thinking I answered, "Yeah, let's go home. Too much of a good thing will rot your teeth." As soon as the words were out of my mouth I cringed, knowing full well he wouldn't understand.

His voice heavy with concern, Prasert asked, "Captain Tom have toothache?" I smiled in spite of myself, feeling a little like George Burns talking to Gracie Allen.

"Yeah, a bad toothache," I answered, figuring the path of least resistance would be easier on both of us.

Back at Ubon, Prasert and I agreed on a rendezvous time for the next day and said good-bye; then the white Toyota pickup whisked him away. Hot and sweaty, in a foul mood to match, I trudged the mile from the flight line to the hooch.

That night I tossed and turned, running instant replays of the day's mission in my mind. As I mentally reviewed the balance sheet, I totaled more screw-ups than atta-boys. I kept thinking, maybe it's me, maybe I'm just not taking control of the situation. In my short combat career, I seemed to be mixed up in one weird event after another—the fake truck, the check ride target, the 23mm hit, the phone booth caper—and now a near midair and the indecisive performance at PS-38. It all boiled down to being able to anticipate the unexpected, something I wasn't sure could be learned. I finally drifted off into a fitful sleep, my last conscious thoughts wondering whether I ever would learn.

On my second full day as a U.S. Air Force captain, I felt better about everything in general. For one thing I was twice as experienced as I had been the day before. Even the weather cooperated, producing a brilliant blue sky with only a few white puffies hanging at the six thousand foot level.

Prasert and I got airborne on schedule and flew directly to PS-38. Dev sounded genuinely glad that we were there, explaining that Pathet Lao troops had launched several heavy probes during the night. The Laotian defenders had managed to hold their own but with several casualties. Dev speculated that they were nervous and scared, possibly on the verge of folding. If the Laotian Army bugged out, there was nothing between the bad guys and the airstrip.

After talking to Dev, the next step was to make direct contact with the ground commander. Prasert finally got him up on Fox Mike. In a nerve-wracking conversation punctuated by frequent translations for my benefit, my back-seater fed me the map coordinates for both the friendlies and the bad guys. The ground commander's position roughly correlated to the word picture Prasert translated; the Pathet Lao coordinates plotted out five miles to the east, an obvious mistake in light of the continuing exchange of sporadic small-arms fire. I had to be sure of the positions, especially since the ground commander wasn't. The worst thing imaginable would be to run an air strike involving a "short round," the term used to describe the accidental bombing or shelling of friendly troops. As the FAC, the responsibility was totally mine.

At my insistence, Prasert instructed the friendlies to mark their position with colored smoke, just the way they'd taught us to do back at FAC U. The voice on the other end of the radio refused, claiming the smoke would reveal their hiding place, a good point. The ground commander did agree to help us by spreading a bright colored cloth panel on the ground. We quickly identified three orange panels and could even see troops waving as we flew overhead. Getting a fix on the enemy position was tougher.

To hear the ground commander tell it, the bad guys were storming the walls, yet his voice sounded remarkably calm—too calm. In spite of his pleas to "drop bomb right now," I kept badgering him for more accurate information. First we made him reconfirm the map coordinates, which he insisted were correct. Next I had Prasert ask him for a compass bearing and an estimated distance to the nearest enemy position. By his calculation the position was northeast at fifty meters. When we pressed him about the distance, he waffled, changing first to two hundred, then to three hundred meters. As a last resort, we asked if he could lob a couple of mortar rounds on the target and talk us in from there. Much to my relief, he said yes and told us to stand by.

Fifteen minutes later the commander announced he was ready. Making sure we stayed well away from his line of fire, I orbited at two thousand feet, a good altitude for taking in the whole scene. As I focused on the target, I assumed the mortar crew would use a white phosphorous round, similar to my willie pete rockets. When nothing showed up after several minutes, it was clear they had used something else or had fired into a completely different quadrant.

With sweat dripping into my eyes, feeling frustrated by the tedious translation process, I irritably asked for another round. This time we saw it, a dirty gray explosion much smaller than I had expected, about four hundred meters from the friendlies. When the ground commander confirmed the mortar round was on target, I felt ready to put the wheels in motion for an air strike.

Just as on the previous day, Hillsboro responded instantly to my request to hit an X-Ray-validated target, only this time the answer put me in a good news–bad news dilemma. Hillsboro's good news was that fighters were immediately available; the bad news, at least to me, was that they were Royal Laotian Air Force T-28s. If yesterday's performance was any indication, I could look forward to having my hands full. Actually, the old single-engine recip trainer, modified to carry guns and bombs, had a good reputation as an accurate dive bomber, but the thought of controlling non-English-speaking pilots and of relying on Prasert's comprehension and translation abilities left me in a cold sweat.

Four stub-winged T-28s appeared over PS-38 at four

thousand feet, circling warily for five minutes before we finally established radio contact. From what I could gather, Lead and Three carried 250-pound general-purpose bombs while Two and Four packed high-explosive rockets. All four pilots listened politely as Prasert translated my instructions, and then it was time to put up or shut up. I warned the friendlies to take cover and then rolled in for the mark.

All the way down the chute, Prasert carried on a running dialogue with the ground commander. As we pulled off, I knew we had to be near the target when Prasert informed me excitedly, "Commander tell us to be careful. Many NVA shoot everything at you."

Looking down at my white smoke, I figured that if we could just get Lead's ordnance in the ballpark, the other flight members would dump their stuff on his. If Lead missed badly, especially in the direction of the Royal Laotian troops, I shuttered to think what might happen. Driving that thought from my mind, I set up a tight figure-eight pattern over the friendlies with the long axis parallel to the north–south run-in heading assigned to the fighters. As Lead rolled in, I broke hard to the right in a 180-degree level turn, ending up on a parallel course between him and the friendly position. When I felt certain his line-up was good, I cleared him in hot. As Lead pulled off, I reversed the process with a hard turn back to the left. Once established in the figure-eight pattern, it was possible to keep it up indefinitely, always turning into the fighters and always keeping them in sight.

Much to my relief, Lead's bombs literally blew my smoke away—a perfect bull's-eye. When I directed Two's rockets into an adjacent clump of trees, nothing happened. Instead, everybody went around the pattern until Lead rolled in for a second run. When Lead finished, Two joined in with several consecutive rocket runs, followed by Three's dive-bomb passes. As I waited for number four to do his solo act, Lead said something on the radio, the whole gaggle rejoined, then flew off to the west without so much as a goodby, thanks, or see you around. They didn't even acknowledge when I tried to pass along their BDA.

With the departure of the T-28s, I felt mentally exhausted. On the one hand, we'd accomplished the job under less-than-ideal conditions, and for that I was thankful. On the other hand, I couldn't seem to shake a nagging doubt about who had been in control of the air strike. My first close-air-support mission wasn't nearly as satisfying as I had imagined it would be.

On the way back to Ubon, we checked in with Art, Bill, and Dunc at the other PS sites. Prasert chattered away merrily, telling his old friends how we'd just saved PS-38 from the entire North Vietnamese Army. In truth, we didn't find a single thing on the bomb damage assessment, much less any sign of the NVA. Not that the lack of tangible damage made the air strike a failure. On the contrary, the bombs and rockets probably gave a very positive psychological lift to the Royal Laotian Army. Hopefully, the bombs had just the opposite effect on the bad guys.

After landing back at Ubon, Prasert and I said good-bye for what turned out to be the last time. In the end he'd been invaluable to me, and over the past two days of flying together, I'd developed fondness and respect for the wiry little X-Ray. As he disappeared down the road in the white Toyota pickup, I helped the crew chief refuel my OV-10 for the return flight to Rocket City and to the Coveys' secret war over the Ho Chi Minh Trail.

JULY

Prairie Fire

Over the past two months, everybody had preached the same sermon: "Thou shalt never fly below fifteen hundred feet; always stay above the small-arms-effective range—you'll live longer." Yet in total disregard of that most sacred of FAC commandments, here we were skimming along the Ho Chi Minh Trail at treetop level in an O-2.

There was no denying how much more detail was visible from down low. I could actually see the texture of the trees and small ridges and hills under them. Staring out the right window of the Oscar Deuce, I fully expected to see bad guys blazing away at us from behind every bush. But the only human to be seen was the Prairie Fire pilot sitting in the left seat, grinning at my obvious discomfort. Feeling more than a little boxed in, I kept thinking to myself, "What a squirrelly way to start the month of July." Other confusing thoughts bounced around in my head as I recalled the strange events of June 28, just three days earlier.

I should have suspected something when Captain Frank "Fuzzy" Furr, commander of the super-secret Covey Prairie Fire flight, headed straight for me as I walked through Covey Operations. The Prairie Fire types rarely associated with the rest of us; they even had their own mission briefing room in the intel shop, a top-secret place we could not enter. Judging from Frank's expression, I had a sneaking suspicion he had something more than idle chatter on his mind.

Fuzzy Furr was a short, stocky man, built like a fireplug but solid as a rock. The front of his half-unzipped flight suit revealed a gray T-shirt with a picture of an OV-10 and the slogan, "Fly the friendly skies of Laos." As he walked up, he looked around the room as if to make sure we were alone, then grabbed me by the arm and pulled me off into a corner.

In very measured tones, he said, "Tom, all of us have talked it over, and we want you to come into Prairie Fire." That was it. No buildup, no hard sell, no explanation, just the equivalent of "Uncle Fuzzy wants you." It reminded me of a fraternity rush, yet from the look in Fuzzy's eyes, it was clear he wasn't joking. There was a brief, awkward pause while I waited for him to add something to his original statement. When he didn't speak up, I did.

"Fuzzy, I'm not sure what to say. Hell, I don't even know what you guys do. Could you give me an idea what I'd be getting myself into?"

Smiling, he said, "Sorry. I can't tell you anything except that it's the most exciting FAC mission going. If you sign up, we'll tell you the whole nine yards. I can promise you'll love it."

Since my first question had led nowhere, I hit him with a second one. "Why me? I thought you guys only took people with six months of experience flying the Trail. I've barely got two months'."

"It's simple," he answered. "You're a little older, you're one of the few Coveys who's ever worked a TIC, and you've been shot at and hit—and handled it well. We just think you'll fit in."

Trying to digest Fuzzy's words, I wondered why being shot at and hit was important to him. I also remembered the old adage about never volunteering for anything.

"Listen, Fuzzy. I just can't see diving into this, especially since you won't even tell me the square root of fox alpha about it. Besides, in another couple of months, I should upgrade to IP, and that's something I really want, sort of a personal goal. Can you see my point?"

"Sure, I hear you," Frank said, seemingly not in the least put off by my answer. "But maybe we can work something out. After a couple of months with us, I'll talk to the boss and see if he'll authorize an instructor slot in Prairie Fire. By then you'd be ready to take over as training officer anyway. This'll work great."

I could see the wheels in Fuzzy's mind turning. He figured he had it all sewn up. His face lit up with a smile, then he grabbed my arm again. "You think it over, and I'll talk to you again tomorrow afternoon. Prairie Fire is the best job there is, no shit. And we really do want you with us." As Fuzzy walked away, he looked back at me over his shoulder and said, somewhat melodramatically, "Don't mention this conversation to anyone, okay?"

That night I fidgeted around my room, trying to concentrate on a volume of the Squadron Officer School correspondence course, but I kept thinking about Prairie Fire. Fuzzy had said it was the most exciting FAC mission going. I knew the Prairie Fire troops got twice as much flying time as the other Coveys, so how could it be a bad deal? Yet there was something just as compelling in the argument that the only pilot I'd ever known who'd died in combat bought it on a Prairie Fire mission. Still, that could happen to anyone on any given mission, so I tried not to blow that aspect out of proportion. As I continued to stare at the text in front of me, the words could have been Greek for the amount of comprehension that soaked in. Instead, I kept hearing, seeing, pondering Fuzzy's words to me: "The best FAC mission going . . . you'll love it . . . we want you in Prairie Fire . . . we think you'll fit in."

It wasn't much to go on. Frank had alluded to TICs and to getting shot at, probably a hint that the job entailed lots of action involving troops on the ground. My only other clue centered on the mysterious "no bomb line" grids on our big wall map in the intel shop. Those boxes seemed to change daily, but they always showed up along the most heavily defended areas on the Trail or the DMZ. The rumor mill had it that Prairie Fire pilots controlled some kind of secret war inside those NBL grids. Since there were no U.S. or ARVN troops assigned that deep in enemy territory, I couldn't imagine who or what was fighting there. Before the night was over, I had almost convinced myself that a Prairie Fire FAC and a Raven FAC had to be one and the same thing. The lure was irresistible. Besides, Fuzzy and the other Prairie Fire types seemed like normal guys—aside from their penchant for secrecy.

By the next morning, I'd made up my mind. That afternoon when Fuzzy came walking toward me, I didn't have to say a word. Grabbing my hand and shaking it, he smiled and said, "I knew you were hooked from the very beginning. Welcome to the club."

Some club. Watching the Trail rush by under the wing of our O-2, I still didn't know what it meant to be a member. At our destination it would be explained, but until we arrived, wild speculation would blot out most other thoughts.

In spite of my preoccupation, one visual cue did catch my attention, however. As we flew farther north, the jungle and foliage beside the Trail opened up, revealing wall-to-wall bomb craters. Along the main segments, hardly a tree remained standing. The whole area had really taken a beating. The sheer tonnage of bombs dropped out there was beyond any reckoning, and it was a wonder anything or anybody had survived. But survive they had, as evidenced by the steady stream of enemy troops and supplies moving down the Trail each night.

At the triborder area where Laos and North and South Vietnam joined, my pilot hung a right and headed for Quang Tri Air Base, a busy field built along the beach just a few miles south of the DMZ. As part of my tour, we flew east along the DMZ, following the Song Ben Hai River to the point where it emptied into the South China Sea. There on the north bank of the river, a tall pole sported a huge, red ceremonial flag—the North Vietnamese flag!

Flying over the North generated all sorts of ominous thoughts, and for me the sensation of looking south at that flag was like taking a left turn into the twilight zone. It was one thing to fly combat missions in South Vietnam or Laos; flying over North Vietnam put a whole new spin on things, made the pulse speed up. For some reason I remembered a training film we'd seen in jungle survival school, a supposedly factual portrayal of the experiences of an F-105 jock shot down over the North. Called *Here There Are Tigers,* the film's title made reference to ancient maps that warned travelers to stay clear of the region because of tigers and other predatory animals. As I looked down at the flagpole two thousand feet below me, the hair on the back of my neck stood up, telling me the tigers might have changed but the ancient warning was still worth heeding.

Several minutes later we landed at Quang Tri and taxied to Barky Operations, headquarters for the FACs who supported the U.S. Army's Fifth Mechanized Division. As I climbed out of the O-2, I could see a sinister-looking black jeep waiting for us. An army staff sergeant in fatigues and a Special Forces green beret nodded and motioned for me to climb into the back seat. He and the O-2 jock talked quietly as we bounced off down the dusty, rut-filled road.

Five miles west of the airfield, we approached a large, heavily fortified perimeter with a barricade gate. Two guards, each with a CAR-15 slung over his shoulder, raised the barricade and waved us through. Although they were clearly Oriental, the guards didn't resemble any of the Vietnamese I'd become accustomed to seeing around Da Nang. These men were taller and more fair-skinned, almost Chinese in appearance.

Several hundred yards in front of us stood a cluster of five one-story frame buildings, three on the left side of an open yard and two on the right. The buildings were long shotgun affairs with no windows. The upper half of each wall appeared to be a top-hinged panel that could be propped open to let air in. Behind the left set of buildings, an assortment of UH-1 Hueys and Cobra gunships were parked in a large, cleared field.

Our jeep chugged to a stop in front of the second building on the left. Again without speaking, the SF sergeant motioned me in with a gesture that reminded me of an usher in a fancy theater. Once inside, I found the room totally unremarkable. The sparsely furnished office contained two desks, a few chairs, and a fairly sophisticated bank of radio equipment. The two Americans in the office stood up when we entered.

An all-American looking young captain, reminiscent of the "Jack Armstrong" radio character, walked over and extended a huge right hand in greeting. He introduced himself as Jerry Stratton, commander of Mobile Launch Team 2—MLT-2 for short. Then he introduced his first sergeant, Ken Budrow, a balding, pleasant-looking senior NCO who had an air of complete calm about him. As with all first sergeants, most folks called him "Top."

With the amenities out of the way, Jerry asked me, "How much do you know?"

"Nothing," I admitted. "Fuzzy Furr said someone at Quang Tri would fill me in. I'm assuming that's you."

"I'm your man," Jerry answered. "Grab a cup of coffee and let's go next door. It'll be easier using the maps."

Once in the next room, we settled into chairs in front of several acetate-covered wall maps, mostly 1:50,000 scale. The intricate assortment of grease-pencil markings and color codes on the map meant absolutely nothing to me; most of the marks appeared to be concentrated in the DMZ and in a section of Laos due west of Quang Tri.

Much to my relief, Jerry started the briefing using the broadest possible verbal brush to paint the picture for me. He explained that Prairie Fire was the code name for a sensitive joint-service project whose mission was to gather intelligence by putting small, long-range reconnaissance patrols on the ground in Laos and the DMZ. From the Vietnamese border, the Prairie Fire AO extended thirty-three kilometers into Laos and the same distance north.

The command structure got complicated in a hurry. Jerry explained that operationally, an organization in Saigon called "MAC-SOG"—Military Assistance Command, Studies and Observation Group—ran the show. Jerry chuckled as he pointed out that the Studies and Observation Group was about as thin a cover as had been devised. Instead of the academics and scientists the name suggested, the personnel were really Green Berets borrowed from the 5th Special Forces Group. To emphasize his point, Jerry proudly tossed me my own MAC-SOG shoulder patch showing a surrealistic human skull wearing a green beret, with fire flickering out of each eye socket and blood dripping out a corner of the mouth.

Jerry went on to tell me that SOG further divided the organization into three geographic operational regions, north, central, and south. The area in which I'd be working was known as Command and Control North, or CCN, with its headquarters at Da Nang. CCN reconnaissance teams, called RTs, worked all cross-border operations from Chu Lai to the DMZ. Within CCN several mobile launch teams operated, including Jerry's MLT-2.

The sensitivity surrounding the whole project stemmed from the use of Americans leading teams of Oriental mercenaries into areas where U.S. ground forces were not allowed. Heavy losses among the SOG teams created political problems requiring elaborate secrecy. For that reason each mission had to be approved by the Joint Chiefs of Staff and the White House. The whole setup was right out of a James Bond story.

At the tactical level, CCN assigned targets to a specific recon team, then shipped the team off to the MLT for the actual mission. The objective might be anything from bomb damage assessment of a B-52 raid to pinpointing logistics supply lines to counting trucks moving down the Trail, sometimes even an NVA prisoner snatch.

Getting the teams safely in and out of enemy territory presented the biggest problem, and that's where I came in. My job was to be airborne commander of the "package," the name given to the helicopter and fixed-wing assets needed for the mission. Usually the package consisted of four UH-1 Huey "Slicks" carrying the team, two Cobra helicopter gunships, and two Air Force A-1 Skyraiders for close air support. In really hot areas, we'd order up a set of fast-movers, usually F-4s, to suppress flak and to act as a MiG cap.

In theory, I was supposed to neutralize the landing zone for the insert, cover the team while they were on the ground, then run the extract. Jerry was quick to point out that the operations never quite worked that smoothly. Invariably the small teams engaged in firefights at point-blank range, requiring an experienced FAC to direct ordnance from the A-1s and Cobras well inside minimum safe distances. A slow-thinking or panicky FAC could get himself or the team killed instantly.

As he talked, Jerry squinted and stared deep into my eyes, apparently searching for the qualities and attributes required of a Prairie Fire FAC. His gaze became so intense that I finally had to look away. His visual third degree shook me up. At that moment I honestly didn't know if I could hack it. I just knew I wanted to try.

Jerry finished by emphasizing that most of the time the team extracts became classic search-and-rescue operations, or SARs, with all the attendant difficulties and dangers. To be effective, I would have to fly right on the trees. Prairie Fire FACs observed no minimum altitudes—my OV-10 would be fair game for any bad guy, with a gun or a slingshot.

After the briefing, I could understand why Fuzzy Furr was so enthusiastic about the Prairie Fire mission. It had all the ingredients for one hell of an adventure: high drama, intrigue, danger, Special Forces, clandestine operations. We were talking real-life "Terry and the Pirates." If the flying was one-tenth as exciting as I expected it would be, I knew I'd found a home. My earlier dream of becoming a Raven FAC faded completely.

On the flight back to Da Nang, I had a lot to think about, but my O-2 pilot took up where we had left off. He eased us down to just a few feet off the beach and pushed the throttles up for a speed dash of 125 knots. The super-heated midafternoon air provided just enough turbulence to keep the ride challenging. Just as I was beginning to feel comfortable, the engines let loose with several heart-stopping sputters. I shot a quick glance at the pilot, thinking to myself that at such a low altitude his only choice was to crash-land on the smooth beach fifty feet below us. As if to confirm my suspicions, he muttered a single "Damn!" Simultaneously his right hand shot out and turned a couple of levers. A lifetime later— actually only a few seconds of real time—the engines caught and wound back up to speed.

Grinning a little sheepishly, my pilot confessed, "I forgot to switch fuel tanks."

A few minutes later, as my pulse settled down, we spotted a large ship several miles offshore. My pilot pointed us in that direction and dropped down even lower over the water. Coming up from the rear, very close to her starboard side, the pilot observed, "It's that German hospital ship. Watch this."

I figured he planned to buzz the unsuspecting ship. Instead, he leveled off deck high, then pulled the nose up and executed a perfect aileron roll to the right. As we rolled inverted, the sight of all that water only a couple of wingspans below pushed my pulse rate back into overdrive. The O-2 theoretically wasn't certified for aerobatic maneuvers, but the crazy Prairie Fire pilot easily disproved that notion by rolling us back to wings-level, exactly deck high, directly abeam the ship's bow. Smiling broadly, the pilot gave me a thumbs up and announced, "Piece of cake."

On July 3 two experienced Prairie Fire pilots, Bob Meadows and Gary Pavlu, piled me into a jeep and drove me over to CCN headquarters near Marble Mountain, just south of China Beach. After only a few days in Prairie Fire, I instinctively liked these two veterans of the program. Each was completely different from the other, which encouraged my hope that stereotypes weren't the rule in our super-secret operation. Bob Meadows was a short, prematurely balding young man with a take-charge, almost cocky attitude. In contrast, Gary Pavlu was tall, slender, with a laid-back, easygoing manner. He had an interesting habit of calling everyone "Slick." Both Bob and Gary had reputations for being fearless and totally composed in the heat of battle.

Watching both men, I developed a monumental case of hero worship.

The heavily guarded compound at CCN resembled MLT-2 at Quang Tri, only it was much larger. Bob and Gary introduced me around the command section, had my picture taken, then gave me a tour of the facilities. We ended up at the all-ranks club, a small but well-stocked bar and recreation hooch. Several SF NCOs joined us for ice-cold beer served by a Vietnamese waitress. In short order the conversation turned to recent missions. At one point one of the NCOs showed me the strangest ID card I'd ever seen. In addition to his name and picture, the following words appeared:

MILITARY ASSISTANCE COMMAND VIETNAM
STUDIES AND OBSERVATION GROUP
APO SAN FRANCISCO 96307

The other half of the card contained the following explanation:

SPECIAL IDENTIFICATION AND PASS
The person who is identified by this document is acting under the direct orders of the President of the United States!
DO NOT DETAIN OR QUESTION HIM!
He is authorized to wear civilian clothing, carry unusual weapons, transport and possess prohibited items including U.S. currency, pass into restricted areas and requisition equipment of all types including weapons and vehicles.
IF HE IS KILLED OR INJURED, DO NOT REMOVE THIS DOCUMENT FROM HIM. ALERT YOUR COMMANDING OFFICER IMMEDIATELY.

I thought the ID card was the closest thing to a license to steal that I'd ever seen and said so, but the conversation drifted to other topics. Eventually I commented about the number of mercenaries we'd seen around the compound, many of whom wore surgical bandages over what I assumed to be wounds received in combat. Everyone at the table laughed, then the SF troops filled me in.

"In the first place," the NCO corrected me, "we don't call 'em mercenaries. We call 'em 'little people' or 'indig'— short for indigenous troops. A few indig might have been hit on a recent mission, but most of 'em did it to each other. See, we taught 'em how to play poker, and they take it real serious, especially on payday. At the end of the month, they get into marathon card games, somebody accuses somebody else of cheating, and before you know it, it's like Dodge City around here. Firefights all over the place."

Everybody at the table laughed again. I wasn't sure whether to believe the guy or not, but based on other weird things I'd heard about and seen at CCN, there was probably as much truth as exaggeration to his story.

The next day, the Fourth of July, passed without any particular observance of the holiday. For the Coveys it was business as usual. But the date took on special meaning for me. After a little over two months with Roomie, I finally had the opportunity to switch rooms. In a bit of random luck, Roomie was transferred to another FAC unit, and I moved to the other end of the hall, into a room with an old friend, Captain Evan Quiros. Evan and I had first met as freshmen in college, our paths crossing later at several other places, including Cannon and Hurlburt. Evan came from a family of prominent ranchers in Laredo, Texas, and because his name had a distinctly Latin flavor, I teased Evan unmercifully about being a "blond-haired blue-eyed Mexican." His wife, Mary, was one of the sweetest, prettiest ladies you'd ever want to meet, and Evan was totally devoted to her and his children.

Over the next week, I flew every day, with Fuzzy Furr and Bob Meadows taking turns teaching me the tricks of the Prairie Fire trade. At first we concentrated on low-level techniques and on learning the prominent landmarks throughout the AO. Next, we watched while one of the other Prairie Fire pilots ran actual inserts or extracts. Surprisingly, they all went like clockwork. Instead of the melee I had expected, I had the benefit of watching several textbook missions, complete with running commentary by my instructors. I found it fascinating to observe an actual combat operation as a student without being involved in it.

During those first missions, the sequence of events followed the script verbatim. The pilot running the show teamed up with one of a small number of experienced SF NCOs known as "Covey riders." Together, they flew every mission, the pilot controlling the airborne assets while the Covey rider helped with map reading and radios, talked to the team on the ground, and interpreted the tactical situation for his pilot and for the MLT listening on the same radio frequency.

After a final look at the preselected landing zone, or LZ, the Covey FAC gave the go-ahead for helicopter assets to launch. Simultaneously, he contacted and set up a rendezvous with his A-1 Skyraiders, Korean War–vintage prop fighters capable of carrying huge loads of ordnance and fuel. Using the call sign "Spad," the slow-moving Air Force A-1s were perfect for the Prairie Fire mission, able to thread a needle with their bombs, orbit forever, and absorb incredible amounts of punishment. As an added bennie, we lived in the same building with the A-1 jocks, thus developing super rapport with these outstanding pilots.

When everybody reached the rendezvous, usually some ten klicks away from the target area, the FAC led the package to the LZ. Contrary to normal procedures, Prairie Fire FACs didn't use willie petes to mark the LZ because the exploding white phosphorous could easily set the whole place on fire. Instead, the FAC rolled in for a shallow dive on the target, all the while giving the helicopters a running verbal update on what he saw. In addition to the verbal description, the long, low run-in to the target served the additional purpose of drawing ground fire from any bad guys in the immediate area. The pilots called it "trolling."

With all eyes glued on him, the FAC would continue to tree-top level and, when directly over the LZ, would call out,

"Mark, mark," then pull up sharply to a loose orbit over the area. Once the choppers confirmed a positive ID on the LZ, the operation shifted into the next phase.

Before committing the vulnerable Hueys, the FAC turned the Cobra gunships loose on the LZ to neutralize the area. Instead of using conventional ordnance, the Cobras fired fléchette rockets directly into the LZ and surrounding tree lines. Each fléchette round contained thousands of one-inch steel darts resembling nails, each capable of penetrating several inches of solid wood. At approximately the halfway point on its flight to the target, the rocket warhead exploded in a cloud of reddish smoke, releasing a shower of "nails" traveling at a tremendous velocity. The actual impact was barely visible from above, with only some dust and splintered wood swirling through the air; no chance of risky fire or telltale smoke. When a Cobra pilot squeezed off a fléchette rocket at approximately three thousand feet slant range, the resulting destruction could cover the area of a football field with one fléchette per square inch.

After "nailing" the LZ, the FAC would clear the lead Huey Slick for the approach, trailed by one of the Cobras to provide suppressing fire if needed. For the orbiting FAC, the trick involved orchestrating everyone's flight path so that the Slicks maintained optimum spacing and were always covered on final approach by a Cobra, ready to bring his guns to bear at the first sign of trouble. Assuming all went well, the Slick touched down briefly, deposited the first half of the team, then pulled off to a prearranged safe orbit area. As Lead lifted off, Slick Two would touch down with the rest of the team.

At that point the insert was far from over. The plan usually called for some old-fashioned sleight of hand. The package would move to another LZ and repeat the whole show at least two more times, for a total of two dummy inserts and one real one. The choice of which was the actual insert in the drama was purely random.

The extract always involved more complications and variables than the insert, since there could be absolutely no ordnance dropped into the area until the FAC could pinpoint the team's position, a nerve-wracking process requiring plenty of low, slow trolling over the often hostile terrain. Once he found his team, the FAC called in the Spads and Cobras to blast anything that moved or looked the least bit suspicious.*

After watching two inserts and one extract, I felt ready to try it myself. With an experienced Covey rider in my back seat, and under the watchful eye of Bob Meadows circling above the show, I successfully managed to pull one team on July 8 and insert another one the next afternoon. As with the missions I had observed earlier, mine went off without a hitch.

The following morning, July 10, the charm wore off. The plan called for an insert on top of a prominent ridge called Co Roc, located just across the Laotian border about fifteen klicks southwest of Khe Sanh. Several years earlier NVA artillery firing from Co Roc's heights had pounded besieged U.S. Marines at Khe Sanh. Enemy activity along the ridge still made people nervous, so MAC-SOG was assigned to check out the situation.

Co Roc's sheer eastern cliffs made for an impressive sight from the air. The steep walls rose some twelve hundred feet above the muddy Se Pone River. The scene reminded me of a miniature version of half the Grand Canyon. Scrub jungle covered the top of the five-mile-long ridge whose axis was oriented roughly north to south. At the southern end of the amoeba-shaped formation, the terrain sloped gently down to the west for several miles before it flattened out into a large plain containing a major segment of the Trail.

For the morning mission, I found myself teamed up with

---

*To avoid confusing the reader, the various components of the package are identified throughout the book by a generic nickname, i.e., Spad, Slick, Cobra, rather than by actual tactical call sign. In Prairie Fire, each component used a different two-letter identifier each day. For instance, on a given day, the call signs might be as follows: MLT: "Alpha Delta"; Team: "Mike Kilo"; Huey Slicks: "Tango Zulu"; Cobras: "Lima Oscar"; Spads: "Romeo Bravo"; FAC: "Sierra Mike." For security reasons the call signs changed daily.

a brand new Covey rider, Sergeant First Class Charlie Gray. As a couple of rookies, we were to observe the operation and to act as backup to the Covey running the insert. Based on my brief Prairie Fire experiences, I expected to watch another milk run.

On this occasion two dummy inserts preceded the real one. They went off with no difficulty, so I positioned us up-sun at an altitude of thirty-five hundred feet, well above the package but two thousand feet below the orbiting A-1s. Sergeant Gray and I watched as the Cobras nailed the LZ, both of us wondering out loud how anybody could live through that deadly hail of killer fléchettes.

Next, Slick Lead started his descent to the target, setting himself up on a south-to-north run-in. At approximately fifty feet in the air, just as he started increasing the angle of attack to go into a hover, the Huey shook violently as a B-40 rocket snaked out of the tree line at his ten o'clock position and exploded in the rotor assembly.

Sergeant Gray and I watched in horror as the Huey pilot fought to regain control of his crippled bird. Immediately, the radio filled with excited yells. Slick Lead shouted, "We're hit, we're hit bad! She's pulling hard to the left!"

From the Covey, "Lead, go for the clear area to the west. Stay with it! We'll cover you all the way. Cobra Two, get on him, get on him, goddamn it!"

Trailing a thin stream of black smoke, Slick Lead managed to roll out on a westerly heading, all the while descending at about the same rate as the terrain sloped down. Without even realizing it, I found myself diving toward the struggling Huey, as if by getting closer I could somehow help. Through my helmet earphones I heard voices shouting, "Stay with it! Just a little farther! You've got it made, just keep her flying a few more seconds!" The shouting voices were Charlie Gray's and my own.

After clearing a final tree line, the chopper appeared to hover momentarily, then flip on its side and fall the remaining twenty-five feet to the ground. The bird bounced once, then broke in half as it crashed back to earth. At impact, the

Huey disappeared in a huge, mushroom-shaped fireball. Somewhere, someone keyed a mike and said, "Sweet Jesus!"

Several seconds of ominous quiet followed before the package commander came up on frequency. "Okay, everybody snap out of it. Let's set up a tight orbit while I go down and see if there are any survivors."

I didn't think anyone could live through that inferno, but out of habit I reached for my binoculars to get a closer look at the fire-engulfed wreckage. After focusing, I was amazed to see figures moving around the burning Huey. Within a matter of seconds, Slick Three, carrying the medic, or *bac si*, the Vietnamese word for doctor, swooped in to pick up five dazed survivors who had miraculously been thrown clear on impact. The pilot and copilot, probably still in the twisted, burning wreck, were unaccounted for.

Late that afternoon, Charlie Gray and I returned to the crash site with a full package, including a special recovery team code-named "Bright Light." The insert went unopposed, allowing the larger Bright Light team the luxury of setting up a perimeter defense while the remaining team members sifted through the burned-out wreckage. As we suspected, they found the pilots still strapped in their seats.

Once the Bright Light team secured the bodies and reboarded, I sent the helicopter package back to Quang Tri. It was time to give the long suffering A-1s their chance. Under the rules of engagement, at sunset we had the option of using any unexpended ordnance the Spads had left over. I knew just where I wanted them to drop their stuff. In the last rays of light, the white smoke from my willie pete billowed out of the tree line that had been the hiding place for the bad guy with the B-40 rocket. All of us felt the same way, and there was no need for a lot of conversation.

"Okay, gents, set 'em up and push 'em up and hit my smoke. Give me a pass with the nape for starters."

Coming low out of the west, the two lumbering A-1s dumped their canisters of napalm onto the top of Co Roc. Then they came back around and blasted the area with high-explosive rockets and for good measure raked the jungle with mini-gun fire. In the dim light from the burning nape, it was hard to tell if we'd hit anything, but the raging fires and explosions were a kind of catharsis for all of us, a release of the tension we'd been feeling since the crash.

Charlie Gray and I flew back to Quang Tri in silence. We touched down on the dimly lit runway and taxied to Barky Ops. Following a quick debriefing at MLT-2, I returned to the airfield to climb into my OV-10 for the fifth time that day. As I slipped on my harness over my survival vest, one of the Barky crew chiefs walked up and tapped me on the shoulder.

"Sir, I think there's something you ought to see." I followed him to the right wing tip, where he focused the beam of his flashlight for me. "Looks like an AK-47 round," he said. "Went in through the wing tip and came out over here on the right aileron. No real damage, but you were lucky."

Immediately I thought about Bennie, my old crew chief back at Da Nang who had also commented on my luck after the 23mm round did a number on our airplane. As with that earlier incident, I didn't have the faintest idea when the AK round had found its mark. As I tried to reconstruct the four sorties I'd flown that day, they all blurred together. The only clear picture I had was of the chopper breaking in half and of the mushroom-shaped fireball. It had been a long day, never to be forgotten.

That night back at Da Nang, I tumbled into my bunk, physically and emotionally drained. That stuporlike feeling was rapidly becoming the rule rather than the exception. With my daily trips to Quang Tri, the main compound at Da Nang became just a place to sleep. At night I'd land on Runway 18 Left and more often than not stumble back to my room, turn the air conditioner on high, and climb into bed. The multi-sortie sixteen-hour days left me limp as a rag. Through bleary eyes I began to see my fellow Prairie Fire pilots in a new light. They weren't so much antisocial or secretive as they were dog tired. The pace, particularly my heavy training schedule, was a real bear, and I looked forward to getting on the regular rotation—or at least to getting used to the grind, whichever came first.

As tired as we were, there always seemed to be time for at least one good meal a day, and in that department we had no problem. The main compound dining hall had to be one of the best-kept secrets of the war. Anyone from colonel to airman basic could eat three great meals a day there, all for practically nothing: breakfast, twenty-five cents; lunch, sixty-five cents; dinner, fifty-five cents. My favorite was breakfast. The cooks turned out eggs and omelettes cooked to order, pancakes, waffles, sausage, bacon, toast, fruit, sweet rolls, and plain old cold cereal. Anyone who complained about that food had to be crazy.

Of course, with Murphy's Law fully operational, we all had a sneaking hunch that our dining hall was too good to be true. Sure enough, toward the end of the month, the VC came through with a particularly heavy 122mm rocket attack, right into our backyard. Most nights the incoming rockets landed on the west side of Da Nang Air Base or sailed completely over us into the city. But on that particular night the bad guys really found the range on the main compound. It was bad enough that one rocket blew the front off our small post office; the real insult came when another rocket exploded just behind the dining hall, riddling the refrigeration unit and freezer with several dozen shrapnel holes. The Combat Support Group chose that occasion to shut the dining hall down for a complete remodeling, for about six months. There was still a dining hall two miles down the road at Gunfighter Village, but it wasn't the same, it wasn't convenient, and most of all, it wasn't ours.

According to my personal log, I flew each day between the twelfth and the twenty-second of July, for a total of twenty-two sorties. On most of those days my Covey rider was Sergeant First Class Marty Martin, a multiple-tour veteran of Southeast Asia and one of the most experienced backseaters in the program. Like most of the SOG troops, Marty went by his personal code name, "Satan." Unlike his code name, Marty had a friendly face and a kindly manner, and although he wasn't much older than the pilots he babysat, the gray touches in his hair and his vast experience made him seem more mature to us.

Satan had one peculiar habit I could never quite get used to. Any time we were flying, he would address me in the third person and only as "Sir." If Marty saw something he thought should be brought to my attention, he'd announce on the intercom, "If Sir will look out the left side at ten o'clock low, he'll notice. . . ." Or he might say, "If Sir will listen up on the Fox Mike radio, I'll call back to the launch site for a status report." Throughout the nine months we flew together, he never switched tenses.

Satan more than made up for that minor quirk with his instant grasp of hot tactical ground situations. When he talked to team leaders, he seemed to have a sixth sense, an uncanny ability to interpret their predicament by listening to their inflections and tone of voice. He could read a man's fear level by hearing him talk on the radio.

Satan had another habit that was equally odd and highly appreciated. During the really hairy extracts, he'd easily pick up on the tension I felt. At just the right moment, he'd key the intercom and very softly begin singing "The Ballad of the Green Beret":

> Fighting soldiers from the sky,
> Fearless men who jump and die.
> One hundred men will test today,
> But only three win the Green Beret.

Every time Marty started his singing, the tension broke like a crack of thunder. No matter how bad the situation, I'd always stop and smile when I heard those lyrics, loosen my grip on the control stick, and relax. To this day I'm convinced Satan's sixth sense helped me keep my cool and fly better. Without my being aware of it, he probably saved my neck on any number of occasions.

On the morning of July 23, Satan and I teamed up to run an insert at the extreme western limit of the Prairie Fire AO.

We inserted the team on the top of a steep karst rock formation a few miles north of Highway 9, a key infiltration route
from Laos into South Vietnam. Right away I got on the horn
to Hillsboro, passing along the prearranged code words to let
them know the team had been inserted and that the no-bomb-
ing rule applied to a six-kilometer square box around the
team's position. Only a Prairie Fire FAC could expend ordnance inside that NBL.

"Hillsboro, Covey 221, over."

"Covey 221, Hillsboro. Go ahead."

"Rog, Hillsboro. We just played the Gray Cloud ball
game. The area's hot as of 1025 Hotel."

With the administrative business out of the way, Marty
and I cruised around the area on a listening watch, just in
case the RT ran into trouble and came up on the radio. During our excursion we overflew the Khe Sanh area, with Satan
giving the history lesson. He showed me the old Lang Vei
Special Forces Camp where, in early February 1968, enemy
tanks attacked along Highway 9. As Satan pointed out the
overgrown perimeter of Lang Vei and the still visible hulks of
several burned-out Soviet PT76 tanks, I studied the scene
with the same kind of detachment one might have on a visit
to any famous Civil War battlefield in the States. For me, the
names Khe Sanh and Lang Vei conjured up vivid images of
great, surging battles where heroics and sacrifice were the
order of the day. But looking down at the ordinary dirt road,
the dilapidated camp, and the deserted airstrip, I felt somehow cheated that the scene below me didn't measure up to
my larger-than-life expectations.

Several miles northwest of Khe Sanh, Satan pointed out a
small burned patch of ground, almost completely insignificant
except for the pieces of debris scattered about. As we circled,
Satan explained that the scar on the ground was actually a
recent crash site, the impact point where Rick Meacham and
his Covey rider had died two months earlier. We circled in
silence, then Marty summed up the whole war, more poi-
gnantly than any poet or philosopher ever could have. To no
one in particular, he mumbled softly, "This whole area is

good country, prime real estate, bought and paid for with American lives.'' I took a pencil and scribbled Satan's words on my clipboard, then I banked sharply around to the east and headed back to Quang Tri.

Back at MLT-2, we sat around killing time. After lunch I had stretched out on an empty bunk to read a magazine, only to fall asleep in the afternoon heat. Waking with a start, I opened my eyes to find Ken Budrow shaking my shoulder. As I swung my legs onto the hooch floor, Top filled me in. ''We just picked up a call from the radio relay. The team's in contact, but they figure they can hold on with some air support. You and Satan are gonna take a couple of Cobras out to see what the problem is.''

Within minutes we were strapped in, cranked, and taxiing. Even with only a half-full centerline fuel tank, the Bronco would need every inch of Quang Tri's three-thousand-foot runway to get airborne. The outside air temp registered a typical one hundred degrees, so I back-taxied into the overrun for an extra hundred feet. At brake release we seemed to crawl forward, eating up runway without much corresponding increase on the airspeed indicator. To compensate for the strong right cross wind off the ocean, I held a healthy dose of right aileron into the wind and a little left rudder to keep us tracking straight down the sixty-foot-wide runway. After an eternity, we reached minimum safe single-engine flying speed, and I yanked us into the air just as we ran out of concrete.

We rendezvoused with our Cobras at Khe Sanh, then pressed out along Route 9 toward our team. When we arrived overhead, the team leader, known as the ''one-zero,'' told us they were taking some harassing fire from a small enemy patrol trying to climb the steep north face of the karst. The one-zero felt his position was secure, but a little insurance would make him feel better. He asked us to hose the north face just to be on the safe side. I fired a couple of willie petes for reference, and using corrections from the team, the Cobras blasted the brittle limestone rocks with mini-guns and high-explosive rockets. On the first few passes, we took a moderate amount of small-arms fire, but by the fourth pass, the only firing was ours.

Since we had plenty of bullets and fuel left, I pulled the Cobras off to the east and set up an orbit, just in case one-zero needed our services again. After two trips around the flagpole, the mission began to take on a completely different complexion when Cobra Lead notified me he was in trouble.

In a calm voice, he announced, "Boss, this doesn't look good. I think we picked up a few souvenirs back there. We're getting some surges and heavy engine vibrations. Let's take up an RTB."

Shortly after we started back to base, it was obvious Cobra Lead had throttled back trying to take the strain off his malfunctioning engine. He held a shallow descent, but all of us recognized that he'd run out of altitude before we could get out of bad guy country. As he passed through a thin broken layer of puffy clouds at twelve hundred feet, the engine gave out. It couldn't have happened at a worse location. We were directly over the 1032 ford, a major intersection where Route 9 crossed the primary north–south segment of the Ho Chi Minh Trail. Even a rookie knew the place was crawling with NVA regulars.

Cobra Lead dropped like a rock, still heading east and trying to stretch his glide in a maneuver the helicopter jocks called auto rotation—roughly similar to a dead-stick landing in a fixed-wing bird. Lead managed to cross Highway 1032 before turning south into the wind toward a large clearing five hundred meters south of Route 9. Cobra Two and I followed him right down to the deck. At the last possible moment, Lead honked back on his controls to break the descent, then he let her settle into a safe but bone-jarring landing. The Cobra bounced a few times before skidding to a halt.

Right away I started feeling the panic and pressure begin to grab just below my rib cage. An acid, burning feeling seemed to move slowly up from my guts, through my chest, and then into my throat. It was up to me to get those two pilots out. But how? As I took a gulp of water to neutralize the burn in my throat, I heard Marty's rendition of "The

Ballad of the Green Beret" come drifting over the intercom. A quick look in the mirror at his calm face told me instantly that the man had faith in me. I winked at his reflection and said, "Hang on, Marty, and keep singing."

To keep us in close, I slammed the stick against my right leg, pulling us around in a steep four-G turn at weed-top level. When the downed Cobra came back into our field of vision, we saw the two pilots out of their chopper, running full speed toward a small gully about a hundred meters to their east. Before we could tell whether they made it, a hail of tracers flashed by us, evidently fired from some scrub bushes on the southwest corner of the large open field. As several more volleys streaked around us, I felt like a duck in a carnival shooting gallery, but I held the high-G turn for all I was worth. At what I guessed to be the right point, I unloaded the Gs and rolled us out, heading directly for the bad guys, hoping the head-on run would present the smallest possible target under the circumstances. We passed over their heads at about ten feet before I zoomed the Bronco into a climbing, jinking turn back to the east. No tracers followed us, prompting Satan to comment sarcastically, "I think Sir's low pass scared them."

From our altitude of one thousand feet, we had a reasonably clear view of the whole area. Cobra Two flew a tight orbit several hundred feet below us, ready to roll in on anyone moving. We caught a glimpse of the downed crewmen huddled against the red-dirt embankment nearest the chopper. In spite of my repeated radio calls to them, neither had yet come up on the survival radio each carried. They seemed intent on watching the tall elephant grass immediately in front of them. From our vantage point, the grass swayed gently in the breeze, easily masking any movement by enemy troops who might be crawling around in it.

In those first hectic minutes, most of my conscious thoughts centered on how to rescue the downed fliers. Through training and conditioning, my instincts told me to contact Hillsboro and lay on a full-blown SAR using Air Force "Jolly Green" rescue helicopters. Under the pressure of the moment, I totally forgot our clandestine operation and our self-contained ability to handle the situation with SOG assets. Instead, I called Hillsboro repeatedly, desperately trying to get anybody on the radio. When we couldn't raise them, I even began climbing to a higher altitude, hoping to improve radio reception.

As I reviewed the bidding, I broke into a cold sweat, thinking about the one-hour-plus reaction time of the Jolly Greens, assuming Hillsboro had even heard my urgent call. I kept asking myself, could we cover these guys that long? Did I have enough gas? Was it a mistake not to fill my centerline tank? Would Cobra Two have enough ammo to keep the bad guys pinned down? Before I had time to whip myself into a complete frenzy, the ground situation heated up, forcing me to do something other than worry and fret.

Cobra Two picked out two separate enemy patrols about four hundred meters west of the gully, all converging in that direction. As he strafed the closest bunch, I felt myself snap out of the fog and indecision that had been clouding my judgment. For some strange reason, the sight of the bullets kicking up the dirt acted like a tonic. At that moment I realized the idea of using the Jolly Greens had been a bad one. Time was critical, and necessity really was the mother of invention.

I yelled to Satan, "Call the launch site and tell them to scramble every Slick and Cobra they've got." Then I asked Cobra Two, "If things get really bad, can you guys lift them out, even if it's only for a short distance?"

"We can do it," he answered, "but you'll have to give us some covering fire. Stand by while we fire off the rest of our rockets. There'll be more room after we jettison the pods."

I couldn't be sure how much time we had, and it was very unsettling not being in radio contact with the two pilots in the gully. To make matters worse, I wasn't at all sure about how effective my covering fire would be. Willie pete rockets were certainly deadly, but I would have given anything to have the four M-60 machine guns the OV-10 normally carried. Months earlier, in a very controversial decision, Seventh Air Force removed the guns from the Bronco, claiming FACs relied on their own ordnance too often, flew too low on strafing runs, and generally took too many chances when armed with machine guns. It would have been sweet revenge to have the responsible staff weenie along in my back seat for a firsthand look at the real world.

I calculated that the reinforcement helicopters would need about twenty minutes to get to us. If we could just keep a lid on things till then, we might get through this. The situation was far from rosey, but at least we had a plan.

While Cobra Two sprayed HE rockets around the large field, I pulled out my binoculars and focused on the gully. Our boys crouched just below the rim, out of the direct line of fire. But as I watched, a steady barrage of bullets kicked up dust along the crest. We were definitely out of time.

Cobra Two and I got our signals straight. He followed us down the chute while I pickled off several willie petes to keep everyone's head down. I reefed us around in a hard turn and fired two more rockets into the area adjacent to the Cobra's intended touchdown point. The white smoke billowed out, only to be caught by a gust of wind and blown directly across the helicopter's flight path. Suddenly, the Cobra disappeared, engulfed in the blinding white smoke.

Seconds later Cobra Two cobbed the power and climbed away from the fiasco I had created. Before the angry pilot could say anything, I said apologetically, "Sorry about that. Let's set up again. I'll keep the rockets farther out this time." All I got in response was an indignant "click, click" from his transmitter.

On the second try, I moved a little farther west and came in right on the deck. With Satan calling out the Cobra's position for me, I put the pipper on a grove of small trees concealing one of the patrols. As we closed at practically zero dive angle, puffs of smoke dotted the length of the grove as everybody and his dog took his best shot. We were so low that my first rocket hit the ground with its motor still running.

The rocket snaked wildly through the weeds like a big Chinese firecracker. The second rocket hit a glancing blow and ricocheted back into the air, sailing over the target and finally exploding several hundred meters away.

My radio blared. "We're almost in. Keep it up, Covey. You've got 'em all shooting at you!"

As we came back around for another run, the downed pilots bolted from the gully just as Cobra Two touched down. It seemed to take them forever to cover the twenty-five yards to their waiting salvation. As they ran, I continued to pop off a steady stream of willie petes. By then, smoke obscured most of the field. Tracers filled the sky, but fortunately, most of them were wild shots, probably directed at our engine sound.

When we bottomed out on that last rocket pass, Marty and I witnessed an incredible sight. In the waiting Cobra, both pilots had their right-side canopies open, merrily blazing away with handguns. Besides having huge brass balls, the two helicopter pilots had to be certifiably insane!

A split second after the running pilots had jumped on the skids, Cobra Two lifted off and began hedge-hopping to the east as fast as they could fly. Satan and I hosed the area one last time, then took out after the Huey Cobra. In the slow climb back to altitude, we flew alongside the gunship turned troop carrier. Perched on each skid, the rescued fliers were all smiles and waves. I felt elated too, like a kid on the last day of school before summer vacation. To celebrate, we did multiple barrel rolls around Cobra Two.

Late that afternoon, Satan and I returned to the crash site with a new load of rockets and a new mission. The downed Cobra contained classified equipment and documents. Our job was to blow it away.

I briefed the orbiting Skyraiders and cleared them in hot. Spad Lead demolished the chopper on his first pass, and Two blasted it a second time to make sure. We naped and strafed the large field for good measure, but with no apparent results. For BDA I gave the Spads one AH-1G Cobra destroyed.

Marty and I were tired but still on an adrenalin high. As the sun set, we took one last swing over the karst hiding our team. After I gunned the engines to get their attention, the one-zero gave us a coded "team okay" over the radio. They were secure in a night-defensive position, so we headed back to the barn. Climbing through thirty-five hundred feet, my VHF radio came back to life.

"Covey 221, Hillsboro. How do you read, over. We've been trying to talk to you for the past hour. If you copy, say the nature of your problem."

I couldn't bring myself to tell the controller the whole story. "That's okay, Hillsboro. The problem went away. We're RTB to channel 103. Catch you tomorrow."

AUGUST

Rescue at Route 966

The dog days of August at Da Nang gave new meaning to the concept of high summer. Not only did we fight Charlie, the grunts' nickname for the VC, but everybody suffered under the sweltering heat. On those incredibly clear, hot days of 1970, the temperature creeped up to over one hundred degrees on a regular basis, with the humidity not far behind. Far offshore in the South China Sea, we all watched the daily buildup of storm clouds, hoping they'd drift our way with some cooling rain. But in a monsoon climate, it was feast or famine. In another two months, we'd give a month's pay for just one day of dry weather.

In early August we said good-bye to Fuzzy Furr, our very capable leader and affable friend. Fuzzy's new job was taking him to a staff assignment at the 504th TASG at Cam Ranh Bay. We hated to see him go, but during our one-year tours, new guys arriving and good friends leaving was the natural order of things.

The job of Prairie Fire boss fell to Mike McGerty, my old teacher from the Ubon X-Ray mission. Now Mike would become the FNG, and his education and training would take center stage. To facilitate McGerty's training, Bob Meadows, our training officer, shifted me south of Da Nang to the MLT operating out of Chu Lai. McGerty would receive his training in the more active northern areas of the Prairie Fire AO, just as I had.

Shortly after I made the shift to Chu Lai, a terrible aircraft accident jerked us all up short, forcing us to reflect on the brutal, fickle nature of war. One of our A-1 jocks, returning from a mission, experienced engine failure en route from Chu Lai to Da Nang. As the big Spad lost altitude, the pilot went through all the emergency procedures in a desperate effort to restart the huge twenty-seven-hundred-horsepower recip engine. In retrospect, he probably should have bailed out earlier, but all of us felt a strong desire to save our aircraft if possible. When the pilot finally realized that further efforts were futile, he activated the Yankee ejection mechanism, a system in which a powerful rocket attached to the pilot's parachute harness literally snatched him out of his seat and clear of the aircraft. For whatever unfair force was at work, for whatever cosmic circumstance had to be satisfied, the rocket didn't fire. The pilot was already too low to bail out over the side, and had no choice but to ride the Skyraider in.

No one could determine exactly what happened in those last few moments. Just a few feet above the trees, the Spad apparently went out of control, cartwheeling into the ground with a shattering explosion. The pilot died instantly. None of us talked about it much, but there seemed to be an unspoken feeling that if fate had willed our friend to die, he had been cheated—he should have been allowed to die in combat instead of in a stupid aircraft accident.

The intensity of operations at Chu Lai quickly forced the A-1 crash to the back of my mind. SOG's cross-border effort from Chu Lai was short but intense, partially dictated by the mission but also shaped by meager resources and the rapidly approaching wet season. I personally had my hands full getting used to the new AO and a different group of people. One of the necessary but dull administrative chores involved assembling and arranging the twenty-five pounds of extra maps required to work the new area. Throughout that early breaking-in period, we always seemed to be pressed for time or behind schedule.

In spite of the pace, the Chu Lai missions gave me a chance to see a couple of old friends flying as Helix FACs for the Americal Division. On my first visit I was astounded. The Helix FACs lived in pleasant, four-man hooches practically on the beach. To me it had all the makings of a really plush setup—comfortable hooches located in a shady grove, a beautiful beach just on the other side of a small embankment, and the South China Sea for a backdrop. The setting made our own China Beach look tacky by comparison. It was easy to see why most Helix FACs hated to come to Da Nang.

Living so far from family, it was a special treat to see a friend from "back in the world." I made a point of searching out Helix 16, Captain Carl D'Benedetto. Carl and I had been to school together and were later stationed together at Cannon AFB and at Hurlburt. My wife and I were good friends with Carl's wife, and the four of us shared lots of good times. Carl's dark good looks and friendly personality made him popular with everyone.

When I ran into Carl, we had only a few minutes to talk. He was understandably confused about a Covey FAC flying missions out of Chu Lai. I felt odd and more than a little underhanded at being unable to tell him, but he took my feeble explanation in stride and didn't press me. Instead, Carl gave me the good news that we'd soon be neighbors at Da Nang, that he'd been selected to be one of the 20th TASS Stan/Eval pilots, and that we'd be seeing a lot more of each other.

On the morning of August 10, I made the fifty-five-mile flight south to Chu Lai. I hated the takeoffs and landing on their runway. The airfield was set up much like that at Da Nang, with two long, parallel runways. A Marine fighter outfit used the conventional concrete runway on the west side of the complex. Everybody else, including the Helix FACs, used the east runway, a temporary affair made of pierced steel planking, or PSP. Bouncing over the PSP felt like driving over a washboard. On takeoff roll or landing, my instrument panel vibrated so violently that it was impossible to read the individual gauges. My eyes suffered a similar fate, fluttering up and down with each bounce. At the midrange speeds, I worried that my airplane and my eyes would be the victims of simple harmonic motion, about to tear themselves apart.

Charlie Gray and I teamed up to run the mission, the insertion of a road watch team just across the border into an isolated area that was being heavily infiltrated by the North Vietnamese. Charlie seemed a little skiddish about the operation for a couple of reasons. First, the Chu Lai AO was new to him also, and neither of us was very familiar with the region or the landmarks. Second, Charlie shared my nervousness about working with the untried helicopter assets from the Americal Division. I knew by reputation they were good, but we were used to working with the troops from the 101st Screaming Eagles stationed at Hue Phu Bai. Finally, Charlie's real feelings about being a Covey rider began to show. I never knew his motives for getting into the program, but I began to sense that he didn't like to fly, that he didn't have that much confidence in the hotshot fighter pilots in whom he was forced to entrust his life.

After the bouncing takeoff out of Chu Lai, we leveled off at two thousand feet above the terrain for the flight to the Laotian border. From our vantage point, all we could see was one steep mountain ridge after another. Each long ridge, running roughly north to south, was completely covered by incredible varieties of lush vegetation. On our westerly flight path, the scene reminded me of an endless series of huge, emerald green ocean waves surging onto a beach. In several of the valleys between the highest ridge lines, we could make out patches of dense early-morning fog, giving an eerie effect to the panorama below us. In spite of the rugged beauty, the terrain seemed somehow sinister, like a dark alley late at night in a tough neighborhood. Nobody would stop you from entering the alley, but you instinctively knew you'd have to fight your way out—and the thugs hidden in the shadows invariably carried razor-sharp switchblades, chains, and brass knuckles. It was their turf, and they fought dirty. As Charlie and I looked down at the jungle, we both sensed we'd probably end this day fighting our way out of some no-name Laotian valley—an old-fashioned, dirty rumble—all because we had to find out who or what lay hidden at the end of that dark alley.

Thirty minutes before the package arrived, we located the

LZ, a small clearing nestled in the crotch of two small inter-
secting ridges. The only approach to the football-sized field
was from the west. The swaying yellow-green elephant grass
gave the illusion that the LZ was flat, but if our maps were
correct, the field sloped up at least fifteen degrees. With the
steep hill directly in front of us and another one to our immediate right, there wasn't a lot of room to maneuver. We knew
it would be risky getting the helicopters into that partial box
canyon, but once on the ground, the team would have a great
view of Route 966, just four hundred meters to the west.

At 0900 we linked up with the package and led them to
the target area. As I flew in to mark the LZ verbally for the
waiting Cobras, it felt strange to dive lower than the target
and then fly up hill to get there. After calling "mark, mark,"
with the hill looming right in front of us, I sucked the stick
back into my lap to start an upward vector climb, then stood
the protesting Bronco on her left wing tip in a hard, rolling G
turn to the north. From the back seat, Charlie complained
loudly, "Christ, that was close!" I took a quick peek at
Charlie in the mirror and could see that his eyes were the size
of saucers.

We continued to bank around to our left, eventually setting up an orbit directly over the LZ and just a few hundred
feet above the tops of the two hills. From our vantage point,
we watched while the Cobras worked the area over with a
hail of fléchettes. We could also see our Slicks orbiting about
a mile to the east, impatient to get in and out.

The moment of truth arrived. It certainly wasn't the time
for a Knute Rockne pep talk, but I felt compelled to let the
Americal pilots know what I expected of them. "Listen up,
gents. The approach and pull-off to the north are tricky, so be
on your toes. There seems to be an unpredictable wind swirling around near the crotch joining the two hills. Be alert for
prop wash. Slick door gunners, when you're in the hover,
watch the slopes above you. The bad guys could easily be
firing down on you. We've got to have a good, tight pattern,
so Cobras, keep it tucked in and your guns ready to bear.
Everybody arm 'em up and let's do it."

There was no radio chatter as Slick Lead flew down final with his Cobra escort. A thousand feet above me I could see the sunlight reflected off the canopies of the circling A-1s. At least a dozen pairs of eyes focused on the LZ as the Huey eased into the tall grass and let his precious cargo of four team members jump out the left troop door.

All of us saw it at the same instant. Before the Huey got ten feet off the ground, the air filled with small-arms and machine-gun fire. The Slick belched several clouds of black smoke from its exhaust, then began to serpentine, first to the right, then back to the left. Two seconds later, the chopper dropped out of the sky and smacked into the ground with a shattering force. The Huey flopped over on its right side and simply lay there like a dead fish.

There was no fire or explosion. At first I thought the chopper had fallen on the team, but Charlie spotted them scurrying up the hill for the cover of a nearby tree line.

Quickly, I thought through the key elements of the predicament we faced: one downed chopper and crew, one small team wandering around the woods, bad guys firing at us from two sides, and a tricky approach into the LZ. On the plus side, I had the assets in place to do the job, good weather, and lots of gas. There was nothing left to do but get on with the rescue, yet I couldn't help wondering where all the NVA had come from. How was it that they just happened to be positioned in force around that particular LZ?

I wasn't sure how Charlie was holding up in the back seat, so as calmly as possible, I said, "Charlie, see if you can raise the team on Fox Mike. Find out what they see and hear and tell them to dig in as close to the LZ as possible. I'm gonna work over the south face with the Spads, then we'll go for an extract."

I ventured a quick look at Charlie's face in the mirror. He appeared stern but composed. He was back in his element and answered crisply, "Roger that. Here's where we earn our combat pay."

While Charlie tried to raise the team, I briefed the Spads. "Okay, Spad Lead, here's the drill. I need a couple of passes from you guys against that southern hill. Let's start off with HE rockets and strafe. I'd like you to plan your runs north to south with a pull-off to the west. Keep a sharp look out 'cause the Cobras will be just below you on a perpendicular flight path suppressing fire on the other hill.''

Next, I turned my attention to the Hueys. "Slick Two, as Spad Two comes off his second pass, I need you touching down on the northeast corner of the LZ. You scarf up the team. Cobra Lead will cover you. Slick Three, land as close to the crash as possible. Have the *bac si* and door gunner do a fast check for survivors. Cobra Two will cover you.''

I armed two rocket pods and rolled in on the south face, spacing four willie petes along the length of its slope. I racked us around in a tight 270-degree right turn and gave the eastern hill the same treatment. There was just time for one final set of instructions. "Spads, hit anywhere between my smokes on the south hill. Cobras, anywhere between my smokes on the east hill. You're cleared in hot.''

I climbed a couple of thousand feet and set up an orbit slightly west of the LZ. A thousand feet below, the Slicks milled around waiting for their turn. Just when I thought we had it wired, one of the Hueys yelled over the radio, "Covey, break left! Somebody's shooting big stuff at you!''

Without waiting to confirm it, I cobbed the power, stomped hard left rudder, and slammed the stick to the left. Down we went in a series of tight aileron rolls. For a split second during each revolution, I could see the string of 23mm air bursts following us. Then, as fast as it started, it stopped. As we leveled off on the trees and circled back into position, I realized I hadn't been paying attention and had drifted out over the Trail. The gun was down there somewhere, more of a nuisance than a real threat, so we avoided the issue by keeping our orbit directly over the LZ.

As Charlie and I watched, the big A-1s and the Cobras began their intricate weave, spraying the jungle slopes with high-explosive rockets and 7.62mm mini-gun fire. As the Spads pulled off their last pass, the Slicks were in perfect position on short final with the Cobras coming off their runs and back around to cover. For added insurance, I had the Spads drop M-47 smoke bombs along the south face. I hoped the thick, white smoke would give the vulnerable Hueys some masking cover as they ran the gauntlet of fire into the LZ.

So far, so good. The Slicks touched down in the tall grass and seemed to sit there for an eternity. I saw two figures leap out of Slick Three, run to the crashed chopper, and climb up on its side. I shot a quick glance toward the tree line, hoping to see our team, but my attention was diverted when a long stream of tracers came pouring out of the jungle about halfway up the hill. Before I had time to say anything, Cobra Lead rolled in and hosed the area, silencing that threat at least temporarily.

When I looked back at the LZ, both Slicks had lifted off, straining for altitude and airspeed. I asked Charlie, "Did you ever see the team?"

He answered, "I never saw them. I don't think they got out. Something must have happened."

We knew the chopper pilots had their hands full, but I couldn't wait. "Slick Two, Covey 221. Say status of the team. Over."

Somewhat irritably, I thought, the pilot responded, "Stand by, Covey." A few seconds later he keyed his mike again. "We've got all four on board, smiling and laughing!"

Elated at that news, I checked in with the other Huey. "Three, were there any survivors?"

"Rog, Covey. We got the door gunner. He's shook up but okay. The two pilots are dead. We couldn't get them out of the wreck."

On that sad note, I rounded up the package and pointed them toward Chu Lai. Charlie and I remained over the crash site for fifteen more minutes, making sure we had all the landmarks memorized, because we both knew we'd be back later with a stronger team in an all-out effort to recover the bodies of our friends. We hated to go off and leave them, fearful that the enemy troops might tamper with the wreckage while we were gone. More out of frustration than conviction,

I fired off all my remaining rockets into the trees around the LZ. Maybe the sound of the explosions would make the bad guys think twice before coming out of hiding to investigate the downed Huey. With any luck we'd be refueled, rearmed, and back on the scene before they got organized.

Back at Chu Lai, it took the rest of the afternoon to get the twelve-man Bright Light team down from Da Nang. While we were waiting, Charlie and I flew one more sortie across the fence, trying to determine if NVA units were moving to reinforce the area around the fight of earlier that morning. During their brief time on the ground, our team thought they might have heard motorized equipment moving out on the Trail. Charlie and I combed every inch of that section of Highway 966, but all we got for our trouble was a good hosing from yet another 23mm gun.

After refueling again, we finally got the package airborne at 1630. This time I kept the chopper force orbiting while the Spads saturated both hills with CBU-25, rockets, and strafe. When they finished, I let the Cobras nail the whole area for good measure.

Covered by the Cobras, Slick Lead eased into the LZ unopposed and deposited the first four men of the Bright Light team. As he lifted off, the Huey shuttered under the heavy force of multiple machine-gun hits as automatic-weapons fire poured out of two pockets halfway up the southern hill. I had a sick feeling in the pit of my stomach as I began talking to my package.

"Slick Lead, take up a heading of 045 if you can and say your condition."

"Covey, we're all okay but the transmission sounds like it could come apart any second now. I've got the RPM beeped up about as much as she'll take. We'll never make it all the way back to Chu Lai."

After a long swig from my water bottle, I answered him. "I got a good copy, Lead. I'll send Cobra Two and Slick Four with you in case you have to set her down. Your best bet is Kham Duc, northeast for thirteen miles. Break, break.

Cobra Two, give us an update on Lead's status every few minutes.''

As the mini-package headed for Kham Duc, Charlie laid some more bad news on me. "Are you listening up on Fox Mike Two?" he asked. "The One-zero says they're taking small-arms fire from that south hill. He'll try to stay put if you can turn off the heat."

Despite all our efforts, the hill was obviously still crawling with bad guys. It was time to pull out all the stops. Switching over to the UHF radio, I told the Spads, "Let's burn 'em out. Give me the napalm along that south face. You're cleared in hot, but for god's sake, don't drop short."

The nape would do the trick, but the one-zeroes generally didn't like us to use the stuff. The residual fires were unpredictable, often moving toward the team and flushing them out of otherwise good hiding places.

While the A-1s splashed the target, Charlie and I talked over the situation between conversations with the team. They could still hear lots of ground fire, but it was all directed at us. By the time the Spads finished, the team reported all quiet. I felt uncomfortable committing the rest of the Bright Light team without the spare Huey, but we had to recover those bodies while there was a lull, and there wasn't time to wait for the rest of my package to make it back to our location.

Once more we double-teamed the targets, with Cobra Lead suppressing to the east and the Spads beating up on the southern hill. In all the confusion, Slick Two started his run into the LZ. On short final he aborted, riddled by AK-47 fire. Badly shot up but with nobody hurt, the UH-1 limped out of the area and headed back to Chu Lai.

With half my package shot to hell and nothing to show for it, I decided to call off the recovery. We had clearly stumbled into a big hornet's nest, a lot bigger than we could handle in the one hour of daylight remaining. Charlie estimated we were up against battalion strength and that the cagey NVA regulars were using the crash and our team as bait. It made sense. During those long hours while we were away, the bad guys had apparently moved half of North Vietnam into prepared positions around the crash. They probably let the team onto the ground before opening up, knowing full well we wouldn't give up until we had our troops back.

In light of what had already happened, it was embarrassing to ask the last Huey to try for a pickup, but there was no choice. When I asked Slick Three if he'd give it a try, he answered, "No sweat, Covey. Just give me lots of cover." I could have hugged the crazy fool.

We were all short of gas and ammo, so this one had to count. As the Slick made his run, the Spads and the remaining Cobra strafed both hills, now almost totally covered in deep afternoon shadows. In the twilight, tracer ammunition crisscrossed the sky. I dropped full flaps and flew formation with the Huey all the way down final, hoping the sight of the low-flying OV-10 would keep a few heads down. It didn't work. Before we made it over the LZ, Slick Three pulled up sharply and broke hard to the north, his gunner slumped half out the door in a lifeless heap.

I thought to myself, what a hell of a mess. No gas, no choppers, no daylight, and four men down there counting on us to get them out. As I was about to ask Charlie to call back to Chu Lai for another Huey, one-zero began whispering on his radio. I'd never heard that sound on a radio before, but it could only mean the worst kind of trouble. His heavy breathing and muffled words sent chills down my spine.

"They're coming in for the kill," he hissed. "Heavy movement twenty meters to our northeast. For reference, they should be about fifty meters due east of the crash site. Put some hurt on them!"

I listened to that pathetic whisper, but I couldn't figure out what to do. The only relevant thought I had concerned my FAC training back at Hurlburt. For some reason all I could grab hold of was a classroom lecture about minimum safe distances for dropping various types of ordnance. I honestly couldn't remember anything that could be delivered around friendly troops inside one hundred meters. Without thinking about what I was saying, I finally blurted out, "I can't take the responsibility for dropping stuff that close to your position. You'll have to move and give us some room to work."

The team leader's response felt like somebody had punched me in the stomach. In firm but quiet tones, he retorted, "Son, forget your goddamn rule book and get on with it. I'd rather take my chances with you killing me than let the VC get us."

A man that eloquent had to be saved. I took another gulp from my water bottle before I answered. "Get your heads down. I'm in from the west, and when my rockets hit, you bug out north as fast as you can run. The Spads will be in fifteen seconds behind me."

As we came down the chute, both hills lit up with small-arms fire. Fortunately, I was so preoccupied with lining up the target in my gunsight that there was no time to worry about it. From a shallow dive angle, I squeezed off two willie petes before racking us into the tighest G turn I could pull without stalling. The Bronco buffeted all the way through the turn, but she kept climbing and flying like the thoroughbred she was. At the 180-degree point in our turn, the one-zero sang out, "You're right on! You're right on! Fire for effect!"

With the heavy G forces giving my voice a funny, wavering sound, I grunted out to the Spads, "Hit my smoke." As we continued the circle, they blasted the area with HE rockets and strafe. In the growing darkness, the explosions made for a spectacular light show. The team wasn't answering Charlie's request for a correction, so I could only hope they were moving. To keep the pressure on, the Spads made one more pass, then advised they were low on fuel and heading home. To complicate matters, my remaining Cobra started home also. Now it was up to Charlie and me, and we only had a few more minutes before we'd have to leave.

It was almost completely dark. The sun had set behind the higher mountains to our west; in a few more minutes, we wouldn't be able to see anything. To complicate the situation further, a small patch of ground fog had developed along a streambed just off the LZ, in exactly the direction our team had moved. As Charlie and I circled forlornly over the scene, the muzzle flashes down below, now plainly visible in the growing darkness, confirmed our worst suspicions; as we counted at least 130 separate flashes, we knew we could never get the team out, at least not that night.

It was a long five minutes before the one-zero reestablished radio contact. As he talked and simultaneously gasped for breath, I could hear steady exchanges of gunfire over the radio. "We're off the north edge of the LZ and about fifty meters down the slope in the first big tree line. Chuck is right on the crest in the elephant grass firing down on us. They're in the open, so blast 'em!"

Since my rockets were the only game in town, I rolled in to do as the man said—blast 'em. I only had the vaguest notion of where the team was, but there was no time to sort it out. I put the pipper on the edge of the LZ and fired one willie pete. I couldn't see the impact, but as we pulled off the run, the one-zero shouted, "You're long. Tell the Spads to go about one hundred meters short of your smoke."

As I maneuvered for the second pass, I said to my backseater, "Charlie, tell him there aren't any Spads. Tell him to keep the corrections coming."

The second rocket was better. The one-zero yelled encouragement. "Bull's-eye. They're screaming up there! Keep pounding that area!"

Just as I was wondering how best to use my last two rockets, the UHF radio crackled. "Covey 221, Spad 03 and 04 are back with you. We've been monitoring your freq and came back to help out. We can give you two twenty-mike-mike passes each, but then we've got to get out of here."

I passed on the good news to the one-zero, but I let the other shoe drop with it. Trying to sound as optimistic as possible, I explained, "There's no way we can pull you out tonight. If the Spads beat up that crest just above you, do you think you can move into a solid night-defensive position and hold on till morning?"

After thinking it over for a few seconds, he answered,

"We can hear 'em up there, and they're hurt and disorganized. If you break the contact for me, we'll be here at first light waiting for you."

I asked Charlie, "How in the hell can he be so calm about spending the night in the middle of an NVA battalion?"

"He's one of our best one-zeroes," Charlie replied. "As I recall, he got a DSC about six months ago on a mission similar to this one."

For the final time that night, I dove the OV-10 into all those winking muzzle flashes. In what turned out to be a piece of blind luck, my smoke hit twenty meters above the team's position. The Spads did the rest, raking the edge of the LZ with a deadly hail of cannon fire. When it was over and the A-1s had departed for the second time, we climbed to a safe altitude and contacted the team. In a whisper the leader told us all firing had ceased and that he had dug in for the night. Charlie and I both promised him we'd be back to pull him out at first light. Then we headed for Chu Lai, running on fumes and feeling totally dejected about having to leave those poor devils out in the jungle.

We didn't have a lot of time to feel sorry for ourselves. I was genuinely concerned about our fuel since we only had three hundred pounds remaining, by far the lowest I'd flown with in my brief career. As we neared Chu Lai, the pucker factor went up a little more when I couldn't raise the tower and couldn't make out any runway lights. My heart sank when a passing C-123 answered my radio calls, informing us that Chu Lai was Condition Red, under attack, and that the field was closed.

I briefly considered landing on the blacked-out runway, but instead turned north on a direct line to Da Nang. Several minutes later, just as I contacted Da Nang Approach Control and explained our minimum fuel situation, the fuel-low caution light blinked on, indicating something less than 220 pounds remaining. Approach Control wasn't thrilled when I asked for a straight-in against traffic, but they finally agreed and handed us over to Da Nang tower for a landing on Runway 36 Right.

When we touched down, I sneaked a peek at the fuel gauge. In the dark cockpit, the needle fluctuated on the very bottom of the graduated scale. It had been close.

After taxiing to the Covey revetments, I shut both engines down and took off my helmet while the props were still turning. As I sat there in an exhausted stupor, all I could hear was the whishing sound as the props wound down and the crackling and pinging noises as the engines cooled off. When everything had stopped, Charlie and I climbed stiffly out of our seats and onto the concrete ramp. As I stood there facing him under the bright flight-line lights, I hoped I didn't look as bad as he did. We had taken off fifteen hours earlier, flying four sorties and spending nine and one-half of those hours in the air. And we weren't through yet. Bob Meadows met us with a jeep and a beer and drove us directly to the Prairie Fire briefing room so we could plan the rescue for the next morning.

None of us slept much that night. When we launched the package at dawn, we went out loaded for bear, fully expecting the NVA to have reinforced throughout the night. The first clue to the contrary came when Charlie tried to make radio contact with the team. Every man in the package was on pins and needles waiting for the reply. At the sound of the one-zero's voice in my earphones, I felt myself exhale loudly; I'd literally been holding my breath since Charlie had first keyed his mike button.

The team was in good shape but needed a few minutes to move up the slope to the edge of the LZ. They reported all quiet—no noise, no patrols, no sounds from the bad guys since just before midnight. As a precaution, we surrounded them with a concentrated saturation bombing and strafing of the hills overlooking the LZ.

Slick Lead made it down final and into a hover without incident. We held our breath again as the team scrambled out of the concealing tree line and into the open troop door of the Huey. As the UH-1 lifted off and turned to the north, the

Cobras plastered the faces of both hills with rockets and mini-gun fire. Strangely, we never saw or heard a shot fired in return. With no apparent opposition from the NVA, we talked to the launch site about going back in to recover the bodies in the wrecked helicopter, but they made the decision to cancel the whole show. We never returned to the LZ overlooking Route 966.

A few days later, the Spads were kind enough to invite me to one of their "hail and farewell" parties. It was just the sort of distraction we needed. Uniform of the day was the party suit, a garish copy of our flight suits tailored and fitted in an outlandish assortment of colors. The A-1 jocks wore either a black or an olive-drab suit. My Covey party suit, in royal blue, clearly upstaged anything there. Individualism was expressed in the various patches on the party suit—Yankee Air Pirate; Participant, Southeast Asia War Games; the Covey patch, depicting that world-famous beagle, Snoopy, dancing a jig over crisscrossing tracers; the Covey Prairie Fire patch, showing Snoopy astride a machine-gun-firing doghouse, diving into a wall of red flames. As accessories, I wore the traditional Covey scarf, black with yellow polka dots, and a brass chain and medallion with the letters WAR.

As I entered the private room of the Da Nang officers' club, the scene appeared tame enough. A U-shaped banquet table dominated the room. In the far corner, most of the Spads and invited guests congregated around a small bar. Predictably, the conversation focused on flying and recent adventures or war stories. The setting reminded me of the dozens of other fighter pilot bashes I had attended over the years.

Then the tenor of the evening began to change. The head Spad invited all of us to order the drink of our choice from the bar. Someone produced a large stainless-steel pot into which everybody dutifully poured his drink—beer, scotch, Bloody Mary, crème de menthe, brandy. Each of us dipped his glass into the vat. When everybody had a brimming glass full of "Spad Sauce," the head Spad lifted his glass in a toast, "To the Spads," to which all of us responded by chug-

ging the nasty, potent, olive-drab concoction. From there, the
party rapidly went downhill.

Shortly after we sat down to dinner, one of the Spads
tossed a dinner roll across the room at some unsuspecting
soul, to the rousing cheers of his buddies who shouted the
warning "In coming!" Periodically throughout the meal, vol-
lies of rolls arched back and forth across the tables.

Following dinner, some enterprising Spad grabbed the
remnants from a sour cream bowl and drew a large bull's-eye
on the back of the closed door. Next, he handed me the bowl
of "ammo" and instructed me to sling a handful of the stuff
at our target. From wherever the "mark" splattered, I issued
corrections to the Spads who stood at the far end of the room
and tossed their drink glasses at the target. In no time we had
broken every glass in the place. The party took a definite
downturn when the irate club manager refused to bring in
another tray of glasses.

As a fitting cap to the evening, the head Spad shouted,
"Anybody who can't tap-dance on the table is queer!" To a
man, all thirty of us in the room leaped on the U-shaped
tables and proceeded to do individual impressions of Gene
Kelly. Under the heavy weight, the tables collapsed, sending
pilots, dishes, and leftovers crashing to the floor in a twisted,
broken heap.

With good cause, the club officer unceremoniously booted
us out. Our understanding flight surgeon patched up the
bruises and stitched up the cuts, then shuffled us all off to
bed, battered but relaxed after letting off the dangerous head
of steam that had been building.

In the days that followed the bash with the Spads, we
returned to the Prairie Fire mission ready to tackle whatever
came our way. Operations took a decided turn toward the
routine. For the remainder of August, most of my flights
involved escorting supply helicopters to a remote mountaintop due west of Da Nang and just across the border into
Laos.

The object of our supply effort was a SOG radio relay site
perched precariously on top of a seventy-two-hundred-foot

mountain. From its commanding heights, the highly trained commo troops stationed there could intercept most line-of-sight radio transmissions from SOG teams in the area, then pass them on to the MLT or to CCN headquarters at Da Nang. Technically, the plan was a good one; realistically, the technicians on the mountaintop fought a never-ending battle against isolation, boredom, limited supplies, and determined assaults by NVA units in the area who wanted nothing more than to wipe out the flagrant little camp operating in their backyard.

Small enemy patrols harassed the relay site regularly, but they never had the strength to mount a frontal attack against the mountaintop perimeter. Instead, the bad guys decided to disrupt the vital supply line by shooting up our supply-laden choppers as they tried to land on the postage-stamp-sized LZ. My job was to direct the fire of supporting Cobras, hopefully pinning down the enemy troops long enough for our choppers to slip in and out unharmed.

On a normal day, we'd fly several round trips escorting huge CH-54 Skycranes with large cargo nets full of supplies suspended under their weird-looking fuselages. The combination of high heat, high-pressure altitude, and heavy loads strained their big engines to the limit and cut the Skycranes' maneuverability to practically nil. Without the help of the Cobra gunships, the big birds were sitting ducks as they lumbered into the relay site with their precious cargo.

Our tactics of spraying suspected positions with rockets and machine-gun fire were generally effective, although results were arguable. For starters, the relay site would brief me on enemy activity during the preceding night. Usually the commander passed on his best guess about directions and distance to sounds, movement, or actual fire received. "Pretty quiet last night. We did hear somebody stomping around just before dawn. Sounded like the noise was on a bearing of 130 degrees, maybe two hundred meters out."

Based on the relay site's estimate, the Covey rider and I would survey the area, pick out the most likely spots, then fire a couple of willie petes into the target. Keying on our smoke, the Cobras worked the areas over while the CH-54 made his run onto the mountaintop. For all we knew, the sounds at which we fired could have been some animal rooting around in the tangle of vegetation, but this was no time to be cautious—anybody moving up the side of the mountain was considered the enemy. Besides, the relay site could hear the bad guys shooting at us on every resupply sortie, so we knew the threat and the danger were real.

These missions seemed easy compared to inserting a team on the Ho Chi Minh Trail. Since there was never any doubt about where the friendlies were, controlling air strikes was a snap. Most of us began to regard the daily resupply missions as milk runs. We knew the NVA fired at us, but we tended to dismiss the danger as minimal. Of course, it was always possible to get hit when the bad guys emptied clip after clip in our direction, but fortunately, the sky is a big place, and most of us felt that if we were to get blasted, it would be the result of a lucky shot, what pilots called the "golden BB."

On August 22 I had a welcome break from the routine resupply missions. South Vietnam was a veritable crossroads for Air Force flyers, and I should not have been surprised to run across yet another buddy from the world, but I was happily surprised to see my roommate from pilot training, Captain Norm Komich, show up at Da Nang. The best part was that Norm had been assigned as a Jolly Green helicopter pilot living on the ground floor of the Covey hooch. Norm was the kind of tonic we all needed. He had a great sense of humor and was one of the most naturally upbeat people any of us would ever meet. Norm took a lot of good-natured kidding over his very meticulous eating habits, stemming primarily from an unquenchable desire for "greens and grams of protein." Norm took the teasing graciously because none of it was vicious—nobody dared to be nasty because he was a world-class body builder and former Mr. Massachusetts. His biceps were about the size of an average man's leg. Throughout the tour, Norm tried, in his heavy Boston accent, to convert us to better health through proper diet, rest, and no booze. He never succeeded, but it was always fun letting him try.

Fortunately for me, I had friends to fall back on when the action heated up, such guys as Evan Quiros, Carl D'Benedetto, and Norm Komich. On the morning of August 31, I slept in since I was on the afternoon resupply run to the radio relay site. At about 10:30 that morning, Evan walked into our room, acting sort of stiff and tentative. I figured that something was bothering him, that he would get around to telling me in his own time. Finally, Evan took a deep breath and said, "I guess you didn't hear about Mike McGerty. The word just came in a little while ago. He got shot down out around that mountain you guys are always flying to."

I felt myself recoil from Evan's news. At first I was angry with him. I'd been in the room all morning. How could I know about McGerty? What a goddamn dumb thing to say. Then I took a close look at Evan's face. It was drawn tight with tension. He probably felt as awkward about telling me as I felt about hearing it. None of us knew how to handle circumstances like that, much less express them. My reaction had been classic—shoot the messenger.

When I finally trusted my voice enough to speak, it sounded hollow to me, as it had when I'd heard that Rick Meacham had been shot down. "Did he eject?" I asked.

Evan simply shook his head no, then added softly, "The back-seater didn't get out either."

We flew the afternoon resupply run as scheduled. After the last chopper dumped his load on the LZ, I circled down the northeast face of the mountain to the crash site. Through the heavy foliage, we could just make out the disintegrated mess that had once been an OV-10. The Bright Light team had already recovered the bodies of Captain Mike McGerty and Sergeant First Class Charlie Gray. Nobody could shed much light on what had happened. The relay site said Mike and Charlie were checking out some movement in a small ravine. The troops on the mountaintop heard a long burst of automatic-weapons fire, followed by a sputtering engine and a loud crash.

Flying back to Da Nang, I remembered that Mike had been in the Prairie Fire program for only three weeks. He'd just been fully checked out a couple of days before. And Charlie Gray, veteran of God only knew how many scary missions on the ground, hated to fly with us. So we teamed the two of them up and sent them out to cut their teeth on resupply missions to the radio relay site—a regular milk run, laced with golden BBs.

SEPTEMBER

Combat Instructor

I assumed we'd have a hard time recruiting new pilots into Prairie Fire after the word got around about Mike McGerty's death. I couldn't have been more wrong. Mike's death uncorked a river of sentiment as well as volunteers, all wanting a chance to fly for Prairie Fire. Each had his own reasons—adventure, curiosity, revenge, even a desire to win a few medals. Whatever the reasons, the head Covey, Ed Cullivan, had the unenviable job of picking a new Prairie Fire boss. While he sorted through the applicants, we kept flying missions.

I had the early morning go on the fifth of September. At Covey Ops, the briefer brought me up to speed on the current and forecast weather. In what amounted to a preview of the coming monsoon season, the coast from Da Nang north was socked in with low scud and drizzle. The weather man expected a gradual burnoff by late morning, but until then, everything along the coast was instrument flight rules (IFR).

Just before dawn, I finished preflighting and completed loading several crates of fresh vegetables and a bag of mail, referred to as "Pony Express," into the cargo bay of aircraft 661. Whenever possible, we tried to help out the MLTs by hauling a few goodies to them. When they had to rely on the normal supply system, the wait tended to stretch out.

Right after lift off, the horizon disappeared into a swirling gray mass of clouds. Totally engulfed in the thick soup, I had no choice but to concentrate on flying precise instruments. While the departure controller vectored me via radar to various altitudes and headings, I stayed glued on my instruments, fighting off a slightly claustrophobic feeling and the uncomfortable sensation that my OV-10 was in a diving right turn when my instruments indicated the Bronco to be climbing on a steady heading. An untold number of pilots had bought the farm over the years because of vertigo, an unreliable feeling deep in the inner ear. I had no intention of being one of them, so I fought the sensation and settled into the mental discipline needed to speed up my somewhat rusty instrument crosscheck.

Tracking outbound on the Da Nang TACAN 310-degree radial, I kept climbing, hoping to break out of the soup. Passing through five thousand feet, the inside of the clouds took on a lighter cast, and at six thousand feet I broke out into the bright morning sunshine. Regardless of my mood when starting out, flying instruments inside the dirty gray clouds always seemed to depress me. But the pilot who doesn't get an instant thrill when he breaks out of the weather and into the dazzling sunshine set against an incredibly blue sky has yet to be born. Climbing into the clear was almost like a rebirth, a new lease on life. After a couple of quick aileron rolls in celebration, I leveled off at seventy-five hundred feet and headed for Quang Tri, thirty miles in front of me, hidden somewhere under all that weather I had just climbed through.

I had hoped to find a few breaks in the clouds for a VFR descent, but the deck was solid. When I contacted Hue Approach Control, the news was even grimmer. Quang Tri was reporting below aircraft approach minimums, with a three-hundred-foot ceiling and half-mile visibility due to rain and fog. To top it all off, Quang Tri's TACAN, channel 103, was off the air, leaving only a low-powered beacon for navigation and instrument approaches. Reluctantly, I set up a holding pattern over the beacon in hopes that the crud would burn off enough to put the field above minimums.

As I ginned around the holding pattern, I talked to Sergeant Budrow at MLT-2. Top didn't sound particularly happy with my report. He respectfully but pointedly reminded me that we had teams on the ground who needed our attention and that I wasn't any use to the war effort in a holding pattern over Quang Tri. He was absolutely right, and the guilt gnawed at me with each successive trip around the imaginary racetrack. More than anything, I wanted to help Top, yet there seemed no legal way out of the weather-inflicted mess. The rules and regulations concerning instrument approaches had been beat into my head from day one as a young student pilot back at Laughlin AFB, Texas. Our bible on flying instruments, *Air Force Manual 51-37*, defined the dos and don'ts; flying an instrument approach into a field below minimums was definitely a no-no. From my perspective at that moment, the rules were absolute, with no provision for interpretation, or God forbid, flagrant disregard. Fortunately, I was about to get another lesson in judgment.

The lesson developed slowly over the course of forty-five minutes in the holding pattern. The first ingredient involved a natural phenomenon. Far to my east, thunder bumpers had already started their ritual buildup over the South China Sea. As the cells gathered strength, they cut loose with an impressive display of lightning. The static discharges were no danger to me, but they did have an unnerving effect on my ADF navigation needle. With each lightning flash, the ADF needle spun around and pointed at the thunderstorms. At least thirty seconds passed before the needle settled down and pointed at the beacon. For all practical purposes, the ADF would be unreliable for an instrument approach.

The second part of the lesson was just as unexpected as the lightning. As I listened up on the five radios we monitored, I heard Batcat, an electronic warfare EC-121 aircraft, talk to MLT-2. Batcat reported heavy sensor movement in the vicinity of one of our teams. The movement could be anything from troops to trucks to water buffalo. Whatever the movement, it spelled trouble for the team.

When Batcat signed off, Top gave me a call. "Covey 221, did you copy that transmission from Batcat?" Top's voice was calm and unemotional as always, but the hidden message came through loud and clear.

I answered, "Rog, Top. I copied. Let me check with Approach Control and I'll get back to you."

Instead, I called directly to Quang Tri tower for a weather update. They confirmed that the ceiling was still below minimums for an ADF approach, but visibility had improved enough to allow a few helicopters to take off under special VFR rules. A lightbulb blinked on in my brain: special VFR might be the answer. Under those rules, certain slower-moving aircraft could take off and land as long as they remained beneath the cloud layer. I'd never heard any of the Coveys talk about flying special VFR, so I wasn't sure whether it was legal or not. More than likely, it was a case of if you're not going to like the answer, don't ask the question.

My immediate problem was to somehow get below the weather. From the holding pattern, I moved a few miles east until I was certain I was over water. I ran through a quick descent check, reduced the power, and started down at 150 knots indicated airspeed. As the Bronco slid back into the thick clouds, I paid special attention to the chatter on the approach control frequency. The name of the game was to maneuver well clear of any IFR traffic moving up or down the coast. The real danger, slight as it was, came from other pilots like myself who were floundering around in the clouds trying to beat the system.

During the descent, I decided to make five hundred feet my hard altitude. If there were no visual references by then, I'd climb back on top. I was flying a modified box pattern, holding each heading for about thirty seconds so as to remain fairly close to an imaginary geographic point over the water. With slight adjustments for the prevailing wind, I would stay in the ballpark.

I leveled off at five hundred feet, still inside the dark clouds. Rather than give up, I decided to fly around the box one last time. Nothing on the first two legs. As I droned northwest on the third leg, I caught a glimpse of white caps below me. The hole closed up almost immediately, but the lure was irresistible. On my attitude indicator, I set up a glide slope of three degrees nose low. A few seconds later I coasted out the bottom of the clouds into a rainy gray drizzle just three hundred feet above the churning water. There wasn't much of a horizon, but off to my left I could just make out the dim outline of the beach.

From there it was uneventful. I crossed the beach searching for familiar landmarks. Finally, the city of Quang Tri loomed directly in front of me. It was easy to pick up the Highway One bridge across the Cua Viet River. At the bridge I hung a right and followed the highway to the airfield, four miles northwest.

Once on the ground, the Barky crew chiefs refueled the aircraft while I waited for the Covey rider to show up. When Satan arrived, we strapped in and started up the engines. The weather still looked lousy, so it came as no surprise when the tower told us that the field was still below minimums. Trying to sound as confident as possible, I countered with a request for a special VFR clearance. Much to my relief, tower cleared us for a special VFR departure. We blasted off to check on our teams.

I followed the same drill three times that day. The experience definitely came in handy, because throughout the remainder of my tour, I flew special VFR on many occasions. Never again did I hold up the war effort while droning around in an instrument holding pattern.

Back at Da Nang, the Covey commander had made his choice for Prairie Fire boss. There was some speculation about my getting the job, but that didn't make sense. With three months in grade as a captain, I was considered too junior. The older Prairie Fire troops would finish their tours the following month, so they were nonstarters. It was no secret that Colonel Cullivan had been hit hard by the Meacham and McGerty losses. He desperately wanted somebody he could count on to control the free-spirited Prairie Fire pilots, perhaps someone a little more senior. He ended up picking a good man—his trailer mate, Major Bob Dennison.

Bob was a hard-flying, hard-playing boss, with many of the same leadership qualities Ed Cullivan had. He had a knack for harnessing our youthful enthusiasm without squashing the independent streak that had attracted us to the Prairie Fire mission in the first place. Bob realized that as young lieutenants and captains, his Prairie Fire troops took on more responsibility on a single mission than many pilots did during an entire tour. He'd look the other way when we stretched the rules, but he was quick to come down hard if we took unwarranted risks.

Early in his checkout, Bob Dennison had the opportunity to meet and fly with one of the truly remarkable characters from the Covey rider ranks. Code-named "Blister," Sergeant First Class Grant was a barrel-chested mountain of man who had forgotten more about being a Covey rider than most men knew. Blister was loud and brash, but on a hot mission, he was efficient and fearless. Over the years, many recon teams and Prairie Fire pilots owed their lives to his fighting instincts.

For the most part, our time with Blister was limited to airborne missions. While we were flying, he'd expound on all manner of subjects. One of his favorite subjects was the solid gold chain he always wore around his neck. The chain was huge and gaudy, somewhat like Blister himself. Each gold link was as big as the end of a man's little finger. The standard measurement for the gold chains came from Thailand, where the weight was measured in half ounces, or *baht*. Most of us wore a one- or two-*baht* chain. Not Blister. His chain contained forty-four *baht* of solid gold.

When Blister and I flew together, he usually called me by the Vietnamese word for captain, *daiwe*. Invariably, the conversation turned to his *baht* chain.

"Hey, Blister. You wearing your chain today?"

"Roger that, *Daiwe*. I never take this baby off. I do *everything* with my chain on. You're really lucky to be flying with me, *Daiwe*. If we get shot down and captured, I'll buy our way out. Then you'll be sorry you made fun of my chain. It's like an insurance policy."

In a mock scolding tone I replied, "Blister, if we get captured, the bad guys aren't gonna ask you for that chain. They'll simply blow your goddamn head off and take the chain. How's that grab you?"

Blister would sputter and fume for a few seconds, then

he'd answer, "You're entitled to your own opinion, *Daiwe*. But I still say the gold will come in handy."

A few nights later at the Da Nang Officers' Club, Blister's gold chain did come in handy. On that particular night the club was full because a USO show was scheduled. For some unexplained reason, Blister showed up at the Covey hooch wearing a sanitized flight suit—no name, no patches, no rank. Instead of leaving him alone, we took him over to the jam-packed club and introduced him as "Colonel Grant." He carried off the charade without a hitch, and in five minutes everyone believed he really was a bird colonel.

Blister's new rank entitled him to a certain amount of preferential treatment, but the best was yet to come. When the Vietnamese waitresses spotted his gold chain, their eyes bugged right out of their heads. They escorted Blister to a table next to the stage. While everybody else had to wait twenty minutes to get a drink, Blister had every waitress in the place hanging all over him, begging to take his drink order. Scheming opportunists, we Prairie Fire pilots crowded around the celebrity table and had "Colonel" Grant order our drinks too.

Just before the show started, a couple of real Air Force colonels came over and introduced themselves. We politely stood up; Blister just sat there glaring contemptuously at the intruders. When Blister started talking, I saw my short career flash before my eyes.

In a surly tone, he demanded, "What do you men do for a living?" The two mumbled something about combat support group jobs. Blister was unimpressed. "Is that right? Well, I fly combat missions with these FACs sitting around this table. They're probably the best and the bravest goddamn pilots you've got on this base. I hope I never hear they're being mistreated, or I'd have to file an official protest. Then unofficially, I'll come back over with a few of my Special Forces troops and we'll kick ass and take names. Dig?" The two colonels mumbled something else before beating a hasty retreat back into the crowd.

Armed with three rounds of drinks each and surrounded

by all the waitresses in the club, we sat back in our chairs as the USO show started. Right away we were disappointed. The rumor going around was that the show starred a couple of genuine "round-eyes" from Australia. Instead, a half-dozen Filipino girls bolted onto the stage, singing and dancing the funky chicken. It wasn't that the ladies weren't pretty. They were exotic beauties with great faces and long, good-looking legs. But like most Oriental women, they were petite and slim, with no real shape. They were flat-chested with no hips. Pretty as they were, practically everybody in the room would have killed for a substantial blonde with blue eyes and lots of curves.

Despite their disappointment, the assembled pilots, gentlemen that they were, decided to make the young ladies feel welcome and appreciated. The shouts began slowly, then built into a deafening roar: "Take it off! Show us your boobs! On your knees, bitch!"

The pretty young entertainers never batted an eye. They'd seen and heard it all before, at camps and clubs from one end of Vietnam to the other. My favorite was a sweet-looking young girl who had the best singing voice of the group. Her rendition of "The Shadow of Your Smile" would have been a real showstopper, except she pronounced the word as "schwadow," to the hoots and great delight of the rowdy audience. I was feeling sorry for her until the end of the song, when she stepped off the stage onto the table next to ours and let some drunk bury his face in her crotch.

The show ended on a predictable note. All the ladies came on stage at once, then led us in a sing-along version of John Denver's popular hit "Country Roads." For a finale, the ladies performed the mandatory anthem familiar to every GI who ever served in Vietnam: "We Got to Get out of This Place."

The morning after the USO show, we piled "Colonel" Grant into an O-2 and sent him packing to Quang Tri, where they badly needed his help. It was clear to all of us that the level and intensity of our cross-border operations had picked up dramatically; we were hard-pressed to find enough warm bodies to keep up the pace. We seemed to be sending more and more teams across the fence, and those teams seemed to get themselves in trouble on a regular basis. Rarely did a team manage to stay on the ground for a full five- to seven-day mission. By the middle of September, our teams were being blasted off the LZ within three hours of the insert.

It was a tough arena for training new Prairie Fire pilots, but there was no other choice. Bob Dennison completed his checkout in record time, yet we were still behind the power curve. Within a matter of weeks, Bob Meadows and Gary Pavlu would finish their tours and head back to the world, leaving us at a loss for experienced pilots. Without realizing it, I suddenly found myself cast in a new and unfamiliar role, that of an old head. One day I was the new guy; the next, I was Prairie Fire's training officer, responsible for getting the new troops combat ready. The time was flying by. Only a few days earlier, my father-in-law, Ken Wood, had finished his tour at Cam Ranh and gone back to the world.

One of my first jobs came as a shock. I knew Bob Dennison had been scouting for new talent, but when he told me my roomie, Evan Quiros, was the choice, the news shook me up. For some reason, I didn't want Evan associated with Prairie Fire. I knew he was a first-rate stick-and-rudder man, so that wasn't the problem. Sorting through my feelings, I narrowed down the reasons to two: first, the mission was too dangerous for such a dedicated family man, and second, for selfish reasons I didn't want to have to worry about Evan. It was okay to train guys I didn't know very well. It became a different ball game when the emotional attachment was more than casual. Initially, I planned to talk him out of it, but Evan was so enthusiastic about Prairie Fire that there was no denying him. In spite of my misgivings, I knew deep inside that Evan was just enough of a nonconformist to be a natural in Prairie Fire.

On September 23, Evan and I flew together for the first time. He had already run a couple of inserts and extracts under Bob Meadows's watchful eyes, so he had a good feel for the mission. There were no teams on the ground that day and no plans to insert any others, so we did a little free-wheeling. After trolling up and down the DMZ several times, we ended up near Khe Sanh. I pointed out "Hickory," our radio relay site located on one of the mountain peaks just north of the abandoned Khe Sanh airstrip.

More to himself than to anyone else, Evan said, "I think I'll go down and introduce myself." With that, he rolled us into 135 degrees of left bank and pulled the nose of our Bronco down into a perfect run-in heading for Hickory. We leveled off one-half mile out, at an identical altitude with the mountaintop. As we streaked over the sandbag fortification at ten feet, Evan slammed the stick into his left thigh and aileron-rolled us down into the adjacent valley. His timing had been absolutely perfect. If he had been just one second earlier on the roll, we would have dinged a wing tip and earned ourselves a number on the weekly casualty list.

To prove it was no fluke, Evan arced back around to the north and rolled in a second time. Evidently our first pass had attracted someone's attention, because as we closed in on Hickory we could see several troops standing on top of the bunkers waving at us. I had a horrible vision of our eight-foot props decapitating one of those poor waving fools, but mercifully, Evan offset just a little to the left so as to miss them. A split second before we buzzed over their heads, one of the troops pointed a pen-gun flare at us and fired it. Before we could even react, the red-hot flare zipped between the right engine and our canopy, about three feet from our warm bodies.

Evan must have read my mind. Instead of continuing the air show, he jinked us down below the relay site's rim and away from the line of fire as fast as we could run.

I was irate. Switching the radio wafer switch over to Fox Mike, I gave the relay site a call. "Goddamn it, Hickory. Your boys almost blew us out of the saddle with a pen-gun flare. Tell 'em to knock that crap off. We're on your side!"

The voice on the other end sounded far from pleased. "Listen up, Covey. I'm sick and tired of you hotshot fly boys scaring the fool out of us with your no-notice buzzing. If

The versatile OV-10 Bronco light-attack aircraft searching for targets over the Laotian jungle. This sweet-flying bird, used by forward air controllers, entered the Vietnam War in 1969. It became my office for 608 combat missions.
(U.S. Air Force photo)

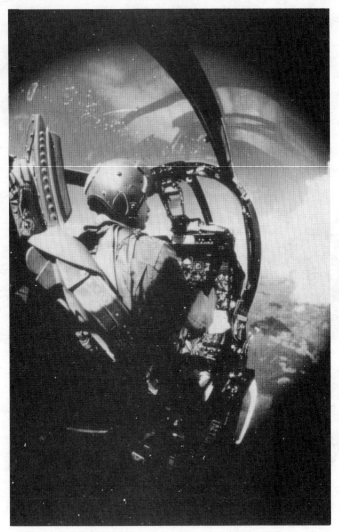

A fish-eye view from the back seat of the Bronco. With its great visibility, maneuverability, and armament, the OV-10 rapidly became the premier FAC aircraft of the war. *(U.S. Air Force photo)*

An AH-1G Cobra gunship escorting Huey Slicks to a secret landing zone deep inside Laos. Cobras routinely provided deadly accurate firepower to within twenty meters of small SOG teams in contact with NVA regulars.
(U.S. Air Force photo)

A UH-1 Huey Slick hovers over the landing zone while an indigenous reconnaissance team off-loads and moves out on its secret seven-day mission. *(U.S. Air Force photo)*

The third member of the SOG airborne package, the incomparable A-1H Skyraider, wings north over Da Nang Bay en route to another Prairie Fire mission. The Spad's awesome load of weapons and long loiter time made it the perfect close-air-support bird. *(U.S. Air Force photo)*

An armed OV-10 parked in the revetments at Quang Tri Air Base, just south of the DMZ. Each morning Prairie Fire FACs flew from home base at Da Nang to either Quang Tri or Hue Phu Bai to support SOG's cross-border operations. *(U.S. Air Force photo)*

Low-level flying became an integral part of the Prairie Fire mission. Here an OV-10 Bronco attacks targets deep in Laos near the Ho Chi Minh Trail. *(U.S. Air Force photo)*

To suppress antiaircraft guns along the Ho Chi Minh Trail, FACs generally called in the "fast-movers." In this instance, an F-105 Thud loaded with five-hundred-pound bombs poses for a photo en route to the target. Note the Daisy Cutter fuse extender on the outboard right pylon.
(U.S. Air Force photo)

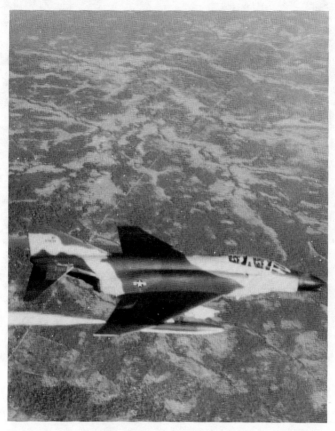

Flying against the big guns in Laos proved to be nerve-wracking as well as hazardous. After being hit by ground fire, the F-4 Phantom in the foreground dumps fuel while returning to home base. *(U.S. Air Force photo)*

For close-in work Prairie Fire FACs called on the tough, daring A-1 pilots. In a near vertical dive, this Skyraider lines up the target in its gunsight. *(U.S. Air Force photo)*

The text visible within the image:
DMGD BNKR
DEST TRKS
DEST TRKS
PREV PHTO DEST TRKS
MERRY CHRISTMAS 1970
DMGD/ DEST SUP
DEST TRKS
DMGD SUP
DEST TRKS

The Covey bomb dump near Ban Bak, Laos, made history as one of the most successful interdiction efforts of the air war along the Ho Chi Minh Trail. This December 1970 reconnaissance photo vividly illustrates the magnitude of the destruction. *(U.S. Air Force photo)*

Once inserted on the ground in Laos, the small Special Forces-led recon teams needed all the help they could get. In this shot a Cobra gunship dives to attack NVA troops moving against a seven-man SOG team. *(U.S. Army photo)*

Subject to frequent enemy rocket attacks, Da Nang came by its nickname honestly—Rocket City. The Da Nang post office suffered this damage in a direct hit from one of the many 122mm rockets lobbed our way. *(Courtesy of Evan Quiros)*

The Muff Divers' Lounge served as the focal point for most Covey FAC social activities. The permanent residents, resplendent in Covey party suits, are, from left to right: Captain Larry "Big Bippy" Thomas; the author; Captain Sonny Haynes. Relaxing in the foreground is our mascot Muff, the Wonder Dog. *(Author's collection)*

A Prairie Fire party in progress at MLT-2, Quang Tri. Standing from left to right: First Sergeant Ken Budrow; Covey rider "Blister" Grant; Major Bob Dennison, the Covey Prairie Fire commander. *(Courtesy of Evan Quiros)*

My old friend and fellow Prairie Fire pilot Captain Evan Quiros saddles up for a combat mission in his OV-10. (Courtesy of Evan Quiros)

During the Vietnam War, Da Nang became a crossroads for Air Force fliers. My roommate from pilot training, Captain Norm Komich, turned up at Da Nang as a "Jolly Green" rescue helicopter pilot, flying the HH-53. The Jollies flew some of the hairiest missions of the war, penetrating deep into North Vietnam to rescue downed pilots. (Courtesy of Norm Komich)

Another good friend, Captain Carl D'Benedetto, was a FAC in the American Division at Chu Lai. After moving to Da Nang, Carl "evaluated" me on an unusual midtour check ride. (Courtesy of Carl D'Benedetto)

The only surviving shot of the Muff Divers' Lounge, an informal social hangout inside the Covey barracks. At any given time, day or night, groups of Coveys similar to this one crowded into the small room to tell war stories or to sip a cold beer.
(Courtesy of Evan Quiros)

you'd like to come around for one more pass, I promise you we won't miss."

As much as I hated to admit it, the voice on the radio had a valid point. We had started it, and they had almost finished it. All of us had been pretty dumb. Rather than leave the whole thing hanging, I passed on a halfhearted apology to Hickory. While I was talking, I noticed Evan had maneuvered around to almost the identical spot from which he had rolled in on the two earlier passes. I had a hunch he was about to roll their socks down with a third pass, so I gently came on the controls and said, "Let me have her for a second." Then I banked around to the north, away from Hickory, and toward the western DMZ.

After pointing out a couple of helicopter crash sites, I turned the controls back over to Evan. As we crossed into the northern half of the DMZ, I asked him, "Were you gonna take a third run at those dudes?"

With what sounded like pure impishness in his voice, he answered, "Who me? Come on, get serious."

I thought to myself, "I bet it would have been one hell of a great low pass."

For no particular reason, I decided to show Evan a new road being built by the North Vietnamese into the extreme western part of the DMZ. Because of the bombing halt, we weren't allowed to hit it. Without any harassment, the NVA road crews had managed to carve out a fairly sophisticated highway, dug into the side of several mountains. The southern terminal of the road ended not more than a kilometer inside North Vietnam.

From our two-thousand-foot altitude over the DMZ, we spotted the road easily. What was on the road watered our eyes. In broad daylight a convoy of six trucks inched southward along narrow cliffs. Under the rules of engagement, the trucks were technically safe from air attacks. It didn't make any sense. It also didn't take a genius to figure out that those trucks weren't hauling toys to the orphans.

Evan and I were thinking the same thought. We couldn't put an air strike in, but the rules didn't say anything about lobbing in a couple of marking rockets—just to shake things up a bit. Evan armed up one of the outboard pods, then pushed the power up to full military. Next, he set up a descending 270-degree turn to the left, finally rolling out in a shallow dive heading straight for the trucks, just over a klick out in front of us. With the OV-10 at full power and 240 knots, Evan pulled us up into a steep, 60 degree climb. Then he pushed the stick forward abruptly, zero "G"ing down to 45 degrees of climb. At what he guessed to be the perfect moment, Evan pickled off four willie petes.

It was easy to follow the four rockets streaking upward during the two seconds of rocket motor burn. At shutdown, the four-foot-long rockets went ballistic, captives of momentum and gravity. As they coasted down the back side, we lost sight of them. I had about given up on our willie petes as duds or unscorables when the first snow-white smoke drifted up. It hit well short of the target, but in succession, number two split the remaining distance, and three and four exploded right in the middle of the convoy.

Both of us let out a howl and started laughing. Any damage done by the rockets was questionable. Still, we would have given anything to see the looks on those smug drivers' faces. Chalk one up for the good guys. We certainly hadn't won the war, but the encounter was still a remarkable piece of flying and shooting by Evan.

A few days later, on the twenty-ninth of September, I flew another mission into the DMZ, but this time I went in fully armed. In a reversal of an earlier decision, Seventh Air Force headquarters in Saigon decided to reinstall the four M-60 machine guns on the OV-10. The intent was to give the FAC a limited attack capability. We had found that in a troops-in-contact situation, the first minutes of the fight were the most critical. Instead of waiting helplessly for the fighters to arrive, the OV-10 FACs could now deliver enough machine-gun fire to keep the bad guys' heads down. The low-level strafing runs were admittedly risky, but nothing compared to what those grunts on the ground had to endure. As often as not, our slow-firing M-60s provided just enough punch to break the contact.

We in the Prairie Fire business found the M-60s especially suited to our mission. When one of our teams got into a firefight in the middle of Laos, it usually started inside of twenty meters. At such close quarters, a well-aimed burst of machine-gun fire was the only option, short of dropping ordnance on top of our own teams. In addition, by delivering our own firepower, we no longer had to try to describe the target to orbiting Cobras or Spads. In the heat of battle, even after we had put down a smoke rocket for reference, we could never be 100 percent sure that the other guy saw the target as we did. Our M-60 machine guns weren't the cure-all, but they did give us added capability when it was needed.

Satan and I had already flown two sorties that morning. At approximately 1500, we took off on a third sortie, due north into the DMZ. Our job was to act as high cover while one of the new O-2 Prairie Fire jocks ran his second solo team insert. If the situation went sour, we were there to help out or take over.

I set up a high orbit a mile east of the LZ, a barren hilltop two hundred meters south of the Song Ben Hai River. The terrain in that area was made up of low hills, ridges, and valleys. Repeated B-52 Arc Light strikes had left little vegetation. From the air the place resembled a moonscape, complete with thousands of craters scarring the surface. In contrast, just a few miles to the north, the countryside looked relatively green, with only a few bomb craters dotting the area.

As the Covey FAC rounded up his helicopters and headed into the LZ, Satan and I were nervous. We were running a partial package with only Slicks and Cobras. For some reason, we had no A-1 support that afternoon. Since the insert was planned for a relatively quiet section of the DMZ, the decision was made to press on. We didn't anticipate going up against any big AAA guns, so the general belief was that the

Cobras could handle the action without the usual help from the Spads.

The dummy insert went off without a hitch. As Satan and I watched, our trainee appeared to have everything under control. When the operation shifted to the primary target, the situation heated up in spades.

The Cobras nailed the LZ with a vengeance, followed closely by Slick Lead carrying half the team. When Lead touched down on the small hilltop, the four team members jumped clear and dashed across the LZ to the western slope of the hill. A split second later, two NVA soldiers popped out of camouflaged spider holes and riddled the vulnerable helicopter at point-blank range with AK-47 fire. Before the door gunner could respond to the threat, an AK-47 round found its mark, blowing his left eye out and killing him instantly. Slick Lead poured on the power and managed to limp out of range of the deadly fire, aided by his flying skills and by the covering dust storm his rotors whipped up on top of the hill.

Looking down on the scene, we could see the spider holes on the northwest sector of the hilltop, roughly one hundred feet from the team crouching just below the rim. The close proximity of the friendlies made for a sticky close-air-support situation. As I was about to offer some advice, my student took charge, shouting instructions and making the right decisions.

"Slick Two, break it off! Abort your run right now. Move back to the holding pattern. Cobra Lead, see those white rocks on the southeast corner of the LZ? Give me one mini-gun pass on a run-in line from those rocks to the two spider holes."

Though the pilot had made a good start, I couldn't resist adding to the instructions. "Cobra Lead, confirm you've got a tally on the team position and acknowledge mini-guns only."

He responded, "Roger on the team pos, and I copy mini-guns only. Am I cleared in?"

"You're cleared in hot," the FAC shouted. Then, forgetting to change his wafer switch to the proper radio, he added,

"One-zero, if you're on frequency, get your heads down. The Cobras are gonna plaster the LZ."

Hundreds of small geysers of dust from the impacting bullets swirled into the air around the spider holes. As Cobra Two rolled in to give the target the same treatment, Satan pointed out several larger explosions in the same area. At first I thought one of the Cobras might have accidently fired an HE rocket, but then we spotted the source. One of the team members was standing bolt upright, firing M-79 grenade rounds at the bad guys. He fired at least a half dozen of the 40mm shells before finally taking cover.

The heavier firepower produced an unexpected benefit. The exploding "blooper" rounds exposed an entire network of holes and tunnels dug into the northern rim of the hilltop. For all we knew, the whole area was linked by passages and tunnels. One thing became painfully clear. Putting the rest of the team on the ground was out of the question. Rescuing the stranded members took top priority.

In the Oscar Deuce with the fledgling Prairie Fire pilot, Blister finally managed to get the one-zero to come up on his PRC-25 radio. As cool as always, Blister exchanged information with the team, then advised them to move around to the south face of the hill and dig in. To cover the movement, the Cobras began continuous attacks against the enemy positions along the northern rim. After multiple strafe passes, the gunships pulled out all the stops by blasting the complex with rockets.

On one of the attacks, Cobra Lead spotted a group of bad guys working their way south along the eastern slope of the hill. Caught in the open, the patrol scattered quickly under heavy mini-gun fire, leaving behind two dead or wounded comrades.

A few minutes later, the situation took a turn for the worse. Within a period of sixty seconds, Cobra Two reported oil pressure problems and Cobra Lead's fire control system went haywire. Under normal circumstances the Spads would have taken up the slack, but with no A-1s, we were out of luck.

Our only immediate option was to have me cover one of the Hueys as he went in for a pickup. I automatically armed up the rockets, then remembered the machine guns. Since it had been so long, I was a little cloudy on exactly how to arm up the M-60s. Carefully, I placed the left-hand gun switch to ready. In that configuration, I'd be firing only the two guns located in the left sponson. Next, I flipped the master arm switch on, then squeezed the trigger. There was an audible "clunck" as the two guns charged themselves. After cycling the master arm switch off and back on, we were ready.

As Slick Three reached the halfway point on the east-to-west run-in to the LZ, I rolled in well behind him and to his right. When he was on very short final, I squeezed the trigger and poured long bursts into the spider holes along the northern edge of the target. My 550 rounds per minute from each gun kicked up quite a dust cloud. The tracer ammunition formed what appeared to be a continuous red line from the machine-gun muzzles to the hilltop. At impact, some of the tracers ricocheted back up into the air, seeming to float as they careened off at wild angles. We passed over the crest of the hill at about fifty feet and kept right on going. I cobbed full power as we climbed straight ahead, then pulled us through a modified chandelle to head us back the other way. On the reverse course, we were head-on with our chopper, which had just touched down. Once more I fired burst after burst into the target area. I could only hope none of the ricochets were bouncing in the helicopter's direction.

By the time I had executed a second chandelle, I could see our chopper lifting off. As I closed in behind him, some movement on the east face of the hill caught my eye. Four bad guys had popped up out of nowhere and were attempting to drag off the two casualties from the earlier Cobra run.

I eased the stick forward to get the OV-10 down even lower. When we were just below the crest of the hill, I put the pipper on their feet and pressed in close. At approximately eight hundred feet of slant range I opened up, pouring a long string of tracers right into them. My aim seemed to be confirmed when all four slumped to the ground. With the hill directly in front and above us, I sucked in the Gs as hard as I could pull. The Bronco practically swapped ends, shuddering and protesting as I asked her to do things she wasn't meant to. Through my tunneled vision, I could see that we would clear the crest by a matter of feet.

Relaxing the back pressure, I let the aircraft zoom into a steep climb. Over the intercom, I gloated to Satan, "Marty, could you see that strafe from the back seat? I nailed their hides!" Before he could answer, I rolled us into ninety degrees of bank to get another look at our target. The scene below wasn't what I had expected to see. Much to my embarrassment, all four bad guys were on their feet, running as hard as they could for whatever spider hole they'd been hiding in.

While I was wondering how I could have missed, with machine guns no less, our trainee had rounded up his package, including the rescued team, and started back to Quang Tri. As we followed the O-2 back into the traffic pattern, Satan tried to console me. Attempting to sound positive, but laughing all the same, Satan announced, "I thought we had them too. Sir's aim was right on the money. It's the damndest thing I've ever seen—dead guys running around like that, not even realizing they'd been shot."

OCTOBER

Battle Damage

By the first of October, the pace of the air war around Da Nang had definitely shifted into low gear. Mother Nature had accomplished what the Viet Cong couldn't. A killer typhoon out in the South China Sea had taken deadly aim at the Vietnam coast. As a precaution most of the flying units had already evacuated to bases in Thailand. From there they would continue to fly missions over the Ho Chi Minh Trail. At Da Nang the remaining pilots and ground crews moved around aimlessly in the uncharacteristic silence, waiting and wondering about the approaching storm. For them the ominous quiet on the flight line roared louder than any J-79 jet engine running up on the test cell.

In contrast to the life and death struggles going on in Laos, those of us who stayed behind to face the fury of the typhoon found ourselves overcome with boredom and restlessness, along with nagging anxiety, probably stemming from fear of the unknown. In the process, the pace of our nonstop, action filled young lives ground to a standstill. With the typhoon-induced slowdown came long, uninterrupted hours during which we contemplated events and people, confronted our innermost thoughts—all wrapped around a single focus, combat missions. With time to reflect, I began considering the only explanation that made any sense. Each Prairie Fire mission seemed to be a self-contained act within an endless drama. Each mission had its own beginning, middle, and end. Its relevance to previous missions was lost in the production. Players tended to appear for a few acts, then disappear without fanfare or applause, to be replaced by other players dressed in the same olive-drab costume. In a future act, I too would take my cue and exit the stage. The bottom-line question was, would I exit standing up or feet first?

When the first typhoon-force winds finally slammed into our compound, the pent-up tension seemed to break in proportion to the wind gusts. Outside on the streets of the main compound, the sheets of rain pulsed and danced in odd geometric patterns across the black asphalt. On our first ventures out into the stuff, panchos flapping in the gale, we found the only way to negotiate the stinging rain was to walk backwards. The soggy experience of fighting the wind and rain just for the privilege of a mediocre meal at the officers' club soon lost its appeal. Like most self-respecting young pilots, we settled for the logical alternative: we camped in the Covey barracks, drank large quantities of Chivas Regal, and chowed down on junk food or care packages from home.

By the second day of the storm, a small group of hard cores began congregating in a room belonging to Captain Sonny Haynes. An easy-going Texan, Sonny was one of the most popular members of the squadron as well as one of the best pilots. Nobody handled pressure better than Sonny. He made a great host too. More and more idle Coveys began crowding into Sonny's place, anxious to be a part of the round-the-clock typhoon party. Sonny's cohost, Captain Larry Thomas, lived in the room next door. A native of Commerce, Texas, Larry had a keen mind and an equally sharp wit. He took a lot of good-natured kidding over his somewhat portly size, and in the vernacular of the popular television show "Laugh In," he acquired the nickname "Big Bippy."

With crowd control becoming a problem, Sonny and Larry sat down over a bottle of scotch, determined to find a solution. They did. They simply took a saw and a sledgehammer and knocked a hole in the wall between their rooms. The two sets of bunk beds were shoved into the "sleeping room" while a sofa, chairs, and a refrigerator ended up in what was to be the party room. The happy arrangement produced only one problem. The irate housing officer curtly informed the assembled drunks that rules were rules—two men to a room and no exceptions. Over another bottle of scotch, Sonny and Larry sat down to resolve this new dilemma.

The three of us had been classmates at fighter lead-in school at Cannon AFB, so we'd been friends for over a year. When they asked me to save the day by moving in with them, I was both flattered and delighted. I felt guilty about moving out on Evan, but I truly missed associating with the other Coveys. I thought moving in might provide a good opportunity to break down some of the barriers between the Prairie Fire pilots and the mainstream Coveys.

Sometime during the course of the typhoon and associated celebrations, I packed up and moved in with Sonny and the Big Bippy. The party room became such a hit, an obvious morale builder, that the housing officer decided to look the other way and not enforce the occupancy rules, as long as the three of us consented to sharing the place with the rest of the Coveys. During that same period we settled on a name for our twenty-four-hour-a-day party room. For the rest of the tour, everybody referred to our place as the Muff Divers' Lounge.

The typhoon eventually ran its course, leaving us soggier and more philosophical than before. In the process of huddling together to ride out the storm, we Coveys had inadvertently created a much-needed social release and hangout—a place to go and enjoy friends when not flying missions over the Ho Chi Minh Trail.

On the third of October, with the remnants of the typhoon pushing well inland, we got back into the war. It was time to start a new act. All of us felt restless from the inactivity. On my first day back at Quang Tri following the typhoon, my Special Forces friends came up with a novel way to get the edge back. The SOG troops called it "coming out on strings." I called it complete lunacy. In a weak moment, I somehow allowed the MLT-2 commander, Jerry Stratton, to talk me into being hoisted off the ground attached to a rope dangling out the door of a Huey Slick. Suspended underneath the hovering chopper, my sole connection to it was by way of a loop in the rope through a series of D rings on the harness I was wearing—something called a MacGuire rig. Hanging there helpless and afraid to move, I began spinning and gyrating wildly in the downwash from the Huey's blades. Cautiously, I extended both arms as Jerry had instructed me to do. Within seconds the spinning ceased. I was out on strings. Suspended about twenty-five feet below the chopper and one hundred feet above the ground, I initially kept my gaze fixed on the far horizon. After the first circle around the large field behind the MLT-2 Ops buildings, I finally mustered the nerve to look around. The wind blast, the engine sounds, and the smells flooded my senses. What a complete change from the sensations inside the closed cockpit of my OV-10. The only experience I could think of to match it might be flying in an open-cockpit biplane.

After another circuit around the field, the Huey went into a hover and gently set me back on solid ground. With the aid of a couple of grinning NCOs, I separated from the string and walked over to Jerry.

"Not too bad for an Air Force puke," he chided. Then, as he helped me out of the harness, he handed me a couple of D rings. "Put these on up here on your survival vest. It's not as good as a MacGuire rig, but if you ever have to bail out, you can hook up to the string and we can lift you out." These tough, highly trained Green Berets weren't big on showing emotion, and I felt the gesture deeply. I had passed the test, had become a full-fledged member of the SOG family. The offer of the D rings involved more than any practical use they might have had. In my mind they represented a passage. At that moment, on the afternoon of October 3, I mentally switched from being a new guy to the role of old head, an accepted combat veteran.

As Jerry and I walked back across the dusty field to the Ops hut, he explained a little more about extracting a team using the strings. In time-critical situations with no LZ available, coming out on strings might be the only option. If done correctly, three men could hook up and be lifted out on the same string. The MacGuire rig left the team members' hands free, enabling them to fire their weapons. As an added bonus, a wounded or unconscious troop could be extracted with no danger of slipping off the rope.

Jerry's explanation made it all sound so simple. Yet in recalling my own brief initiation a few minutes earlier, I remembered how incredibly vulnerable I felt hanging out there in space, little more than a moving target with nothing but my own skin shielding me from a hail of bullets. Doing it for fun was scary enough. Coming out on strings in actual combat had to generate paralyzing, debilitating fear. My hat was off to Jerry Stratton and his recon teams. They were definitely a special breed of warrior. Jerry and his bunch were pros in every positive sense of the word. They knew how to fight, and when called for, they knew how to die.

In a graphic demonstration of all those qualities I so admired in the SOG troops, one of Jerry's reconnaissance teams paid the ultimate price two days later. On the afternoon of October 5, my ex-roomie, Evan Quiros, was airborne, returning from Quang Tri after inserting one team and scouting a number of LZs for future missions. Flying over a solid cloud deck, Evan found himself facing a different kind of storm, every bit as deadly as the recent typhoon, but a lot more personal. As he cruised south along the Laotian border, Evan monitored a transmission from the one-zero of recon team Fer-de-Lance. The team leader advised that he had movement on three sides, clearly a dangerous situation. With no chance of slipping in under the weather, Evan set up an orbit over the team, hoping the sound of his circling OV-10 would keep the bad guys off balance. After exhausting most of his fuel, he had no choice but to return to Quang Tri for gas.

Launching out of Quang Tri at 1810, Evan returned to the team's general location. As he approached, he heard a voice whispering on the radio. Evan's blood ran ice cold. In a trembling, pathetic whisper, the assistant team leader begged Evan to mount an emergency extraction. What was left of the seven-man team was in heavy contact on three sides and low on ammunition. The one-zero had been hit and had fallen off a cliff.

Faced with heavy weather and darkness, Evan knew a

rescue was out of the question. But to keep the team's spirits up, he told them to keep their heads down while he armed up his rockets. Counting on the law of averages and a big dose of luck, Evan began firing blind through the cloud deck, praying his rockets would break the contact without hitting the team. The first few salvos landed well north of the target area, exploding harmlessly in the thick jungle. Even the assistant team leader realized the hit-or-miss tactic wouldn't work. In a perfectly calm voice, he said to Evan, "Covey 220, we're out of ideas and time. Got any suggestions?"

At first Evan couldn't think of a positive answer to the hopeless question. Then he recalled that a few of the teams carried small portable radar beacons. Keying off that signal, sophisticated sensors aboard an AC-119 Stinger gunship could lay down a deadly wall of mini-gun fire, theoretically to within just a few yards of friendly troops. It was their only chance.

Evan told the trapped team, "I've ordered up a Stinger gunship. You've got to hang on another forty-five minutes. In the meantime, I want you to find the beacon and get it set up."

His voice heavy with dejection, the assistant team leader replied, "No good. The one-zero had the instrument on him. He's somewhere down on the rocks below us."

"Your only hope is to find that beacon. You've got to retrieve that beacon!"

After the truth of Evan's words sank in, the voice answered, "I'll give it a try. Here goes nothing—wish me luck."

Evan continued to circle in the darkness for five long minutes, hoping beyond hope that the gutsy Green Beret below would find the all-important beacon. When his radio receiver finally crackled, Evan's heart sank into his boots. In a quivering, weak voice, the assistant team leader said simply, "I've been hit—and in the worst way." There were several groans, then the radio went dead.

The next morning when we got airborne, there was no trace of Recon Team Fer-de-Lance.

For the October 6 missions, we launched the entire Prairie Fire pilot force. During most of the morning, we searched at tree-top level for the missing team—with zero results. With three OV-10s and three O-2s cruising around the same vicinity, we must have made tempting targets, but we couldn't get the bad guys to fire at us. Anxious to turn up any kind of clue, we let our minds play tricks on us. The slightest bit of static on the radio, a momentary fleck of reflected morning light, two rotted logs lying near a trail forming a natural V—we clung to the wildest kinds of possible evidence, jumped to the most amateurish conclusions. Throughout that morning of false hopes and phony optimism, there were two negatives none of us would bring up: we couldn't find the team, and we couldn't bring ourselves to believe that there was no longer a team to be found.

By midafternoon we called off the search and went back to business as usual. The business went sour in a hurry. In what turned out to be a strange bit of timing, I was leading a package out of Hue Phu Bai as one of the other Coveys flew inbound with his package and freshly extracted team. The plan called for us to swap out the A-1s just east of the A Shau Valley. We were particularly careful working around the A Shau, a major infiltration route into the Thua Thien Province and the old walled city of Hue. Ever since the Cambodian incursion in May, the place had been crawling with bad guys. From discussions with the helicopter pilots from the 101st Airborne, we learned that in July the fighting had become so intense that the 101st Screaming Eagles evacuated a key position in the A Shau called Fire Base Ripcord. Now, as Laos transitioned into its dry season, enemy infiltration down the Trail increased dramatically. In the face of heavy NVA opposition, the ARVN First Division was about to be driven out of another A Shau hot spot, Fire Base O'Reilly.

As I tuned in the correct tactical radio frequency, it became clear the situation out over the A Shau was bad. The radio chatter indicated someone in the inbound package was in trouble. Apparently the Spads had taken a lot of ground fire in support of the extraction. A few rounds had found their mark.

Right away I recognized the A-1 pilot's voice as that of one of my friends from back at Da Nang. The stricken pilot, John, was advising the FAC, "The cylinder head temp is off the charts, and she's starting to smoke. I'm gonna have to get out."

The Covey answered, "I copy, Spad Lead. If you can, stay with her until we cross the fence and clear the A Shau. That way we'll have a chopper waiting for you when your feet touch the ground."

In between radio calls, I told the other FAC, "Bob, I'm inbound to you and will be over the east wall in five minutes. We're fat on gas and ammo if you need us."

Switching to his FM radio, the package commander replied, "Keep pressing, Tom. But I don't think we've got five minutes."

Seconds after that transmission, John shouted, "Okay, I can't wait. I'm punching out."

A long pause followed; then the Spad wingman chimed in, "John, get out of it! Get out now!"

"I can't. The Yankee didn't work."

"Don't you have anything?"

In a low-pitched, angry-sounding voice, John replied, "I don't have a damn thing."

As I listened in horror to the drama taking place fifteen miles in front of me, I pushed up the power levers for more speed. My package would have to fend for itself. In a cool voice, the FAC talked to the rapidly descending A-1. "Spad Lead, go for the pass between those two ridges directly in front of you. You've got a good glide going. Hold her steady on a heading of 120 degrees. Looking good."

Then the FAC's voice jumped up three octaves. "Lead, no! No, for Christ's sake. Back to your right! To your right!"

Somebody else came up on frequency. "He went in. Big fireball on the east wall. Negative chute."

Crossing the range of low hills forming the east wall of

the A Shau Valley, I saw it. Bright orange-red flames consumed a football-field-sized area just below the rim of the
small ridge. A pall of sooty black smoke floated straight up
above the inferno. The package commander was still in control but obviously shaken by what he had witnessed. When
we talked on the company FM radio, he sobbed, "If he'd just
stayed on that heading. He had it made. Why didn't he listen? He just went into a left bank and held it. Tom, he
wouldn't listen to me. Why didn't he listen?"

When my package arrived on the scene, I put them in an
orbit just south of the crash site. Fifteen minutes later, the
other FAC rounded up his package and headed home, low on
gas and demoralized. With his departure I became the on-
scene commander. In surveying the crash, I felt certain the
pilot hadn't survived, so a rescue wasn't the issue. But I did
want to get my troops on the ground to recover John's body.
I called the launch site, canceled the planned insert, and received their permission to use the team around the wreckage.
The Cobras and I flew several low passes around the area,
trolling for ground fire. There wasn't any. Next we directed
Slick Three to lower the medic to the ground near the crash.
The fire had burned out, revealing the twisted wreckage of
the big Skyraider. Hopefully, the *bac si* could poke around
the site under our protective cover.

As he sifted through the smoldering debris, the *bac si*
found part of John's helmet, badly shattered and burned.
Strangely, there was nothing else identifiable around what
had once been the cockpit. The real shock came when the
medic dislodged a section of the right wing, approximately
fifty feet away from the fuselage. At first the charred body
was unrecognizable. All that remained was the torso, minus
head and limbs.

The fire had rendered everything at the crash site white
hot. Any recovery would have to wait. I was also concerned
about the *bac si*'s safety. Wandering around down there
alone, he'd make an easy target for any bad guys attracted by
the crash. I was also worried about any ordnance on board
the Spad that could still cook off. Rather than lose another

good man, I ordered the medic out. He did manage to bring out the burned helmet.

My package flew back to Hue Phu Bai while I remained over the crash. I passed along the coordinates and the details to King, the USAF HC-130 responsible for coordinating all search-and-rescues for downed pilots. The controller aboard King accepted the sad news stoically. I advised King of the recovery plan for the following day when the wreckage had cooled, then I signed off and circled down for one last look at the crash. Searching the scene, I could think only about the anger in John's last radio transmission. I tried to imagine the feelings he experienced when the Yankee extraction system misfired. This was the second time I had seen an A-1 pilot's ejection system fail and cost a life.

Pressing in on the deck, I was struck by the irony of the situation. If John had been just fifty feet higher, he would have cleared the crest of the hill and had a shot at a forced landing in some fairly open terrain. Like the other Prairie Fire FAC, I found myself asking, "Why did he turn left? Why didn't he listen?"

We managed to recover John's body the following day. There was barely time for a short memorial service before we suited up again for more missions. Operational requirements left no time for extended grieving. A different Prairie Fire FAC took over in the A Shau Valley, and I moved back north to the MLT at Quang Tri.

On October 10, with thoughts of the missing team and the dead A-1 pilot still churning in my mind, I almost met the same fate. Satan and I had already flown once that morning in marginal weather conditions scouting for LZs. When the sun finally came out around 1500, we launched a second time, heading for a particularly hot area along Highway 9 just east of Tchepone. Flying right on the trees, Marty and I plotted several likely spots for future inserts. As we climbed back to the east, some movement on the Trail below caught our attention. Several hundred meters north of the intersection of routes 9 and 92, we spotted at least a dozen figures on the road. A quick check with the binoculars confirmed a road crew hard at work patching ruts and craters. They seemed oblivious to our presence, so Marty and I decided to ruin their day. From an altitude of fifteen hundred feet, I rolled in on the enemy troops while simultaneously arming up my two outboard pods. Recently we had started flying with fourteen high-explosive rockets in our bag of tricks, in addition to our two pods of willie petes and two thousand rounds of machine-gun ammo. The scene below me seemed custom made for an HE-rocket attack.

Pressing in from the south, I was about to fire when a .51-caliber machine gun opened up from a pit near the road crew. The stream of tracers raced up from our left as the two rockets roared out of the LAU-68 pods. As I sucked in the Gs to start a rolling pull off to the left, all hell broke loose. With a horrendously loud bang, the left canopy disintegrated into a thousand pieces of flying glass. Something red-hot streaked in front of my face and shattered the top of the canopy. Perhaps instinctively, perhaps out of fear, I had released the control stick and moved my right hand upward to shield my face. I winced in surprise as a dagger-shaped piece of canopy imbedded itself in my palm.

In the split second that followed, I seemed to view the hectic action in slow motion. Through my peripheral vision, I watched helplessly as the left canopy frame bowed into a contorted shape, then broke loose and flew up into the wind stream. For some crazy reason, I reached out into the blast to try to catch it, only to be thrown back violently by airstream. Under the tremendous aerodynamic force, aggravated by our nose-low, ninety-degree left bank, the top hinges snapped like balsa wood. The metal frame sailed up and over my glassless canopy on a trajectory that sent it crashing into the right engine propeller. The gnarled three-blade Hamilton prop, badly bent and completely out of balance, began vibrating and shaking us to pieces. The OV-10 felt like it was about to tear itself apart.

At some point in the melee, I managed to get back on the controls. Somehow, I got us back to some semblance of level flight, just five hundred feet above the trees. As we limped off to the west, the bad guys added insult to injury by hosing us until we were out of range. When the tracers stopped, I turned my attention to the problems over which I had control. First, I tried reducing power on the wobbling right engine. It made no difference. It was clear I'd have to shut the engine down. Before going through the emergency procedures for engine shutdown, I reached for my checklist out of habit. It was gone, along with all my maps and my binoculars. The wind stream had sucked them right out of the cockpit. They were probably scattered all over the Laotian countryside. For some reason, the thought of all those maps fluttering down on the machine-gun crew struck me as hilariously funny. They shoot lead bullets at me, I retaliate with a map bomb.

I forced myself to get on with it. Reaching up to the left side of the glare shield, I paused a second, then punched the emergency-stores release button, known as the salvo button. As advertised, the heavy centerline fuel tank and all four rocket pods tumbled away from the aircraft. With the excess weight and drag gone, the Bronco seemed to leap forward. With virtually the same motion, my left hand slipped down on the condition lever and pulled it back into the feather and fuel cutoff position. Within seconds the wounded engine began spooling down, the vibrations decreasing in direct proportion to the turning prop.

In the thirty seconds or so since the nightmare had started, Marty and I had not been in communication with each other. Initially there hadn't been time. Then the wind blast in the cockpit was so incredibly loud that it drowned out my voice as I tried to shout into the boom microphone on my helmet. Finally I lowered my seat to its bottom position and cupped my hand around the mike. I yelled, "Marty, are you okay? Can you read me?"

"Nothing serious back here. How's Sir?" Before I could answer, he followed up with, "Are we gonna make it back home?"

At that moment I honestly didn't know. We were flying, and that's what counted. Physically, we were both okay— peppered and nicked by hundreds of pieces of glass but otherwise in good shape. The Bronco was a different matter. As I nursed us through a slow climb, I took a minute to study the damage. In addition to the missing canopy and the shutdown engine, there was a large, basketball-sized hole in the leading edge of the wing just inboard of the right engine. It appeared that after chewing up the propeller the canopy frame slammed into the wing. There was no telling where it had gone from there—it had probably glanced off and over the wing. With a sickening premonition, I knew where to look next. By twisting in my ejection seat and using the mirrors, I could sight back along the right boom to the tail. From the looks of things, the top two feet of the right vertical stabilizer had been sheared off. I wasn't sure what was holding the horizontal stabilizer in place.

As we made a wide turn back toward Quang Tri, I called the tower for a weather update. The news wasn't good. Since our takeoff, the winds off the ocean had shifted to a direct cross wind gusting to thirty knots, ten knots above the maximum allowable limit for the OV-10. As badly as I wanted to get us on the ground, Quang Tri's narrow sixty-foot-wide slab of concrete wasn't the answer.

The flight southeast to Da Nang's big runway turned out to be trickier than we had bargained for. Halfway there, a solid wall of cumulonimbus towered in front of us. Gingerly picking our way through the CBs, Marty and I were soaked as the rain pelted in on us. Wet and miserable, I forced myself to concentrate on coaxing the single-engine Bronco through the maze of buildups and squall lines blocking our path. Each bump and bounce reinforced my fears for the structural integrity of the crippled OV-10.

As we neared Da Nang, I started looking for holes through which we could descend, since we were still cruising at forty-five hundred feet. After a few more minutes of floundering around, I caught a glimpse of Da Nang Bay off our left wing tip. Carefully, we spiraled down through the hole, always turning into the good engine. Since nobody knew we were coming or what our condition was, I decided to give them a clue by turning the master control knob on the transponder to emergency. Da Nang Approach picked up the distress signal right away.

"Aircraft squawking emergency on the three-five-eight radial at five miles, contact Da Nang Approach on two-forty-three-zero or two-seventy-nine point five."

"Approach, Covey 221. How copy, over."

"Covey 221, read you five by. Go ahead."

"Rog, Approach. I've got battle damage and the right engine out. Two souls on board and lots of gas. I'd like to switch over to tower for a long straight-in with a delayed gear call. I've got a tally on the field."

"Squawk standby, contact Da Nang tower, channel Two. Good luck."

At one mile on final with 130 knots of airspeed, exactly 30 knots faster than normal OV-10 approach speed, I lowered the gear. Because of my uncertainty about the extent of the damage and what effect it might have at low speeds, I kept the airspeed high and left the flaps up. On short final I centered the rudder trim and shoved in on the left rudder pedal to keep us close to a coordinated flight condition. As we crossed the threshold and settled into the ground effect, the extra speed caused us to float. Slowly, I eased the power back, and we touched down with a solid, friendly thunk. We were home!

A large crowd met us when we taxied in. Marty and I were thankful to see anyone, but apparently our welcoming committee felt the two of us looked worse than our beat-up airplane did. Much to my displeasure, the net result was a medical grounding called DNIF—duty not involving flying.

Although I couldn't prove it, I felt certain the flight surgeon and the Prairie Fire commander, Bob Dennison, conspired to keep me from flying. Between the two of them, they managed to keep me off the schedule for six straight days, supposedly for my own good. On the first day, I was probably still on an adrenalin rush, so sitting around didn't bother me. The second day wasn't too bad, since I was tired and did need the rest. By the third day, I started climbing the walls. Sitting around the Muff Divers' Lounge grew old quickly.

My two new roomies were out flying all day long, and there wasn't anyone to talk to. Because of the night schedule, the Covey O-2 pilots and navigators slept all day, so I ended up trapped with my own thoughts. As I sat there sipping scotch and contemplating my circumstances, several long-held but still half-baked notions began to crystallize.

I realized that I had changed radically in my six months of flying combat missions. The mechanics of being a FAC, so complex and mystifying to me in the beginning, had become second nature, almost a reflex. My old instructors, John Tait, Don Jensen, and Norm Edgar, all long since back in the States, would have been pleased with my progress. The things they chided me about, such as listening to all five radios at once, no longer bothered me. In fact, I couldn't even remember why it had seemed so difficult. And the maps. When I got the new set built, I knew I'd be able to reach into the bag and instinctively grab the right one without missing a beat. As for controlling the fighters, the Spads, and the Cobras, I found myself able to do it with a certain rhythm, a kind of natural flow which seemed to relax the pilots and maybe even inspire a little confidence. Most of all, in a really hot situation, my instincts had developed to the point where they could instinctively handle the present while my mind's eye projected ahead, anticipating. Coupled with a confidence in the Bronco and in my own ability to fly her out of the worst of scrapes, I saw myself for the first time as being truly combat ready.

Armed with a clearer picture of my own capabilities and limitations as a FAC, I was genuinely looking forward to strapping into my OV-10 after the long layoff. On the seventeenth I finally got airborne again, only not quite in the way I had expected. Looking down at the Ho Chi Minh Trail from the right seat of an O-2 didn't thrill me, especially since I was only a passenger being hauled from Da Nang to Nakhon Phanom Air Base in Thailand. In what I perceived to be another one of those unexplainable bits of military logic, the head Covey decided I needed a rest from the war and that a three-day pass in Bangkok was just the ticket. Evidently my week of sitting around didn't count. I pleaded my case carefully, since I wasn't at liberty to talk about the pending SOG missions, not even to Lieutenant Colonel Ed Cullivan. That was the real reason I didn't want the pass. But when the boss finally stated that in his view I needed a change of scenery, there was no way out.

The flight to NKP would allow me to hitch a ride the following day on one of the many transport aircraft flying to Don Muang Airport in Bangkok. That night I had a chance to talk to one of the C-123 crews at NKP. Their mission was anything but the typical airlift job. These guys were pilots on C-123s known as "Candle Stick" birds. As unlikely as it seemed, they performed a modified FAC mission. The crazy fools would fly around over the Trail at night searching for trucks. When they found something, the Candle would call in the night fighters, drop flares and ground marks, then direct the air strike. The cargo plane–turned–FAC could carry huge loads of flares and could loiter over the Trail for hours. From all indications, the Candle Stick crews were responsible for busting large numbers of enemy trucks. The old workhorse C-123 Provider finally had itself a glamorous mission.

The following day I linked up with Captain Bill Stewart, a Covey navigator who also needed a rest. A native Californian, Stu Stewart looked the part: tall, blond, a quick smile, and a willingness to party. We hopped a C-130 to Bangkok and ended up at the infamous Florida Hotel, right across the street from the Chao Phya, the U.S. military hotel and officers' club in Bangkok. Using the two hotels as a combined base of operations, we proceeded to attack the city with a vengeance, just like every other tourist GI faced with the dilemma of a huge city and only limited time to take it all in.

There is nothing subtle about Bangkok. It invades your senses with exotic sights, sounds, and smells. Stu Stewart and I immersed ourselves completely. We took in the Grand Palace and the Emerald Buddha. We toured Wat Po to see the Reclining Buddha. We sampled spicy-hot Thai food from noodle carts along the street. We went on the Floating Market tour through Bangkok's famous canals. Sandwiched in among the sight-seeing, we spent lots of time and cash in the count-less jewelry stores on every corner. At night we hit all the bars, always ending up back on the top floor of the Florida Hotel at a steamy place called the Bora Bora Room. During the forty-eight-hour blitz, I don't think we ever slept.

Early on the morning of the twentieth, we hired a Thai taxi to drive us fifty miles south to U Tapao Air Base, home of the large tanker and B-52 force supporting the war effort in Southeast Asia. From there we would hop a military flight back to Da Nang. On the drive south, we hoped to catch a few winks, but our driver turned out to be a frustrated ka-mikaze pilot. In spite of the steady stream of oncoming traf-fic, our boy couldn't resist pulling out into the other lane to pass some slowpoke. With horns wailing, brakes screeching, and our hearts pounding in our ears, our daredevil driver somehow managed to duck back into his lane at the last pos-sible moment. When we finally made it to U Tapao's front gate, both Stu and I were on the verge of hyperventilating. That unforgettable ride was probably the closest either of us came to being killed in the war. After three or four hours at Base Ops, we boarded a C-123 headed for Da Nang. Late that afternoon we collapsed in our rooms back at the Covey barracks, frightened, exhausted and much worse for the wear than when we'd left four days earlier. I wasn't sure about Stu, but I couldn't take another "rest" like the one that just ended. Flying combat missions would be a lot less tiring and probably not as dangerous.

But the Bangkok blitz had served its purpose. During most of that time, I pushed the Prairie Fire mission to the back of my mind. Yet once we were back home, I couldn't wait to get back in the saddle.

NOVEMBER

Outside the Envelope

Even in a combat zone, a certain amount of quality control was to be expected. Since most Covey pilots flew missions over the Trail every day, their opportunities to practice simulated airborne emergencies were limited. To make sure all of us remained current and capable of handling those emergencies, we were required to fly a midtour check ride with one of the 20th TASS instructor pilots. The drill normally occurred six months after a pilot became combat ready. The process included a hundred-question open-book exam on aircraft systems, operating procedures, and limitations. There was also a short test on emergency procedures. Most of us considered the check ride a waste of time and an insult to our prowess as pilots. But there was a good reason for our suffering the indignation. Our leaders saw what we couldn't. For six months the individual FAC had been a free spirit, answering to nobody and generally accustomed to having his own way. At that point we thought we knew it all, that we could handle anything. Our bosses knew better. They had gone through the same euphoric stage years earlier. They knew that young pilots were most prone to get in trouble early in the combat tour when they were green and at the six-month point when they were cocky. The midtour check was a scathingly brilliant way of pulling in the reins.

My chance to excel came on the fifth of November. These check rides were similar to any other graded test, and a certain amount of anxiety was involved. Fortunately, my old friend Carl D'Benedetto would be my flight examiner. After taking the written tests, I preflighted our OV-10 and got us airborne. Looking in the mirror, I could see Carl sitting in the back seat, cool as always, debonair and dashing with his bushy black mustache. Carl had me demonstrate a traffic pattern stall series and some slow flight, then we flew to Hue Phu Bai for some landings. We started off with a simulated single engine. I knew Carl was aware that I had handled the real thing a month earlier under tougher circumstances, but we pressed on anyway. I entered high key directly over the field at twenty-five hundred feet, then executed a shallow-bank descending turn to downwind at fifteen hundred feet. From there we turned final, threw the gear down, and landed.

Staying in the closed pattern, I set us up for a normal landing when Carl came up on intercom. "A beer says I can do a better spot landing than you. The one who touches main gear closest to the top of the runway numbers wins. You first."

"You gotta bet," I responded.

By all rights I should have won easily. From the front seat, I had great visibility. From the back Carl would have to peek around my ejection seat and my helmet even to glimpse the target. Thinking about how easy it should be, I set up a steady glide angle and held one hundred knots as we crabbed down final toward the concrete runway. Just before touchdown I lowered the right wing into the wind and eased in left rudder to align the fuselage axis with the runway. We touched down on the right main tire, maybe three or four feet short of the target.

On takeoff leg Carl took the controls. His pattern was much like mine except his final was a bit more shallow, and he kicked the crab out before we crossed the overrun. Tracking wing low, only a few feet above the surface, Carl had dead aim on the runway numbers. At the point where I thought we would touch, Carl rapidly retarded the throttles, settling us in exactly on the target—not an inch either way. It had been a remarkable piece of flying.

From Hue Phu Bai we flew north to my old stomping

ground at Quang Tri. After a no-flap touch-and-go, I dialed in the MLT-2 administrative frequency to say hello. Top answered right away and asked for some help. He had no idea I was unarmed and on a check ride.

"Listen, that team you put in the DMZ a couple of days ago has a problem. How 'bout swinging over their position and find out what's going on."

"We're on the way, Top. I'll get back to you in a few minutes." Then I said to Carl, "Babe, the check ride has to wait. You ever been in the DMZ before?" I knew he hadn't.

With no maps, no guns, and no rockets, I felt naked. There was no telling what kind of trouble the team had stumbled across, and I wasn't sure what help we could be. Still, it was worth a try. From Cam Lo I pointed the Bronco northwest on track across two prominent terrain features, the Rock Pile and the Razor Back. We flew into the DMZ and crossed the Song Ben Hai River into the north. On a finger-shaped ridge near Dong Cam, I set up an orbit over the last known position of our team. After I gunned the engines a few times to get their attention, the one-zero came up on Prairie Fire Common, UHF frequency 282.0.

In a muffled but clear voice, he asked, "Covey circling my pos, how do you read, over."

"Covey 221 at your service. What's your situation?"

"We've got a lot of movement about four hundred meters to our west. If you can distract them, I want to move one hill to the east. Can you cover us?"

The problem was I didn't know exactly where they were. With no maps the only choice was to have the team mark their location with an orange panel. Once I talked the one-zero into that, it became easy. With Carl sitting silently in the back seat, I made four or five low passes on suspected bad guy positions, hoping the simulated machine-gun passes would do the trick. While we buzzed the bomb-cratered hills, the team moved swiftly and silently to a more secure position. Thirty minutes later, the one-zero came back up on frequency. In a whisper he said simply, "Team okay. Thanks for the help." Carl's only comment was, "Do you guys always fly that low?" When we finally landed at Da Nang, the one-hour check ride had stretched to two hours. With a smile and a shake of the head, Carl passed me with flying colors.

Following the check ride, I spent the next several weeks handling my duties as Prairie Fire training officer. I really enjoyed working with the new recruits, teaching them, worrying about them, and generally carrying on like a mother hen. There was one disadvantage. On early training sorties, I sometimes had to ride shotgun in the right seat of the O-2. While most of the O-2 jocks thought fondly of their war bird, I had a real problem getting used to it. To me, flying the Oscar Deuce in combat seemed to be more of an exercise in energy management. When my eager young trainee would dive on a target to fire a willie pete, things really got interesting. On the pull-up, we didn't go anywhere. The heavy, underpowered Cessna just couldn't zoom back to altitude as my OV-10 could. On each pass we'd end up lower and lower, out of ideas, airspeed, and altitude. In spite of what I saw as a definite disadvantage in equipment, our O-2 jocks took it all in stride and ended up running some of the most hairy Prairie Fire missions of the war.

In between training missions and normal OV-10 sorties, we occasionally got mixed up in off-the-wall episodes. The last half of November turned out to be nonstandard on all counts.

By the eighteenth one of our teams had been sitting around for a week waiting to be inserted. One delay after another had forced a postponement. Not only was the team getting antsy, the indig members were tired of eating GI food. They began complaining and asking for food more to their liking. Since things were slow, we mounted an airborne hunting safari to keep peace in the family. With Satan in my back seat, we drafted one Huey Slick and one Cobra gunship to go with us. Our objective was a marshy area at the base of Tiger Tooth Mountain, near Khe Sanh and the Laotian border. En route our Cobra had the first success when they spotted several wild boar ambling along a trail. With ruthless efficiency the Cobra crew nailed the tail-end Charlie. The Huey swooped in, hovered, and retrieved the small pig.

Several miles east of the marsh, we put our choppers in a holding pattern. Marty and I pressed on, climbing to three thousand feet. As we flew over the rain-soaked ground, we could see hundreds of ducks floating quietly on the seasonal ponds below us. "Marty," I asked, "have you ever strafed ducks?" He replied, "Never have. Does Sir have a hunting license?" Arming up all four machine guns, I ignored Marty's question, eased out to our west, and descended to treetop altitude. As we pressed in on the deck, surprisingly few of the ducks seemed upset by our approach. At point-blank range I squeezed the trigger, spraying hundreds of 7.62mm bullets across the surface of the pond. As the huge flock struggled into the air, we banked hard to our left to avoid the wall of ducks directly in front of us. Between the terrified birds and my machine-gun fire, the placid pond had become a churning sea of water.

For the next twenty minutes, we circled the scene while the door gunner aboard the Slick employed a long stick resembling a shepherd's crook to retrieve the dead ducks scattered about the pond. For all of the rounds I fired, we only managed to bag about fifteen birds. Still, our indig would enjoy a hearty feast of pork and fowl over the next several days.

On a different type of hunting trip late that same afternoon, I teamed up with an ARVN ranger to pick out an LZ for an all-indig mission. We concentrated on the line of hills north of Route 9, just to the east of Tchepone, scene of my recent run-in with an NVA .51-cal machine gun. As we circled one potential LZ, I noticed several flak bursts well to our north. There was nobody else in the area, so I couldn't imagine at whom the gunner might be firing. As we approached, the gunner kept up the tempo, firing clip after clip straight up into the air. He obligingly kept on firing while I plotted his position.

My ARVN back-seater and I weren't looking for trouble, but I couldn't resist asking Hillsboro for some air. To my way of thinking, the 23mm gun crew had gone off the deep end and deserved to be put out of their misery—before they killed someone. Evidently the controller aboard the big C-130 felt the same way. Within minutes, Dudley flight, a four ship of F-4s, checked in with us. I gave the circling Phantoms a quick brief, then rolled in from the south right on the deck. With five degrees of dive angle at a slant range of two thousand feet, I popped off two willie petes as my pipper superimposed on the gun pit. Then I racked it hard to the west for a climb into the late afternoon sun.

Out the top of the canopy, we could see the marks were right on. I advised my fighters, "Okay, gents, hit my smoke. Whoever's in position is cleared in hot. I'll be holding low, about a klick to the south."

The gunfire had stopped. The ranger and I watched as Dudley Lead rolled into a steep dive from the east. At about four thousand feet, Lead pickled off several canisters of CBU-24. Roughly halfway to the target, the bombs split in half, releasing hundreds of spin-armed bomblets. On impact, each bomblet exploded, propelling tiny steel balls in all directions. The overall explosion pattern as seen from above resembled a giant doughnut with a hollow center. In succession, we cleared Two, Three, and Four in to give our gun more of the same. After the smoke cleared, we watched as ten to fifteen rounds of exploding 23mm ammo cooked off inside what had been the gun pit. With the F-4s covering me, we made one low pass over the position. In the dark shadows, the gun sat upright with its barrel drooping, pointing into the ground. There was no trace of the crew.

In the last rays of light, we headed back to Quang Tri. In spite of the darkness, we could see several rain showers in the vicinity of the runway. Coming in from the west, I entered downwind and turned a left base. On very short final, maybe fifty feet in the air, we crossed the perimeter road and ran smack into a solid wall of black rain. My forward vis-

ibility was instantly reduced to zero. For a split second, I
thought to myself, "Just hold this attitude, and we should
touch down right on centerline. You've done it a thousand
times." Instead, I cobbed the power and pulled the nose up
in a desperate attempt to put altitude between the runway and
me. When I had positive climb indications on the altimeter
and vertical velocity indicator, I sucked up the gear and put
us in a gentle bank to the west. Within seconds we were out
of the rain, into the clear night sky. Climbing back to pattern
altitude, I could see that the south end of Quang Tri's runway
had disappeared in the squall. On the other end the dim white
runway lights outlined a clear slab of concrete. This time I
turned a right base for the opposite runway and landed uneventfully. On the roll-out, we coasted back into the driving
rain at the other end of the field. Slowly I taxied us clear of
the active and toward Barky Operations, without even waiting
for the de-arming crew. When we climbed out, my passenger
smiled from ear to ear. I couldn't even force a grin. For the
first time in the war, I looked down to see both my hands
shaking. It was terrifying to think about what a stupid thing I
had almost let myself do.

Following the strange episodes involving ducks, 23mm
guns, and rain squalls, an old-fashioned Prairie Fire mission
would have been a welcome change. It wasn't in the cards.

Several days later Blister, the Covey rider with the gaudy
gold chain, jumped in the back seat of my OV-10 for what
we thought would be a routine baby-sitting mission. A few
minutes past noon, we headed into Laos, with Blister cheer-
fully munching away on his favorite sandwich, raw hamburger meat on French bread. Neither of us anticipated much
action. Unlike the normal five- to seven-man team, the group
we were going to support was large enough to take care of
itself. Early the same morning, a twenty-four-man SOG team
stumbled out of an armada of Huey Slicks and sprinted off
the LZ located in the middle of an area known as the Laotian
salient. On our maps, the salient resembled the business end

of a hatchet, with its blade roughly five miles wide and its body jutting about eight miles due north into Vietnam.

When we arrived overhead, the one-zero complained about sporadic sniper fire from three sides. As I worked a couple of Cobra gunships around the flanks, I heard Blister's voice become deadly serious as he talked to the team leader.

"Mac, I don't like this. You're letting these snipers herd you south. There's lots of cover and well-used trails that way. You've got the muscle, so keep moving east."

Several exchanges later, I heard Blister say, "It's a setup, Mac. I'm advising you to move any direction but south."

The team leader wouldn't listen. He continued the sweep due south for another hour. Shortly after the one-zero reported the sniper fire had ceased, a new voice began screaming at us: "Prairie Fire! Prairie Fire! We're in contact. The one-zero's down. Get us out!"

In the confusion I had no idea where the enemy fire was coming from. Blister, in his inimitable gruff but calming voice, fired off a few questions and gave me all the data we needed to get started. Using directions from the assistant team leader, I turned the Cobras loose on the pocket of small-arms and automatic-weapons fire. From the radio chatter, I gathered the team had begun an organized withdrawal to the north. We pounded the area around the team for twenty minutes, hoping to break the contact and give them a chance to move to a more defensible position, preferably close to a usable LZ.

While Blister called back to the launch site for some Hueys, I asked the team, "How's the one-zero?"

The assistant answered, "The *bac si* is working on him now. It's a flesh wound in the groin. Doesn't look too bad."

Thirty minutes later, we put four Hueys into a nearby LZ for an unopposed extraction. As my package headed back toward Quang Tri, Slick Lead relayed the bad news. The one-zero was dead. After we landed Blister and I talked to the *bac si*. The young medic stood there, rocking back and forth, looking old and drawn. When we asked him what had happened, he stopped rocking for a few seconds, then said hoarsely, "We did everything we could. He wasn't hurt that bad. I think he just gave up. He quit fighting. I've never seen anything like it."

November's strange turn of events kept right on coming. On the morning of the twenty-third, as I cruised around the north end of the A Shau, a mayday call from a battle-damaged F-105 drew everyone's attention. The distressed aircraft, Dallas 01, relayed his position to the search-and-rescue C-130, King, and I knew we were in the same neighborhood. Several minutes later, five miles away and well above me, I saw the burning Thud. Within a matter of seconds, the F-105 veered sharply to its left, and a parachute appeared. The whole sequence happened so fast I never actually saw the ejection.

Evidently I wasn't the only FAC in the vicinity. One of the O-2 FACs supporting the 101st, call sign Bilk, notified King that he had a tally on the chute and was assuming the job as on-scene commander for the rescue. Since we were in his assigned sector, I had no problem with Bilk's initiative. But instinctively, I felt better qualified to run a SAR. It was right up my alley, precisely what I'd been doing for the past five months. Somewhat grudgingly, I kept my mouth shut until Bilk elected to do things the hard way, calling for a scramble of Air Force Jolly Green helicopters from Da Nang. To me time was the problem, not the Jollies. Those aircrews included some of the bravest, most dedicated aviators in the world. The problem was it would take them forty-five minutes to arrive. From experience, I knew I could have an Army chopper on the scene in five minutes.

One quick call to my helicopter buddies in the 101st produced all the help we needed. An OH-6 Loach contacted me for the downed pilot's position, then headed straight for our boy. Somewhat guiltily, I thought about the ramifications of upstaging the other FAC. It wasn't his fault he'd never run a SAR before. He was simply doing it by the book. Reluctantly, I had the Loach contact Bilk.

In the radio exchange that followed, the Bilk FAC seemed pleased to have the help. In a very professional manner, he talked the Loach into Dallas 01, who appeared to be stuck up to his armpits in mud on the bank of a small stream. With no hesitation and no cover, the Loach landed near the pilot, discharged a copilot, and continued to sit there brazenly while the spare crew member tried to pull the pilot free. When the copilot ran back to his helicopter, I could tell there was trouble. While the Loach pilot and the FAC discussed options for freeing the stuck Thud pilot, I got on the horn and asked the 101st to divert a medical evacuation helicopter, known throughout Vietnam as "Dust-Off." Within minutes the Dust-Off contacted the orbiting O-2, and that's when the turf battle got out of control.

Up to that point, King, the orbiting C-130 SAR coordinator, had been fairly quiet, asking a few questions and passing along the progress of the Jolly Green. But when the Dust-Off showed up, King became very vocal. With a definite edge in his voice, the controller aboard King interrupted. "Dust-Off, this is King 24. Request you remain clear of the area. We have a Jolly Green inbound at this time. He's equipped with a hoist and medical help for this rescue."

The Dust-Off shot back, "We're hoist equipped and have a medic on board also. I've got your pilot in sight at this time."

In an even more agitated voice, King countered, "I say again. Remain clear of the area. The Jolly is ten minutes out and will make the pickup. This is an Air Force rescue. Acknowledge."

Nobody said a word for about fifteen seconds. During the silence, the tension was thick enough to cut with a knife. Then, without identifying himself, a voice said disgustedly, "King 24, you're an ass." That comment voiced the sentiments of all of us watching the fiasco. With that, the Dust-Off executed a 180-degree turn and headed back to Hue Phu Bai. Twenty minutes later, the Jolly Green pulled the downed pilot aboard and retraced its flight path back to Da Nang. In spite of everything, the rescue had turned out okay, but it wasn't exactly a red letter day in the annals of interservice cooperation.

Fortunately, the rift wasn't permanent. The day before Thanksgiving, the news in the *Stars and Stripes* captured everyone's attention. In bold one-inch letters, the headlines declared: "RAID ON POW CAMP." Colonel Arthur "Bull" Simons, a legend in Special Forces circles and former commander of MAC-SOG, had led a fifty-six-man team in a daring rescue raid on the Son Tay Prison, twenty miles west of Hanoi. Supported by Air Force H-53 Jolly Green helicopters and A-1 Skyraiders, the SF volunteers stormed the prison in a perfectly executed plan—only to find all Americans had been moved. It was a bitter disappointment. Still, the audacity of pulling off a mission right under Uncle Ho's spiritual nose electrified the SOG community and shocked the North Vietnamese.

On the twenty-seventh I spent the night at MLT-2. As we sat around the newly constructed dayroom/kitchen/party hooch sipping beer, the Son Tay raid dominated conversation. Speculation became the order of the evening. The Green Berets sprawled around the smoke-filled little room took turns guessing which of their SF buddies had been on the raid. Someone would offer, "I'll bet old so-and-so was on it. He always was in the right place at the right time." From across the room, a slurred voice countered, "Nah, he's a jerk and a lousy shot. Bull would never pick him." This type of banter continued well into the wee hours. Through it all, the sense of pride came through loud and clear. Every man in the room would have given up practically anything to have been part of the Son Tay raid.

In my five months as a Prairie Fire pilot, that night was the first time I had a chance to see and hear the personal side of the men with whom I'd been working. Sitting there on their home turf, their inhibitions melted away by too many beers, I listened to them ramble on about friends, ex-wives, gripes, retirement plans. In their maudlin moods, much to my embarrassment, they couldn't say enough nice things about the Air Force FACs who supported them. The bond was genuine and the sentiment, sincere. I was deeply touched by their words, but for whatever reasons, I was too hung up to show it. Instead of accepting their compliments graciously, I retreated behind a facade of jokes and laughing denials.

My SF friends had their hang-ups, too. As we continued to drink and talk, each story became part of a composite forming in my mind. A definite pattern emerged. Every Green Beret in the room was serving on at least his second tour in Vietnam. Most were on a third or even fourth tour. Most had already suffered through at least one bad marriage, aggravated by long separations. All of these men had an abiding love for Special Forces and the values the Green Berets represented. Yet they seemed to be trapped in a push-pull situation. On the one hand, they were drawn by the freewheeling adventure and unconventional war of Southeast Asia. On the other hand, they seemed repelled by the regular army with its spit and polish, garrison duty, and stateside rules. To a man they bemoaned the fate of any of their number who rotated home only to become part of the bureaucracy at Fort Bragg charged with training sullen antiwar draftees. Rather than face that prospect, most of the MLT-2 troops chose to extend their tour in Vietnam indefinitely— until the war ended or it killed them.

Shortly after midnight a change in mood rippled through the hooch. A mischievous feeling replaced the melancholy. Before I could figure out what was happening, my hosts swept me out the door into a jeep. In addition to the five of us crammed into the M-151, another half-dozen limber bodies piled into a three-quarter-ton truck. With beers in each hand and shouts of encouragement all around, we set off down the bumpy road toward Quang Tri Army Base.

Nearing the center of the sleeping base, our drivers turned off their headlights. Everyone in the convoy became deadly quiet. At a snail's pace, we motored silently down several side streets and through a back alley or two. My companions in the jeep became tense and alert, displaying just the sort of composure I imagined they'd have on a Prairie Fire mission. After a few more turns, we stopped behind a nondescript one-story building. A porch light at the far end of the long building seemed to be the only light around. Amid groans and giggles, the men in the back seat with me climbed out and sprinted to the lighted end of the structure. Quickly and silently, they blended into the night shadows. Simultaneously, the crew in the truck moved swiftly to the back door of the building and disappeared inside.

Finally I whispered to the driver, "Will somebody tell me what the hell's going on?"

He whispered back, "Be quiet. Here, have another beer."

Obediently I accepted the can. For the next ten minutes, the two of us sat there, the only sounds coming when we slapped a mosquito or gulped down a big swallow of beer. I couldn't imagine what my SF friends were doing inside that building, but instinctively I sensed they were up to no good. Helped by the alcohol, my mind reeled. Panty raid? Nurse napping? God help us, bank robbery?

A dark figure whistled softly, then the truck started up and backed up to the rear door. Straining, I thought I saw several men load a large rectangular shape into the truck. Seconds later one troop climbed back in our jeep. Again with headlights out, we fell in behind the truck, retracing our route out of Quang Tri Army Base. When I asked about the missing man from our jeep, the driver simply jerked a thumb to the rear. Looking back, I saw another jeep, lights out, in trail behind us.

Once we reentered the MLT-2 perimeter, my jeep mates began hooting and laughing between chants of "popcorn, popcorn." I still didn't have a clue. The pieces fell into place when I saw a shouting, groaning team of men unload a full-sized popcorn machine, just like the ones in movie theaters back in the States. To the cheers of onlookers, the crew carefully carried it inside, placed it in an empty corner, then plugged it in. From the looks of anticipation on their faces, the assembled Green Berets could already taste the fresh, hot popcorn. But, just as quickly, the smiles turned to frowns. Members of the road crew began a frantic search for something, dashing to the truck, then back to the hooch. After inspecting every door, every corner of the popcorn machine, the men slumped dejectedly into chairs. In the darkness and confusion, they had forgotten to "borrow" the bags of unpopped kernels and the oil. The popcorn party would have to wait.

When I finally crawled out of bed in midmorning, the MLT-2 troops were already hard at work. The focus of most of the activity appeared to be a strange jeep bearing the markings of the Eighteenth MASH, the hospital on Quang Tri Army Base. Two men were painting it black while another began filing the serial number off the engine. I decided to ask no questions. I couldn't swear it was the jeep from last night's adventure, and I really didn't want to know for sure.

Late that afternoon as I was preparing for the flight back to Da Nang, several SOG troops jokingly presented me with a hastily framed sheet of paper. Reading it, I found that the part about stealing jeeps struck particularly close to home. The framed document read:

THE FAC

As seen by 7th Air Force: A drunken, brawling, jeep-stealing, woman-corrupting liar with a star sapphire ring, Seiko watch, and a pearl-handled .38.

As seen by himself: A tall, handsome, highly trained professional killer, gentleman idol of women, with a star sapphire ring, wearing a pearl-handled .38, who is always on time due to the reliability of his Seiko watch.

As seen by his wife: A stinking member of the family who staggers into town about every year or so with a B-4 bag full of dirty underwear and fornication on his mind.

As seen by his commander: A fine specimen of a drunken, brawling, jeep-stealing, woman-corrupting liar with a star sapphire ring, Seiko watch, and a pearl-handled .38.

As seen by the Department of the Air Force: An over-paid, over-ranked tax burden who is indispensible because he has volunteered to go anywhere and do anything as long as he can booze it up, brawl, steal jeeps, corrupt women, lie, wear a star sapphire ring, a Seiko watch, and carry a pearl-handled .38.

DECEMBER

The Covey Bomb Dump

As the war eased into the final month of 1970, I found myself on more than one occasion remembering my pilot-training days at Laughlin AFB. The month of December had been a particularly trying time for our instructors. To a man they hated the thought of Christmas break. The IPs complained bitterly that their boneheaded students spent more time daydreaming about the upcoming holidays than learning to fly. The preoccupation with family, girl friends, and Christmas manifested itself in several disturbing statistics. Whether by design or coincidence, December always spawned a rash of automobile accidents and airplane crashes among student pilots. It was the best of times and the worst of times.

On December 4, 1970, I came within a cat's whisker of becoming one of those dreaded statistics, of succumbing to the lack of concentration I supposedly outgrew three years earlier at Laughlin. Instead of channeling my energies into tackling the horrible weather around Quang Tri, I let my mind race toward the end of the month when I would be meeting my wife in Hawaii. We hadn't seen each other in nine long months. On top of that, Jane didn't have a clue about what I was doing in the Prairie Fire mission. Since I wasn't allowed to tell her about it, I gave a lot of thought to how I'd dodge the subject. An instructor at Louisiana Tech University, the lady was no dummy. As an Air Force brat, Jane knew a lot about the flying game. I wasn't at all certain about how I'd handle the situation.

In Quang Tri Province, gloomy gray clouds socked in the

entire area. A low ragged ceiling held steady at about two to three hundred feet. After landing special VFR, I got word through Barky Ops radio that one of our teams was in trouble. Without waiting for a Covey rider to arrive, I launched into the scud. Imitating Army chopper pilots, I elected to remain below the deck as I hedge-hopped toward Laos. For ease of navigation I pointed the Bronco northwest toward Dong Ha. From there I turned west to Cam Lo, then picked up Route 9 as it wound through the hills toward Khe Sanh. As I approached the abandoned airstrip from the east, the cloud deck dropped even lower. Several miles away, the terrain and sky blended together into a dark gray curtain. In an all-out effort to get to the team, but with thoughts of R and R buzzing in my brain, I piloted the OV-10 into the Rao Quan River gorge.

The Bronco seemed alive as we glided through the narrow gorge, just below the rim of the jagged cliffs on either side. Maneuvering space in the gorge was minimal, but visibility proved to be excellent. With only a few clicks on the trim button, I could will the aircraft into gentle climbs or banks. The control stick responded to the slightest pressure from my hand. In addition to the sheer thrill of flying, I took a few moments to enjoy the scenery. In contrast to the swirling gray mist only a few feet above, the gorge was alive with green tropical vegetation, bolders with seal-slick texture, and white water cascading along the bottom, swollen by the monsoon rains. The Bronco and I faithfully followed each S turn of the river, completely absorbed by the primordial scene.

Five minutes after entering the gorge, I rolled into ninety degrees of left bank to negotiate a particularly tight hairpin turn in the river. As I centered the stick, the sight in front of me made me gasp out loud. Approximately a mile ahead of me, a solid wall of rain obliterated the gorge. With less than fifty feet separating each of my wing tips from the rocky sides, a retreat was impossible. I knew that flying into the rain squall would result in a fiery crash against an unseen wall of the gorge. My only chance was lady luck and the climbing power of the OV-10.

Pulse pounding in my temples, I shoved the throttles forward to full military power, then set a twenty-degree nose-high climb on the attitude indicator. Seconds later we slipped into the dark clouds. As the Bronco struggled to gain altitude, I fully expected to slam into one of the many three-thousand-foot mountains on either side of the Rao Quan River. Flying on instruments, I could only guess at my position relative to the mountains. Since the river generally ran to the northwest, I held that heading and watched as the altimeter slowly wound up—one thousand, fifteen hundred, two thousand. I began talking to my mechanical partner. "Come on, baby. Climb. Climb. Get us out of this. A little more back pressure and trim to keep this angle of climb. Twenty-five hundred. We've almost got it whipped. Keep climbing. Don't stall on me."

Passing three thousand on the altimeter, I let out a war whoop. The threat had to be to my right, so I eased in a little left aileron and rudder to give us more room. At thirty-five hundred feet, we broke out of the soup between layers of stratus clouds. Nothing had ever looked so beautiful. Roughly one mile off the right wing tip, the barren, bald top of Tiger Tooth Mountain jutted into the gray drizzle, an ugly reminder of how close I had come to being the worst kind of statistic.

Fortified with a renewed sense of respect for the anonymous sage who coined the adage about keeping your mind on your work, I mentally got myself back in the war. Several days after the close call in the Rao Quan River gorge, I stumbled headlong into a different type of distraction. The day started innocently enough. The head Covey, Lieutenant Colonel Ed Cullivan, hopped in my back seat for a lift north to Quang Tri. When we landed, Ed remained on the airfield to conduct some negotiations with Barky Operations while I pressed on with my secret Prairie Fire mission. I think the whole setup made us both a little uneasy. Even in his position as Covey commander, Colonel Cullivan didn't have operational control over the six Prairie Fire pilots. We operated a completely independent schedule and mission from the Trail Coveys. He didn't even possess the necessary SOG security clearances to enter our top-secret Prairie Fire briefing room at Da Nang. He had a vague idea of what we did, but his knowledge stopped there. Our tactics and standard operating procedures remained off limits. I knew for a fact the convoluted situation troubled him. Since the only Covey combat losses during Ed's command involved Prairie Fire pilots, he felt a genuine sadness and sense of helplessness over the turn of events. On more than one occasion, Colonel Cullivan would shake his head and mutter, "What a way to run a railroad."

By midafternoon the head Covey met me plane-side for the flight back to Da Nang. Out of habit I left all our radios tuned to operational frequencies. Just as we were airborne, a distress call blasted through our earphones. Unaware that Colonel Cullivan was listening, the O-2 jock filled me in over a secure voice gadget known as the KY-28. In between squelch breaks and beeps, Ed heard the pilot announce, "Tom, I've got a TAC E going and no close air support. I'd like to expend your ordnance before I commit the Hueys. How copy, over."

My passenger and I heard it loud and clear. My mind raced as I formulated an answer. The situation sounded hot, and my guns and rockets might make a big difference. On the flip side, playing fighter with the uncleared commander in my back seat presented a different kind of risk, not to mention an unwelcome distraction. With mixed emotions and no real conviction in my voice, I finally replied, "Covey 221 inbound to you with a flight of one. I've got fourteen each willie petes and HEs, and two thousand rounds of pop gun."

As we slipped across the fence, the boss didn't have much to say, and I made no effort to steel him for what lay ahead. Thankfully, we each had the good sense to leave the other alone. Still, I couldn't help thanking the weather gods for a high broken cloud ceiling and plenty of sunshine. The very thought of hugging the top of the triple-canopy jungle made me squeamish. Even at fifteen hundred feet, I could have sworn I felt Ed's dark eyes burning disapproving holes into the back of my head.

The target loomed straight in front of us, a large emerald green field surrounded by scrub brush and scrawny trees. Several low hills immediately to the north, casting afternoon shadows across the landscape, created the illusion of an overgrown crater or a shallow soup bowl. The SOG team had managed to get itself into a firefight at the geographic center of the field, one of those rare occasions when the good guys and bad guys chose to fight right out in the open. As luck would have it, my passenger was going to get an eyeful.

The Prairie Fire O-2 laid down several well-placed white smokes to mark the target, then he cleared us in hot. Out of deference to Colonel Cullivan, I came down the chute a little steeper and higher than normal. With one eye on the smoke and the other on the team seventy-five meters to the south, I lined up the target in my gunsight. Purposely aiming slightly right of the target in the direction of the friendlies, I squeezed off two HE rockets. On the first shot, the one-zeros preferred that we keep the stuff in close, to drive the enemy away from the explosions and the team rather than forcing them to flee into our team. At the sight of the dirty little detonations, I completely forgot about my back-seater.

The orbiting FAC, cheered on by enthusiastic corrections from the team, had me dive in for three or four more rocket passes. Then the fun started. For good measure we flew multiple machine-gun passes, stitching the green field with long bursts of fire. While I kept the bad guys pinned down, two Hueys swept in for a formation landing. We kept up the figure-eight strafing patterns until the choppers lifted off and climbed to a safe altitude.

As the package took up a heading for Quang Tri and I pointed us south, Huey Lead gave me a call.

"Covey 221, the one-zero says it's imperative you return to QT. He's got something you've gotta see."

With a shrug of the shoulders, I banked us around to the northeast. To Colonel Cullivan, I explained, "This shouldn't take long." Then somewhat apologetically I added, "They wouldn't call us back unless it was important."

The MLT black jeep was waiting when we landed. Colonel Cullivan strolled back into Barky Ops while I bounced off down the road to the launch site. When we arrived, the driver struck out across the soggy LZ toward a group of figures standing near the choppers. They seemed intent on watching something or someone. As I walked up, the circle of Special Forces troops and helicopter pilots parted, revealing the object of their attention. Squatting flat-footed, balanced perfectly on his haunches in Oriental fashion, a young NVA soldier sat there puffing on a cigarette. He wore a baggy khaki-colored uniform, the shirt conspicuous by the large blood stain on the left side. An army battle dressing was tied around his left bicep.

Sporting a wide grin, one of the troops explained, "We snatched this character during the middle of your air strike. The *bac si* says it looks like a couple of pieces of rocket shrapnel creased him. We told him you did it. He said he'd like to meet you."

Someone said something in Vietnamese, bringing a weak smile to the baby-faced soldier's lips. In between drags on the cigarette, he rattled off a couple of sentences. The translator said that the kid thought I was a good shot. Partly out of curiosity and partly out of meanness, I asked, "What effect did my shooting have on the rest of your buddies?" After hearing the translation, the kid spoke no words, but his defiant glare more than answered my question.

On the flight south to Da Nang, Ed Cullivan chattered away, never once mentioning the curious little battle he'd observed out in the middle of Laos. In a breezy, casual manner, he confined most of his comments to the Barky operation, discussing their FAC mission and the problems they faced. As he talked, I only half-paid attention. My mind kept framing pictures of the boyish-looking NVA soldier, his dark eyes with no pupils staring at me. I felt a certain twinge of remorse at being responsible for his wounds, yet that same little guy, armed with an AK-47, had been a dangerous adversary only minutes before. Still, I derived no sense of pleasure in shooting him. In fact, the down side to meeting him face to face outweighed the novelty of meeting him at all. In a passing thought, I worried that on my next mission, taking aim through the gunsight, I might see his smooth, expressionless face instead of a fleeting target. Hashing the episode around one last time before we landed, I arrived at only one clear conclusion. Temperamentally, I was much better suited to the impersonal air war than to the close-up, blood and guts side of the fighting.

As if in a self-fulfilling prophecy, for the next few days I had trouble shaking the vision of the baby-faced NVA soldier at Quang Tri. The episode never seemed to bother me during the work day. But at night, during lulls inside the Muff Divers' Lounge, I could visualize the blood-soaked shirt in vivid detail. The preoccupation finally took care of itself as I became absorbed in setting up and trying out my newly arrived stereo gear: Teac tape deck and Pioneer tuner and speakers. That simple diversion did the trick for me. Other Coveys handled the tension in other ways.

To take their minds off the fighting, the troops in Vietnam devised some inspired ways to let off steam. A few of the less rowdy types tried losing themselves in hobbies or in reading. Others opted for marathon card games. The more active ones participated in roughhouse games of volleyball, playing by "jungle rules"—anything goes. The whole idea was to find a distraction to occupy the time between combat missions. This safety valve came naturally to most, as if bred into the soldiers, sailors, and airmen by design. But a few always hung back, almost brooding. The stress ate away at them. Such men tended to lose themselves in a fog of whiskey or depression. One of our own Prairie Fire pilots resigned from the program, claiming too much was expected from him. Unable to cope with the stress, the man became physically ill.

Sometimes a little artificial help was needed to lower the stress level. On December 11 the Coveys instinctively knew the time had come for a rip-roaring bash. From all over the main compound, a crush of bodies packed the Muff Divers' Lounge. Coveys, Spads, Jolly Greens, nurses, intel, maintenance—everybody crowded in. As nominal hosts, Sonny,

Larry, and I picked the theme. We decided on a "Yucca Flats" party. Into a large steel kettle, we poured gallons of vodka and grain alcohol. To mask the awful taste, we stirred in sliced oranges, jars of maraschino cherries, and a little sugar. The potent concoction easily lived up to its namesake in the Nevada desert. One sip could blow the top of your head off.

A simple dip of the cup into the vat would have been the obvious, conventional way of serving our thirsty guests. But in honor of our unconventional war, our Yucca Flats punch needed a unique touch, a bit of flair, a dose of the dramatic equal to the high spirits of the evening. The solution was simple. One of the nurses donated a pair of black silk panties. Someone else chipped in with an old tennis shoe. The Big Bippy did the honors by stirring both deep into the vat. Then we announced the rules of engagement. Anyone wanting a drink had to wring the soaked panties into his cup until it was half full. The tennis shoe became a ladle to fill the cup to the brim. Amid howls of laughter, everyone followed the rules to the letter.

Later in the party, armed with a full cup of punch guaranteed to cure shyness, I struck up a conversation with two of the Air Force nurses. Lieutenant Pat Orowski, a pretty blonde Yankee, had the most intriguing Maine accent I'd ever heard. Her sidekick, Lieutenant Sherdeane Kinney, was a slender, auburn-haired looker from Mobile, Alabama, by way of Woodstock, New York. At first I asked a lot of dumb questions just to hear the two contrasting accents. Then as Pat and Sherdeane began talking about their jobs at the Air Force hospital, I found myself listening for content. Their professional lives revolved around an endless stream of badly wounded GIs, most waiting for medical evacuation back to the States. On each shift the nurses dealt with sucking chest wounds, shattered limbs, mutilated bodies. Along with the gory dressing and bandaging of wounds, the nurses were drafted by their patients into the emotional roles of friend, confidante, pseudo-mother, sister, or even girl friend. I listened as the two ladies described laughing and teasing with a young man with both legs blown off. Then, with knots in their stomachs, they walked out of the ward and into the corridor to cry. And the same scene repeated itself, day after day. If anyone ever deserved a chance to unwind, these very professional Air Force nurses did.

Eventually the conversation lightened up. As we talked, Pat and Sherdeane brought up the possibility of visiting a few nurse buddies at Quang Tri. Rumor had it I flew up there every day, and they wondered if I would give one of them a ride in my OV-10. At first I dismissed the notion as party chatter, but in her deep Southern drawl, Sherdeane persisted, demanding a definite yes or no. As she tried to convince me, it occurred to me who she reminded me of. She could have been the personification of Holly Golightly, the free spirit of *Breakfast at Tiffany's*. And the similarity went deeper than looks. Like the character Holly, Sherdeane struck me as being capable of operating comfortably in the conventional world, then easing right into the flower child scene. She was a hawk on the war, but her heart was in Haight Ashbury. Finally, at two in the morning, with some strong-arm help from her buddy Sonny Haynes, I agreed to fly Sherdeane to Quang Tri.

The Yucca Flats party generated two casualties. The first was my old friend Norm Komich from pilot-training days. On the day of the party, Norm decided to move out of his Jolly Green quarters and into the Muff Divers' Lounge. We knew he wouldn't last. Norm's clean living and spartan habits doomed the experiment to failure. The drinking, the loud music, and the round-the-clock tempo were too much. The next morning, Norm apologetically moved back in with the other helicopter pilots. In his heavy Boston accent, he pleaded, "Hey, it's not you guys. Honest. But Tom, Tom, I just couldn't get any Zs. I gotta have my Zs. It was the noise. I really am sorry." All of us fell over laughing. All by itself, Norm's pronunciation of my name, "TOE-UM," cracked us up.

The other casualty was our maid, Mamma San. When she walked in and saw the mess, she almost cried. Bottles, cups, and potato chips lay strewn about the room. The floor was gummy from spilled punch, and soot from several large candles had blackened the white tile ceiling. Her blood-curdling scream echoed through the place as she dug through the remnants of the Yucca Flats vat. She was calm as she fished out the panties and the tennis shoe. She maintained her composure as she gingerly scooped out someone's partial denture plate. But when Mamma San reached in and pulled out a life-size realistic-looking rubber snake, she ran screaming from the Muff Divers' Lounge. Two days of bribing with food and presents wouldn't coax her into returning.

In the late morning sunshine on the day after the party, I walked nervously across the ramp to my airplane, with my back-seater matching me stride for stride. Suffering from a mild case of paranoia, I searched the faces of the staring crew chiefs, wondering which of them would be the first to recognize Lieutenant Kinney, even with her long red hair cleverly hidden under the helmet she wore. Their expressions revealed nothing. The troops were conditioned to seeing me show up with an oddball assortment of Green Berets or indig, so I hoped they'd pay no attention to my latest passenger. Unfortunately, the young airmen spotted Sherdeane's shape in spite of the baggy fatigues she wore. By the time we reached the plane, half a dozen grinning crew chiefs greeted us, each gushing for a chance to help the Air Force nurse climb into the waiting OV-10.

I growled at them, "Knock it off, gents." Then to the only one of them wearing a shirt, I snapped, "You, help the lieutenant strap in." Without waiting to see the reaction, I climbed into the front seat and began attaching the survival kit fittings, the lap belt, and the shoulder harness fittings. Through the mirror I could see the young crew chief, perched on the side of the plane, warming up to his duties. I had to smile when he told Sherdeane, "You sure do smell good, Sir."

Once airborne, my initial uneasiness disappeared until Lieutenant Kinney asked, "Tom, what happens if we have to bail out?"

"You just pull the ejection D ring like I showed you."
Then I added sarcastically, "Once you're clear, then I'll fly
into the nearest mountain peak, because if anything happened
to you, the brass would kill me anyway."

On the flight north, I let my passenger fly the aircraft
while I gently guarded the controls. I even talked her through
a pretty decent aileron roll. She handled it so well that I decided to give her the acid test.

In an open area a few miles south of Khe Sanh on the
Laotian border, a deserted thatch hooch stood innocently, the
victim of monsoon weather and hundreds of practice rocket
attacks by passing FACs and gunship pilots. Over the months
I had fired at that blasted hooch dozens of times and never hit
it once. As we flew over it, I set the hook.

"Hey, Sher, I just saw some bad guys run into that
hooch. Hold on while I blast 'em."

With a flip of the wrist, I put the Bronco on her back, all
the while feeding in the back pressure to pull the nose down
to the target four thousand feet below. When the hooch disappeared underneath us, I rudder-rolled back to wings-level and
popped off one willie pete as we stabilized in a forty-five-
degree dive. Out of consideration to my back-seater, I executed a weak pull-off of three Gs. When I looked back at the
target, white smoke came belching out a hole in the roof and
through the door. The temptation was too much. In mock
horror I yelled, "Damn! Did you see that? Did you see those
two bad guys run outside? Their clothes were on fire from the
burning phosphorous!"

Not knowing how far to carry the hoax, I shut up to hear
what Sherdeane would say. Her answer floored me.

"Go back for another pass and nail their hides!"

I banked around for Quang Tri instead, not willing to
press my luck. I could have fired at that hooch all day long
and probably never scored another direct hit. Also, I wasn't
keen about the game any more. It suddenly felt tacky to tease
Lieutenant Kinney about something as serious as shooting at
people. Still, she had been a real trooper about it. Who would
have thought that a sweet little Air Force nurse, an angel of

mercy from the Da Nang hospital, could get such a charge out of an ordnance delivery. She was a true warrior.

Several days later I ran into Sherdeane's friend, Pat. I asked if anything had been said about the OV-10 ride. "Not really," Pat answered. "All she said was, 'Tom's a good shot.'"

In the week following my flying Sherdeane Kinney to Quang Tri, I returned to the more familiar turf of Prairie Fire. I found myself relegated to the back seat as part of a new Prairie Fire pilot's checkout. Captain Jim Smith was a pleasure to fly with and a quick study. Jim had already served one tour in Vietnam as a Caribou pilot, so he had a lot of air sense. He was picking up on the mission so fast that I had already mentioned to our boss, Bob Dennison, that Jim would be a good choice as training officer when I left.

Although my Prairie Fire duties had no tie-in to the normal Covey Trail mission, I managed to hear a few war stories by virtue of my residency in the Muff Divers' Lounge. There was a lot a discussion about the heavy truck traffic moving south through the Covey sector of the Trail, VR-6. A sophisticated network of acoustical sensors, code-named Igloo White, could actually hear each truck pass a given point along the Trail. Specially equipped orbiting aircraft picked up the signals and relayed them to Task Force Alpha, an enormous concrete building at NKP Air Base, Thailand. There, intelligence analysts studied the raw data and plotted numbers, times, and locations as enemy trucks motored south each night. The wizards at Task Force Alpha could even track individual trucks as they passed consecutive sensors. More important, the analysts could tell when the traffic pulled off the road before reaching the next sensor. The interruption generally meant one thing—a truck park.

On the night of December 18, the Coveys struck the mother lode. At the controls of his Oscar Deuce, Covey 281 lifted off Da Nang's Runway 18 Left exactly on time. He began a slow climb to the west and leveled off at seventy-five hundred feet MSL. At the Laotian border, he gave the traditional across-the-fence call to Panama, switched off all outside navigation lights, unsinked his props, then called "Moon Beam," the night time version of Hillsboro. Arriving over the Trail, the pilot took up a heading for a geographic reference point called Delta 43, near the deserted Laotian village of Ban Bak. From sensor movements, the intel types swore there had to be a truck park in the area, and Covey 281 was determined to find it.

In the right seat of the O-2, the forward air navigator broke out his starlight scope and poked it out the open right window to begin the search for any movement on the dark trail thirty-five hundred feet below him. He didn't have long to wait. Shortly after midnight, the nav detected "movers." While his pilot radioed Moon Beam for air, the navigator picked out a convoy of twelve trucks without lights running south along a relatively clear stretch of road. A convoy of that size was definitely a juicy target, so it was a bitter disappointment when the trucks suddenly turned off the main road and disappeared beneath the jungle canopy.

The two Coveys knew the convoy had to be somewhere down there in the darkness. Rather than go home emptyhanded, they decided to probe around the area with ordnance from a set of fighters approaching Delta 43. After briefing Iceman flight, Covey 281 dropped a mark that ignited on the ground in the general target area, crossed his fingers, and cleared the fighters in hot. Using the burning log as an aim point, the two F-4s dumped their heavy loads of Mark-82s right on the money. The exploding five-hundred-pounders were always an impressive sight, especially at night, but this time the dark jungle erupted in an old-fashioned fireworks display.

In a matter of minutes, the thick foliage had been ripped and splintered away by twenty-eight secondary explosions. Circling overhead, the Covey FACs also counted seven big fires, including two fiercely burning trucks. Covey 281 thought to himself, "At least part of the convoy will never make it south—chalk up another good mission for the Coveys." As the O-2 crew watched the jungle burn, neither they nor anyone else suspected that the fires and explosions at Ban Bak would continue without letup for another ten days!

At dawn on December 19, the OV-10 Broncos picked up where the Covey night shift had left off. In addition to the daylight, the complexion of the battle also changed. The enemy gunners around Ban Bak reacted fiercely, hosing FACs and fighters with an unusually heavy barrage of 23 and 37mm triple A. Most Coveys were conditioned by regular hampering fire from guns along the Trail, but nobody had ever seen the likes of the flak at Ban Bak. By midmorning the sector FAC reported, "The stuff's so thick you can get out and walk on it." As an added safety measure, the squadron back at Da Nang launched a second FAC to fly high cover. His job would be to call out the gunfire, allowing the primary FAC to concentrate on directing air strikes.

Flying the second OV-10 mission of the day, my roomie, Captain Larry Thomas, ran through the target briefing with Gunfighter 66 flight. As he was about to mark the target for the orbiting F-4s, Larry detected a single truck sneaking away from the area through a small streambed. Using a quick movement he had practiced many times, he selected the left outboard rocket pod on his armament panel, flipped on the master arm switch, turned on the gunsight, and dialed in 28 mils. Then he reefed the OV-10 into a near vertical dive toward the smoke-filled jungle below. When the fleeing truck was lined up perfectly in his sights, Bippy fired two willie petes and then yanked the stick back into an eye-watering five-G climbing right turn. Holding the back pressure, he glanced over his right shoulder just in time to see the white smoke of the first rocket hit short and the second one score a direct hit through the windshield. Jubilant, Larry yelled into the mike, "Hot damn! Scratch one truck and driver!"

Gunfighter Lead began cackling about a lucky shot, but Larry was too busy to trade quips. Three 23mm guns opened up simultaneously, pumping over one hundred rounds at the slow-moving OV-10. No matter how he maneuvered, the guns kept tracking, kept firing, kept following him with deadly gray and black air bursts. At one point, the high-cover FAC observed the Bippy's aircraft totally bracketed and obscured from view by exploding flak bursts. Miraculously, Larry dished out the bottom of the ugly cloud without a scratch.

After spending three hair-raising hours over Ban Bak, Larry turned control over to our other roommate, Sonny Haynes. Before he had a chance to work a single set of fighters, Sonny watched through his binoculars as fires on the ground from Larry's air strike touched off several more large secondary explosions. It was becoming clear that the Coveys had found something a lot bigger than just a twelve-truck convoy. The target area had assumed the proportions of approximately one kilometer square with many fires and detonations visible in all quadrants. The inferno below him boggled the mind. As Sonny studied the destruction, his UHF radio receiver announced the arrival of another set of fighters. "Covey 262, Black Lion flight at base plus 11. We've each got eight Mark-82s, ten minutes of play time. Gimme a hold down, over."

In his easy-going Texas drawl, Sonny began the briefing that had become second nature to him. As he talked, a navigation needle on Black Lion Lead's instrument panel homed on Sonny's voice, pointing directly at the low-flying Bronco. Lead banked his flight twenty degrees to the left and continued homing as the FAC spoke. "Do I have a good deal for you—trucks and supplies right out in the open! Target elevation is 2750. High terrain is fifteen miles east, going up to 4550. Wind is out of the northeast at less than ten knots. There are at least five 23 and 37mm guns in the area, all active. If you get in trouble, your best emergency bail out is the high stuff to the east. If you end up on the ground, stay cool, work with me, and I'll save your butt for mamma. One last thing. These gunners are really good, so whatever you do, keep it moving and don't be predictable."

As with all of Covey 262's air strikes, the attack proceeded like a well-choreographed ballet. Black Lion's bombs touched off thirty secondary explosions. While navigating through the smoke and low clouds trying to determine the nature of those detonations, Sonny ran into an intense barrage of fire from four 23mm weapons, which poured out over three hundred rounds in his direction. Several of the airbursts were so close that the concussion jolted his aircraft. When Sonny Haynes returned to Da Nang and taxied into the Covey revetments, the ground crew and several other pilots noted that his face was totally covered with black cordite from the exploding flak.

Over the next three days, the Coveys continued to pound Ban Bak. Hillsboro cooperated by diverting all available air to the area, advising the fighters to "Rendezvous with your FAC over the Covey bomb dump." The day- and night-shift Coveys directed thirty-five flights of fighters against the bomb dump, setting off thousands of explosions and drawing hundreds of rounds of antiaircraft fire. In one instance the sector FAC observed fuel barrels exploding every few seconds over a period of two-and-one-half hours. During the night of December 22, Covey 276 and his navigator watched in disbelief as their fighters ignited a spectacular fireball, which reached a height of two thousand feet, turning the black night into day. Detonating tracers from the blast shot up to an altitude of nine thousand feet.

On the twenty-third, weather socked in the Trail, shutting down virtually all bombing missions against Ban Bak. But the sector FACs reported seeing the eerie glow of fires and secondaries reflecting through the layers of clouds shrouding the bomb dump. Anyone silly enough to venture under the low ceilings found out that NVA gun crews still seemed well supplied. The rash young pilots always attracted four or five clips of 23 or 37mm fire.

Back in the Muff Divers' Lounge, excitement kept building among the Coveys. The restless pilots stood around talking with their hands and comparing strike results in the best traditions of one-upmanship: "I'll see your two trucks and raise you three more," or "I'll see your five large secondaries and raise you five hundred small ones." There was even a lively debate surrounding reports that NVA gunners were firing red and green tracers, in honor of Christmas. In keeping with the spirit of the season, I had managed to scrounge up one of the tree-shaped acoustical buoys normally dropped along the Ho Chi Minh Trail to monitor trucks. Decorated with tinsel, ornaments, and a star, the pathetic-looking device resembled a surrealistic Christmas tree. It was a perfect addition to the Muff Divers' Lounge, which was doing land-office business, generated partly by sentimental holiday thoughts of family and friends back home and partly by the tension surrounding the life-and-death struggle at the Covey bomb dump.

At six P.M. on Christmas Eve, a twenty-four-hour ceasefire went into effect. Nobody at Da Nang seemed to notice, especially the Coveys, who continued to fly missions in Laos. Yet the atmosphere around Da Nang was festive and upbeat, due primarily to one enduring tradition: the Bob Hope Christmas show. Over twenty thousand troops packed into the Freedom Hill amphitheater and spilled over onto the neighboring hillside for a glimpse of the renowned comedian. The GIs weren't disappointed. In addition to Bob Hope, the show included the lovely and talented Gloria Loring, six gorgeous singer-dancers called the Gold Diggers, and Johnny Bench, the all-star catcher from the Cincinnati Reds. But everyone's vote for hit of the night went to Lola Falana, a beautiful, sultry actress-dancer who stole the show along with everyone's heart. Just one look at the smiling faces of the wounded soldiers wheeled in by their nurses convinced all of us that the Bob Hope show was better medicine than any hospital could administer.

Christmas Day passed quietly. Most of the Coveys felt an undercurrent of melancholy or even homesickness. There was no denying we missed our families. Yet we were among good friends, thrown together by circumstance and chance. The bonds of friendship and common experience in many cases forged stronger ties than we had back in the world. On reflection, I wanted to be home for Christmas with my wife and family, but selfishly I wanted all my Covey and Prairie Fire buddies there with me. It wouldn't have seemed like Christmas without them.

By late afternoon on December 26, the weather over the Trail broke. The pilots radioed back incredible descriptions. The area around Ban Bak resembled a vast landscape on the surface of the moon. The jungle was gone, bomb craters pitted the black, scorched ground in all directions, and smoldering vehicles were scattered about in twisted, contorted heaps. Through breaks in the clouds, pilots could see the billowing smoke and fires from twenty-five miles away. And the stench. The smell of burning rubber, fuel, and cordite permeated everything—cockpit, flight suit, helmet, eyes, nose, and mouth. It was actually possible to taste the smell. Some of the odors were strange and nauseating. The pilots tried not to think about those smells.

For Lieutenant Rick Ottom, the euphoria of three earlier missions against the bomb dump gave way to the grim reality of routine. Tall, slender, introspective, and good at his job, Rick began to feel the grind. No matter where he directed the strike aircraft, their bombs always ignited spectacular secondary explosions. And every time Rick rolled in to mark a specific target, the gunners responded with a vengeance. Rick sincerely believed the missions had become a deadly game, a test of wits and nerve rather than skill. As he pulled off one rocket pass, a pair of 23mm guns opened up with seventy rounds in a classic tail shoot. This time, the play backfired. Tide 71 flight, holding over the target, spotted the gun, and after receiving clearance from Rick, blew the position away with well-placed canisters of CBU-24. In addition to taking out the gun, the exploding bomblets set off hundreds of small secondary explosions and seven sustained fires.

The incredible destruction continued through the night, but by the morning of the twenty-seventh, a perceptible decrease in secondaries was evident. During the remainder of the day, the Coveys used thirteen sets of fighters to destroy seven trucks and seventy-five stacks of camouflaged supplies.

The bomb dump finally played out on the twenty-eighth. During ten incredible days, Coveys logged more than two hundred hours over one of the most heavily defended targets in Southeast Asia. Flying low and slow, the Coveys jinked and maneuvered through thousands of rounds of antiaircraft fire without a single loss. By contrast, the enemy on the ground suffered horribly in lives and treasure. FAC-directed fighters destroyed forty-six trucks, ten thousand rounds of ammunition, countless drums of fuel, and over one thousand tons of supplies. During the bombardment, aircrews counted over 6,500 secondary explosions and 225 sustained fires. By any standard, the Covey bomb dump was one of the largest and most successful interdiction efforts waged against the Ho Chi Minh Trail. In a letter of appreciation, General Lucius D. Clay, Jr., the Seventh Air Force commander, relayed the following message from the chairman of the Joint Chiefs of Staff, General William C. Westmoreland:

> The effectiveness of U.S. air operations in Steel Tiger was most clearly demonstrated by the outstanding success achieved by the TACAIR sorties directed against the truck park and storage complex in the vicinity of Ban Bak. We may never know precisely the degree to which the destruction of this storage complex affected the enemy's logistic capability, however, I am convinced that his capability to support combat operations has been seriously degraded and the damage to the enemy represents one of the most outstanding achievements by TACAIR in Commando Hunt operations. The success of this strike effort is due . . . to the determination of the Covey FACs in their surveillance of the suspected area.

As the last strikes were going in against the bomb dump, my thoughts couldn't have been more noncombative. With my B-4 bag draped across Larry's bunk bed, I happily packed clothes for the R and R flight to Hawaii the next morning. The war was on hold for me. I was putting the finishing touches to the folding and stuffing when a voice yelled to me from the hall door, "Hey Tom, telephone." Shuffling down the hallway, I wondered who could be calling me. In my nine months at Da Nang, I could count on one hand the number of phone calls I'd received.

When I picked up the receiver, the duty officer began talking in a low, apologetic tone of voice. "The Ops officer told me to call you. Evan Quiros just radioed us that Jim Smith is overdue by a couple of hours. Evan thinks he must be down. You want us to get you a plane ready?"

I looked at my watch—3 P.M. Not much time to launch, find Jim, and mount a SAR before dark. "Yeah," I answered. "Get somebody to preflight it for me. I'll be there in fifteen minutes."

On the short jeep ride to Covey Ops, I tried to force myself to stop thinking about R and R. Think about the mission, think about Jim. It had to be a mistake. Jim was too good to be cannon fodder for the bad guys. Even though he had been combat-ready in Prairie Fire for only two weeks, he was a natural. He must have landed at Hue Phu Bai without telling MLT-2. The SOG folks must have their wires crossed on this one. I had trained Jim. I had taught him the fine points. Had I glossed over something important? Had I forgotten something in his training?

In spite of the excitement generated by the emergency scramble out of Da Nang, the afternoon sunshine streaming through the canopy made me feel sluggish and listless. More than once on the flight north, I caught myself thinking about the early-morning report time at the MAC passenger terminal. The reverie didn't evaporate until I heard Evan's high-pitched voice on the KY-28. Evan explained, "There's been no contact with Jim since noon. He can't still be airborne. He had dry tanks two hours ago. Let's spread out and start looking. Any place in particular you want to search?"

I didn't have a clue. For lack of a better plan, Evan concentrated on the area around Route 9. I focused on the real estate on the east side of Route 92. We crisscrossed the terrain time after time for two hours. As the sun got lower, our sense of urgency got higher. A few minutes before sunset, Larry Thomas diverted into the area to help. We couldn't find a trace of a crash, a parachute, a signal mirror, or a flare. The three of us searched until dark with no luck.

Frustrated and tired, I was about to call off the effort when the obvious hit me between the eyes. Jim and his Covey rider, Buffalo, must have been in contact at some point with our only team on the ground. Disgusted with myself for not having thought of it sooner, I attempted to hide the anger in my voice as I asked Evan to get the team up to find out what they might know. Fifteen minutes later, I braced myself as Evan relayed his conversation with the one-zero. The team reported contact with Jim's OV-10 overhead at 12:40. Because of a low cloud deck, there was no visual contact. Several minutes later, they heard several long bursts from what sounded like a 14.5mm ZSU heavy machine. They heard the distinctive turbo prop engines increase to full power, then there was a loud explosion. The one-zero estimated the map coordinates, based strictly on sound, to be about a thousand meters from his position. According to the plot, the impact point was near a steep cliff socked in by mist and low clouds.

Cruising south to Da Nang, I set the OV-10's air vents to scoop up the maximum flow of cool night air. With the refreshing stream blowing in my face, I tried to sort out my feelings. I didn't want to believe Jim and Buffalo had crashed. But nothing else made any sense, no other scenario matched the few facts we had. Reluctantly I concluded our troops really were down. At best they might have ejected and be evading through the jungle. But if that were the case, we would have heard the emergency beepers from their survival radios. Deep inside, I knew they were dead. Emotionally, I felt like a traitor for giving up on them.

The next morning, as I stepped on the R and R bird for Hawaii, guilt riddled me from the top of my head to the soles of my feet. The other Prairie Fire Coveys had already launched to resume the search. They were flying combat missions while I sat in seat 15A of a comfortable Boeing

707 bound for paradise. My stomach churned as I rationalized. My fellow Prairie Fire pilots didn't need my help to pull off the grim task they faced. I wanted to be with them, but after six months of SOG flying, I desperately needed to get away from it for a few days. I couldn't wait any longer to see my wife. Somehow, I knew Jim Smith would understand.

JANUARY

All Points of the Compass

The Army personnel at the Fort DeRussy R and R Center in Honolulu ran an amazing operation, around the clock, 365 days a year. At least three or four times daily, a Boeing 707 or Convair 880 cleared Honolulu International's main runway and taxied to the terminal. Between 165 and 200 tired but anxious GIs filed stiffly out of each bird and onto waiting Army buses for the short ride to DeRussy, located on Waikiki Beach, right next door to the Hilton Hawaiian Village. At each of the daily reenactments, the buses pulled up to a one-story, nondescript-looking welcoming center. Inside, the Army had cleverly stashed the dozens of waiting wives and girl friends; unleashing them at the airport would have caused total pandemonium.

As we piled off the buses and walked inside, none of us was ready for the sight that greeted us. Standing expectantly two rows deep along each side of the long corridor painted latrine green, excited ladies hopped, waved, whistled, and called out first names or pet names to their loved ones: "Bill, over here!" or "Honey, sweetie, here I am!" A dozen confused GIs pivoted first in one direction, then another as they searched the crowd, trying desperately to match the shouts with that one all-important face. As each match occurred, the result was a predictable squeal of delight from both parties, followed by a flurry of tears, hugs, and kisses.

As I inched my way between the rows, two outrageous thoughts filled my mind. First, the scene somehow reminded me of an experience years earlier as a Boy Scout, when for punishment or amusement we ran a gauntlet known as the belt line. The object was to run as fast as possible through two rows of belt-wielding Scouts, each intent on landing a solid blow across the victim's backside. Now, as I looked around the R and R center, the parallel was unmistakable. My other thought was much more worrisome. I hadn't seen Jane in nine months. What if in the commotion I inadvertently walked right by her? Worse still, what if I didn't recognize her? My anxiety intensified as I approached the end of the gauntlet.

That first glimpse of my wife is one of those memories etched permanently on my brain. I spotted her standing quietly toward the end of the right-hand row—small, shy, and beautiful, with long blonde hair and a short miniskirt, looking like a composite of Catherine Deneuve and Grace Kelly. As we embraced, the smell of her hair and the softness of her cheek against mine were overpowering. For a brief second the tears welled up in my eyes. Deftly, I wiped them away in Jane's hair. She might have been embarrassed to see her combat-pilot husband cry in public.

For six glorious days we indulged in a whirlwind of sightseeing, restaurants, and tourist traps. In addition to the obligatory time on the sands of Waikiki, we took in Pearl Harbor, Diamond Head, the Dole pineapple fields, the International Market, and a dinner show performed by the well-known Hawaiian singer Don Ho.

During our time together, Jane and I rarely talked about the war and my specific job. I fended off most of her questions by maneuvering the conversation toward the lighthearted and insignificant events that were part of our existence at Da Nang. I told her about the rowdy hail-and-farewell parties, the cookouts, the funny incidents. Part of my ploy was to hide what I was doing in Prairie Fire. The other was to spare her the details, some gory, of what I actually did. In a nutshell, I didn't want her to worry about me. I desperately wanted to tell her about Jim Smith, about Prairie Fire, about the secret war we were fighting in Laos. But I couldn't. And I didn't. Every time the subject of flying came up, I would look into Jane's beautiful blue eyes and see genuine sadness, a forlorn reflection telling me that she knew I was either lying or purposely evading. She instinctively knew something was eating away at me, yet she never pressed, she never tried to confront me with it. With both of us holding back emotionally, the strain that developed was predictable and inevitable.

After six days with Jane at the Ilikai Hotel, I joined the other troops for the return flight to Vietnam. The long ride provided plenty of time to think. It had been a wonderful trip, but the R and R fell short of being the dream honeymoon we'd both anticipated. No matter how hard I had tried, I could never shake thoughts about the SAR effort for Jim Smith. Jane had picked up on my preoccupation over what was going on back at Da Nang. Although she didn't know exactly what was bothering me, Jane knew competition when she saw it. Predictably, she felt hurt, and I felt like an insensitive jerk.

On January 9 I flew to Quang Tri on my first mission since returning from R and R. In the cockpit on the flight north, I smelled a soothing aroma I had truly missed, a strange blend of leather and JP-4. I felt comfortable, back in my element.

The first order of business after landing was resolved as I expected it would be. The Bright Light team had found Jim Smith and his back-seater, Buffalo, still strapped in their ejection seats. Their OV-10 had plowed into a box canyon not far from the location guessed at by the reconnaissance team. At the MLT, nobody said much about the crash, a sure sign that the episode was eating away at their insides. A tough situation was made even worse by a small, yellow puppy scampering playfully around the compound. The little mongrel ran from one American to the next, only to be kicked away or ignored. The sight of the corkscrew-tailed little dog was more than the SF troops could bear. During the two weeks prior to the crash, Buffalo and the puppy had been inseparable.

Late that same afternoon I flew high cover as one of the new O-2 jocks ran a team insert deep in the western DMZ.

To me, First Lieutenant Larry Hull seemed an unlikely candidate for the Prairie Fire program. Larry was blond and slender, almost fragile looking. On the surface he flaunted a cocky, devil-may-care attitude. Underneath, a boiling anger or resentment about something made him much more dangerous than his boyish appearance suggested. The SF troops evidently saw something of themselves in Larry because they idolized him, partly as warrior and partly as mascot. For a reason known only to them, the Green Berets decided Larry reminded them of Woodstock, the small yellow bird from the "Peanuts" cartoon strip. They even pasted a Woodstock decal on Larry's helmet.

With all eyes in the package watching, Larry dived his O-2 toward the LZ for the verbal mark. From my vantage point he appeared even lower than normal. When he pulled off without keying his mike, I knew something had gone wrong. "Covey 275, this is 221. What's the problem, over."

"No big deal," he answered. "I seem to have brushed the tops of the trees. Actually, part of one looks like it's growing out the leading edge of my right wing."

From my height advantage I pulled the Bronco down and to the inside of Larry's turn. With plenty of speed advantage and lots of cutoff, I rejoined on his right wing in a matter of seconds. Sure enough, several small branches and tree limbs lay draped across the midsection of the wing. There was no way to tell whether the wind stream held the branches in place or if they were in fact embedded in the metal skin. As we climbed to an altitude of two thousand feet, Larry performed a controllability check on the battered Oscar Deuce. He claimed handling characteristics were normal, so I sent him home while I continued with the team insert.

By the next morning, Larry's SF buddies at Quang Tri had already written a short poem to commemorate Covey 275's baptism of fire:

The Ballad of Woodstock

I love to fly the Oscar Deuce from channel one-oh-three.

*I fly that dog through rain and fog in the extreme
   western DMZ,
And no one knows we're fighting there 'cept Charlie,
   you, and me.
So mark my words and heed them well, or you could
   end up like me.
I flew down low and got too slow and hit a goddamn
   tree!*

While Woodstock's brush with the trees made him a celebrity within Prairie Fire circles, another Prairie Fire Covey managed to achieve unwanted notoriety on a much larger scale. January 10 turned out to be Evan Quiros day, and a memorable one at that. Shortly after noon, the team Larry and I had inserted the day before ran smack into a large NVA patrol. The team one-zero reported his situation as a "TAC E," or tactical emergency. By using that particular phrase, the one-zero was letting us know that his situation was tense and fluid. An emergency extraction might be necessary, but with some close air support, the mission might be able to continue.

Evan pinpointed the team's position, then he began working over the enemy patrol with his M-60s. Like virtually all our other sorties, this one required placing ordnance well inside the prescribed safety margins. Since Evan was an old pro, he didn't even flinch at the prospect. He dived his OV-10 on multiple strafing passes to within only a few feet of the friendlies. His deadly aim broke the contact quickly, allowing the team to move to a safer hiding place. After things settled down, Evan asked the team if his machine-gun fire had been close enough for them. The one-zero replied, "Let's put it like this. If I'd wanted to smoke, I could've held a cigarette at arm's length, and your tracers would have lit it for me. Great shooting."

The Prairie Fire pilots always got a tremendous charge out of laying it in really close when one of our teams was in trouble. The invisible bond between that team on the ground and that pilot with his finger on the trigger is beyond explanation. People such as Evan Quiros and Larry Hull would break every rule, take any chance to help a reconnaissance team. When the action was super-hot, the one-zero never gave a second thought to friendly machine-gun fire or rockets kicking dirt up at his feet, as long as it came from one of his Prairie Fire FACs. That mutual respect and commitment formed the lifeblood of our operations so deep in the secret parts of Laos.

On that same afternoon, off the coast of the DMZ, a U.S. Navy destroyer moved in close on a naval gunfire mission. The USS *Lynde McCormick*, DDG-8, had recently arrived in the South China Sea by way of Hong Kong. On her second day in the war zone, the *Lynde McCormick* had already fired one early-morning mission from her five-inch deck guns. As she was about to fire a second mission late that afternoon, Evan Quiros decided to give the crew a thrill.

Evan was still keyed up from his own gun mission in the DMZ. He knew he'd made a difference. He felt good about himself. When he spotted that large gray ship off the coast, he saw the perfect opportunity to let off some steam. Without considering the ship's possible mission, Evan dropped to wave-top level and headed for the *Lynde McCormick*. With his Bronco's engines cranked up to full power, he pressed in to a wingspan's separation while flying the length of the ship. Reaching the bow, Evan pulled up and reversed course with the first leaf of a Cuban eight. For the next five minutes, he dazzled the crew of the destroyer with a series of perfectly executed aerobatic maneuvers. Unknown to Evan, the *Lynde McCormick* had been forced to abandon her fire mission because of his air show. That fact finally sank in when the ship broadcast a warning on the emergency radio frequency. Through his helmet earphones Evan heard, "Air Force aircraft operating in the vicinity of the U.S. Navy warship off Ha Loi. You are interfering with a naval gunfire mission. Depart the area immediately!"

I was standing in front of my aircraft, getting ready to fly back to Da Nang, when Evan's OV-10 touched down on the Quang Tri runway. He taxied in, shut down, and walked straight toward me. Something about his gait, something about the way he carried his shoulders and head, signaled that all was not well.

Evan poured out the whole story in a briefinglike manner. When he finished, he looked at me with those light blue eyes and asked forlornly, "What do I do now, coach?"

For the next several minutes, we stood there conspiring, trying desperately to invent some plausible explanation for what had happened. We ended up settling on an absolutely absurd rendition of the facts. In our panic to save Evan's rear end, we decided that he was signaling the destroyer trying to get their attention. He needed their gunfire for a target, and since he didn't know their radio frequencies, buzzing the ship at close quarters seemed to be the only choice.

The plan survived about thirty seconds until logic and guilt took hold. We knew lying wasn't the answer. We also knew that in the screwed-up world of Vietnam the episode would probably end up buried in the ship's log. We decided to forget about the incident unless the Navy made an issue of it, in which case Evan would confess and take his medicine.

In the remaining twilight, I climbed into my Bronco. Once airborne, I dropped down on the deck and eased out over the sandy beach. The trip was part of our training route for new Prairie Fire pilots. To accustom them to low-level flying, we'd use the beach as an altimeter check for absolute sea level. Once the new guy felt comfortable at one hundred feet, we'd ease down to fifty feet. When he could handle that reasonably well, we'd move inland to mix absolute altitudes with the real world—trees, hooches, hills, power lines. Graduation came with flying nape of the earth over the deadly hills and mountains in Laos.

Flying low-level demanded complete concentration, and I needed that mental stimulus to shake myself loose from Evan's problem. Once over the beach, I dropped to twenty-five feet, then to ten feet, then down to just inches above the mild surf washing up on the sand. Over the past month, I had pushed myself to fly lower and lower, perhaps just to prove that I could hack it. Part of it was an ongoing game with the crew chiefs at Da Nang. When I'd land, several would run over. The old head would say to the relatively new crew chief, "See, I told ya." Then to me he'd say, "Captain, I don't know where the hell you fly, but I keep telling these guys every time you come in there's saltwater spray all over your centerline tank."

Larry Hull's close call and Evan's predicament still concerned me, no matter how hard I tried to block them out of my mind. Of all the Prairie Fire pilots, those two were special to me. Like an old mother hen, I hovered around, preoccupied that something bad might happen to my brood of chicks. Still, I had to back off enough to let them do their jobs—and I had my own to do. Through it all, the missions kept coming and the sorties continued to mount for all of us.

On the fourteenth I logged a healthy 9.2 hours in the OV-10, with a routine insert along Route 9, then an emergency extraction. All the missions seemed to be running together in my mind. The normal tour for a Prairie Fire pilot was about six months. So far, half our pilots never lived that long. And here I was, into my seventh month in Prairie Fire, with two more months to go. The nonstop pace began to take its toll in subtle ways.

At 1400 a new Covey rider jumped in my back seat for my fourth sortie of the day. I felt dog tired, and the low scud and rain moving in made the flight even trickier. Our mission was to find one of our teams in the DMZ. Unlike most teams, this one had been on the ground for a complete term of seven days. By now, they were probably out of food and exhausted.

As we leapfrogged across the rain-soaked ground at treetop level, I somehow missed the Song Ben Hai River, where I needed to hang a left to navigate to the team. My backseater noticed but said nothing, figuring I knew what I was doing. As we pressed farther north, the scenery didn't look right. At first subtly, then more rapidly, the terrain changed from moonscape bomb craters to cultivated green fields. I realized with a shock where we were when I saw two hooches just in front of us and figures running toward three 57mm gun positions. We were well into North Vietnam.

I jammed the stick to the left, racking us into ninety degrees of left bank. Then I fed in the Gs to keep the turn as tight as possible. As the OV-10 shuddered through the near-stall-producing 180-degree turn, I kept my eyes riveted on the soggy terrain only a few feet below us. I could just make out the four red spoiler plates on top of the left wing, each sticking out in the wind stream to kill lift on the low wing, enabling me to keep the roll and high-G turn going.

Once we returned to a southerly heading, I rolled us out abruptly, then added several spirited jinks to throw off the aiming solution of any would-be gunners. As I rolled back to wings-level, the view through my gunsight sent my pulse into overdrive. A quarter of mile in front of us, a long column of North Vietnamese troops marched south along a muddy road. They were strung out along the trail in three long files. I estimated at least three hundred troops were down there. From our height of fifty feet, and with a fast closure rate at full power, there wasn't even time to charge my machine guns. This was the best target I'd ever seen, and I wasn't even in position to strafe them out of existence.

The sound of the Garrett AiResearch turboprop engines running at full military power finally reached the rear of the enemy column. The figures looked like falling dominoes as the sound traveled the length of the procession. From rear to front, row after row of troops tumbled or dived to the ground as the roar of our OV-10 registered in their brains. As we streaked overhead, tracers came at us from all directions. Unlike some of the other times I'd been hosed and hit, this time I heard the impact. A series of sharp thumps registered somewhere in the nose section. Through the rudder pedals, the bottom of my feet felt the vibrations as the bullets found their mark.

As fast as it started, it was over. Within seconds the firing troops were behind us, masked from view by veils of drizzle and low clouds. My back-seater was philosophical about the ordeal. As we retreated back to Quang Tri, he mused, "Wish we could have iced those little bastards." Then as an afterthought he added, "Even a camera would have been okay.

I'd love to have just one eight-by-ten glossy to toss on the table the next time some antiwar creep shouts all that dribble about how the North isn't the aggressor or doesn't infiltrate troops south." He received no argument from me.

After we landed the Barky crew chiefs needed only about an hour to work their magic. From somewhere they scrounged a spare nose-gear door to replace the ragged one unceremoniously dumped on them. Three well-placed AK-47 rounds had done a number on the original. Miraculously, there was no other damage. For the third time in the war, a crew chief, noting the battle damage to my airplane, told me how lucky I was.

That evening at Da Nang, I dropped into the Covey intel shop to talk with our intel officer. Normally the Prairie Fire pilots handled their own debriefings via a top-secret events log maintained in their special room. Since my mission contained a few peculiar twists not having much to do with Prairie Fire, I decided to share them with the Covey intel officer. I gave him my best guess on coordinates for the three gun positions. Then I told him about the troop column moving south. After copying the information, he looked up with a smile and said, "Actually, unless you were on a mission number fragging you into the North, you really shouldn't have been up there. Your report might generate a few questions along those lines. Just out of curiosity, what were you doing up there?"

Smiling back, I told the intel officer, "If anybody asks, just tell them the weather was bad and that I got lost."

Shaking his head from side to side, he responded, "They'll never buy that one."

"It's the truth," I said, shrugging my shoulders. Then I turned around and walked out the door. We never heard another word about that mission.

A week later Evan and I got mixed up in another strange episode, this time involving the cargo-carrying capacity of our OV-10s. We had several teams on the ground along Route 9, one of the primary east—west infiltration routes into Quang Tri Province. The team working the south side of the road encountered no problems. They did, however, find an odd assortment of NVA supply items. They found several tins of processed meat from Czechoslovakia. In an even more bizarre discovery, they stumbled across a bootleg cache of empty Coca-Cola cans and a worn pair of Keds tennis shoes. Ironically, the Communist meat tins had been discarded unopened.

The team on the north side of Route 9 ran into a buzz saw. In the heavy fighting, they suffered two indig killed in action, or KIA. Through the team's heroics and the bravery of the chopper pilots and the A-1 jocks, we managed to extract the team, including their KIAs.

Back at Quang Tri, the MLT troops placed the body bags in a secured building near the runway. Dedicated SOG airlift from Nha Trang would pick up the remains and return them to the grieving families. Unfortunately, four days passed with no airlift in sight. The families at Da Nang were beginning to raise a stink equal to the one emanating from the makeshift morgue. In a fit of desperation, somebody remembered the cargo bay in the OV-10.

When North American Rockwell designed the OV-10, they included a small cargo bay as part of the fuselage behind the cockpit section. Covered by a tapered, side-hinged clamshell door, the cargo bay measured roughly three by three by eight feet, for a total of about seventy cubic feet of space. The ingenious Special Forces troops quickly calculated that the cargo bay was the perfect size for a coffin.

Evan agreed to give it a shot. Even though this particular situation wasn't covered in the FAC mission description, he genuinely wanted to help out. And how much could the dead soldier weigh, maybe 120 pounds? Evan knew he was in trouble when a truck backed up to his bird and a small army of SF types began straining to lift a wooden box into the cargo bay. As they slid the coffin inside, the Bronco's main landing gear struts compressed noticeably from the heavy weight. For a guess, the SOG troops estimated the coffin tipped in at five hundred pounds. To cover the overpowering stench, they had doused the body in formaldehyde, then filled the coffin with sand.

On his takeoff roll, Evan used every inch of Quang Tri's runway. As the last few feet of concrete disappeared under the aircraft nose, Evan pulled the protesting bird into the air. With the Bronco staggering forward at just ten feet off the ground, Evan carefully milked the flaps up in increments. A full mile off the end of the runway, he finally gained enough flying speed to begin a slow climbing turn to the south.

The next day, I had my chance. Learning from Evan's experience, I carried empty rocket pods and only enough gas to get us to Da Nang. As the troops loaded the heavy coffin, we all knew the extra day had been a mistake. Even with the light breeze blowing off the ocean, most of the loading crew became nauseated in a matter of seconds. My only hope was that the ram air effect during the flight would keep the stench behind me.

We got airborne without incident. Cruising southeast along the coast, I soon realized the ventilation system wasn't going to work. For some reason, that sickening sweet formaldehyde aroma circulated through the cockpit. During the remaining twenty minutes of flight, it took all my concentration to keep from gagging and retching.

After landing, with absolutely no reverence or ceremony due a fallen warrior, I turned the remains over to the waiting CCN delegation, then made a beeline for the Covey barracks. It took three long showers before I felt relatively free of the death smell. Repeated washings of my flight suit never did rid it of the smell. I finally gave up and threw it away.

By the end of the month, I was well into the training program for Jim Smith's replacement, First Lieutenant Henry Yeackle III. A baby-faced cherub, Henry's good nature and even-keeled outlook masked his aggressive, tenacious approach to flying as a Covey FAC.

Early on the morning of the twenty-eighth, Henry and I got airborne and took a detour into the normal Covey AO to look at a large enemy truck convoy trapped in the open during the preceding night. The sector FAC had wisely directed his fighters against the lead truck and the tail-end charlie. Stranded on the face of a cliff with no way to move around the burning roadblocks at either end of the procession, the helpless enemy trucks sat awaiting their fate.

Since the Trail Coveys rarely flew low and almost never used their machine guns, I decided the convoy would be good practice for Henry. With a little coaching from me, Henry dropped down to an altitude level with the road cut into the ridge. Only a few days earlier, my front-seater had been a Trail Covey, cruising over this same sector at three to four thousand feet.

As we pressed in perpendicular to the line of trucks and at precisely their level, Henry armed up all four guns. While he chose an individual target, I reminded him, "Henry, to compensate for our forward momentum, keep your tracers impacting on the bottom of the truck. The other four ball rounds will be hitting a little higher, probably right on the money. You'll actually be bunting forward with the stick to keep that sight picture."

Our M-60 machine guns weren't known for their hitting power. As Henry opened fire, I wasn't sure what effect our pop guns would have against a heavy truck. We got the answer fast. To my surprise, the truck vibrated and bounced up and down in a pronounced fashion as Henry poured long bursts into it. It was clear our 7.62mm bullets were beating the hell out of that truck. Our target never did explode à la World War II gun camera films, but the truck would never run again. Rather than press our luck, we scooted out of the area with a new-found respect for the firepower of our OV-10.

That afternoon at Quang Tri, I came to a decision about something that I had been kicking around in my mind for a couple of weeks. Buffalo's golden puppy had grown pretty large. He was a good-looking animal as Vietnamese dogs went, but he still got a cold shoulder from everyone at the MLT. Now, instead of romping around the compound looking for friends, the little dog would lay off to the side, chops resting on crossed front paws, watching each passerby with sad brown eyes, which under other circumstances would melt an iceberg. I was convinced the SF troops didn't realize how they were reacting to a situation that wasn't the puppy's fault. I also knew the treatment was breaking my heart.

Without revealing my motives, I casually asked if they'd mind if I took charge of the puppy. I laid it on a little thick, explaining that I wanted to take the dog to Da Nang to be the Covey mascot. They thought it was a great idea.

The next problem was getting our new mascot to Da Nang. I wanted to take him with me in the OV-10, but that squirming bundle of fur inside the cockpit would be more than three handfuls. The SF medic came up with what seemed like a workable solution. While Henry and I held the puppy, the *bac si* grabbed a handful of skin on the back of the dog's neck and injected him with some sort of knockout drug. Within a few minutes, the pup was sound asleep. Next we took gauze and tied the dog's front legs together, then the rear legs together. As a final precaution, we wrapped several layers of gauze around the animal's eyes to form a blindfold. With no small amount of trepidation, we climbed in a jeep and headed for the airfield.

After I strapped in the back seat, Henry and a crew chief lifted the sleeping puppy up and laid him across my lap. As we taxied out, I said to Henry, "Keep it smooth, and no emergencies. In case he starts wiggling around, I'm gonna have to leave the pin in my ejection seat."

Halfway to Da Nang the little beast started coming to. For several moments he became violent as he tried desperately to use his front paws to swipe at the blindfold. All of the movement and banging into the control stick made it tough for Henry to keep us in level flight. In a last-ditch effort to regain control, I reached out and pulled the blindfold away from the puppy's eyes. As another precaution, I slid it down and tightened the gauze around his mouth in a makeshift muzzle. Right away he settled down, looking around the cockpit curiously. He even stood up in my lap and looked outside. With his legs still tied, he wobbled and lurched badly but would have no part of my attempts to make him lay down. When he started gasping and whimpering, I became concerned he couldn't breathe. Cautiously, I removed the muzzle. Again he settled down, but first rewarded me with a series of wet licks across my face.

Once he could pant and look around, our furry passenger took to flying like a natural. The only other tense moment came when I looked up to see him happily chewing away on one of the fire T handles. Pulling one of those would have shut the engine down instantly.

Following Henry's smooth landing, we taxied into the de-arming area. Before the crews would go under the aircraft to install safety pins in the guns and rockets, they insisted that pilots hold up both hands to show that nobody was moving switches around on the armament panel. The drill was designed for the ground crew's protection. Trying to control the dog's movements, I wasn't able to put my hands up, prompting several angry signals from the de-arming team leader. It was a Mexican standoff, and tempers were getting short. Finally, I lifted the dog above the canopy rails so everyone could see the problem. The crusty old crew chief shook his head in disgust, then waved his troops under the aircraft.

When we had shut down in the revetments, Henry and I began tossing helmets and map bags to the waiting crew chief just like after any other mission. As the young troop walked away with our gear, I yelled to him, "Wait a minute. I got something else." When I handed the wide-awake puppy over the side, the crew chief's eyes bugged right out of his head. From the corner of my eye I saw the line chief get out of his jeep and trot over for a firsthand look at the strange scene. While I climbed down out of the back seat, the line chief stared at me for a few moments, then he announced, "If that dog crapped in that airplane, you're gonna clean it up yourself. And Sir, I just gotta tell you this. You pilots might be college graduates, but you don't have a lick of common sense." Henry and I just smiled as we loaded our dog into the jeep for the short ride to Ops.

The puppy took to the Muff Divers' Lounge as if it had

always been his home. There was no end of Coveys to spoil him, and the little rascal seemed deliriously happy, running from one outstretched hand to another. By acclamation we decided to name him Muff. Only a few people ever knew the sad story of Muff's original owner at Quang Tri or how the Covey mascot made the trip to Da Nang. But I felt certain about one thing: Buffalo would have been pleased with the puppy's new home.

The next morning, at 0400 hours on January 29, units of the U.S. Army's First Brigade, Fifth Mechanized Infantry Division pushed out of Dong Ha along Route 9 westward toward Khe Sanh and the Laotian border. They constituted the lead elements of Operation Dewey Canyon II, the last major American combat operation of the war. The objective of the long column of M-48 tanks, M-551 armored reconnaissance assault vehicles, and M-113 armored personnel carriers was to secure Khe Sanh, Lang Vei, and all the real estate up to the Laotian border. Once under U.S. control, the border area around Khe Sanh would become the jumping-off point for a massive, though temporary, ARVN invasion of Laos, code-named Lam Son 719. The ARVN force hoped to push out along Route 9 to Tchepone, with the stated objective of disrupting the whole NVA logistics network flowing down the Ho Chi Minh Trail.

When we heard about the plan, all of the Prairie Fire pilots and most of the SOG troops smiled nervously and began fidgeting. The consensus of opinion was that the ARVN troops were in for a rough time. The SOG teams were the only ones who had any firsthand knowledge about Laos. From personal experience, they suspected the ARVN force was about to walk into a buzz saw.

We figured a sense of humor would help. Since Laos was our stomping ground, we decided to make the Fifth Mech troops feel welcome when they reached Khe Sanh. With two Cobras and my OV-10 providing the cover, we escorted a UH-1 directly to the deserted Khe Sanh airstrip. Under our watchful eyes, the Slick landed in the middle of the old runway. Several figures darted from the chopper to the edge of the strip. Carefully, the two Green Berets planted a large sign in the red dirt. Then they hustled back aboard their chopper for the ride back to MLT-2. For grins, I made a low-level pass the length of the east–west runway, just to savor the effect of the sign. In big letters it said:

WELCOME TO CCN COUNTRY

FEBRUARY

Valley of the Shadow of Death

February 1 literally came in with a bang. Around Da Nang things had been relatively quiet, due in all probability to the Tet ceasefire from January 24 through 26. Then, at midnight on the first and again at 2 A.M., the VC lobbed several rockets in, probably to let us know they were still around. They saved the best for last. At 0405, eight deadly 122mm rockets crashed into Da Nang Air Base, lighting up the perimeter like day. We were helpless against the barrage, so to shake off the tension, somebody in the Muff Divers' Lounge passed out the shot glasses, poured the scotch, and offered a toast to combat pay. We sat there quietly, sipping and looking at each other, wondering how bad things would get. Everybody had expected the action to pick up with the beginning of the dry season. Maybe the increasingly frequent rocket attacks were telling us something.

Approximately an hour before sunrise on February 8, I took off into the darkness and began a gentle turn to the northwest. The day was destined to be a special one. The night before, CCN had briefed us that the eighth was D-day. A large force of ARVN infantry and armor was scheduled to move out on Operation Lam Son 719, the invasion of Laos. Although MAC-SOG had no role in the actual assault, their recon teams had performed all preinvasion intel along Route 9. Now I would have the chance to carry the SOG banner, figuratively, on the initial thrust across the border. Somebody must have figured that it might be handy to have a Prairie Fire FAC on the scene.

Lam Son 719 kicked off on schedule at 0700 hours. As

the lead elements prepared to cross into Laos, my Covey rider and I circled over Co Roc, waiting for the Huey Slicks carrying the pathfinder troops of the ARVN First Infantry Division. Our job was to mark the LZs verbally for our helicopter buddies from the 101st Airborne. Since Co Roc was the prominent terrain feature south of Route 9, it made sense to secure the ridge with its commanding view before the armored units pushed west. There were plenty of old heads around who remembered the murderous enemy artillery fire three years earlier when NVA gunners, shooting from the top of Co Roc's steep cliffs, zeroed in on the U.S. Marines at Khe Sanh. A repeat performance against ARVN tank columns in the open would have finished Lam Son 719 before it started.

The first batch of six Hueys checked in with us right on time. As the serpentine procession flew over Co Roc east to west, I dived in from the opposite direction so they could see us as we overflew their LZ. There was no ground fire as we trolled along at treetop height, but there was an anxious moment pulling off the LZ. It took some fast stick-and-rudder work to avoid colliding with several command and control Hueys darting around the area. They seemed to be everywhere.

When Slick Lead confirmed he had a tally on the LZ, I climbed above the traffic to watch the drama unfold. While we circled, chopper after chopper touched down uneventfully, off-loaded its troops, and then flew back for another load. The shuttle continued throughout the morning, lifting ARVN troops to a number of LZs on either side of Route 9. By the end of the day, helicopters from the 101st had carried over six thousand troops into Laos. By contrast, my single mission in support of Lam Son 719 had been tame and insignificant. Still, there was an indescribable sense of satisfaction and pride in being even a small part of a history-making event.

While the ARVN forces fought their way west along Route 9, we inserted several reconnaissance teams roughly twenty miles to the north to get a feel for how fast the NVA might try to reinforce the area. We got our answer on February 12. When the ARVN columns closed in on the intersection of routes 9 and 92, they ran into the first sustained heavy fighting of the invasion. Everyone except the SOG teams seemed surprised by how quickly the enemy was able to move in reinforcements. They were also shocked by the toughness of the NVA soldiers and their willingness to stand and fight.

We got our first chance to see big enemy troop concentrations on Valentine's Day. At 1300 I got airborne from Quang Tri for the return trip to Da Nang. Rather than go home by way of the beach as usual, I decided to swing out over the triborder area. As soon as I crossed into Laos, one of our teams began yelling for help. Four days earlier, I had inserted the eight-man team on a karst ridge overlooking Route 92 near the North Vietnamese border. On our maps the place was named Ban Chay. I recognized the one-zero's voice and headed straight to him.

When I arrived overhead, the team leader explained, "They've got us pinned down with mortar and .51-cal fire. There's a company-size force climbing up a draw three hundred meters northwest of us. It should be real prominent from the air. We need some stuff all along that gully."

I had no trouble spotting the little wash he described. But from my altitude of three thousand feet, I couldn't see any movement, only the scrub brush and trees growing along either side. To do the job right, I needed a set of fighters with lots of soft ordnance. When I relayed my request to Hillsboro, the controller had absolutely nothing available. He offered to scramble a flight from one of the Thailand bases, but it would be at least thirty minutes before the cavalry would arrive. Judging from the high pitch in the one-zero's voice, we didn't have that kind of time.

Arming up the high-explosive rocket pods, I began a fast spiral down to working altitude. From the insert I recalled that the run-in was going to be a little tricky. Another karst ridge just to the north of our team severely limited our maneuvering space. The only low-altitude approach was through the valley between the two ridges. To keep from firing in the team's direction, it was necessary to make each pass from east to west. Directly abeam the team, I'd bank sharply left into the karst, pickle off a rocket into the gully, then execute a hard rolling turn back to the north.

After the first few identical passes, the bad guys caught on to the plan. From then on, they threw up everything except the kitchen sink. A pair of 12.7mm machine guns were pouring out the lead. The situation got even hotter when a 37mm gun joined in the fight and began firing flat-trajectory shots at me. The exploding flak bursts at eye level sent the one-zero into convulsions. He'd never seen anything like that before. He pleaded with me over the radio to "be careful of the big stuff," but I was much more concerned by the machine-gun fire. To counter the 37mm, I dropped down to the bottom of the valley floor. I doubted that he could shoot down on me. And rather than pull up after each pass, I merely set up a low-level race track by flying one valley farther to the north. Now, on the eastbound leg of each circuit, the intervening ridge protected me from the ground fire.

In between passes, I asked the launch site to send a package for an emergency extraction. With the help of the HE rockets, the team's situation seemed to be improving. They were no longer in contact, and the attacking force was moving back down the gully. We needed to pull our troops while there was a break in the action.

The lull only lasted a few minutes. Pulling off the final rocket pass, I spotted an unnerving sight. On the valley floor, a group of about one hundred enemy troops had fanned out for a dash across the open area between the karst ridges. Our team was obviously their objective. No longer constrained by restrictive run-in headings, I armed up all four M-60s and rolled in west to east. Using a ten-degree dive angle, I poured burst after long burst into the advancing troops. In all, I made four strafing runs before the survivors melted into the vegetation at the base of the karst. As I lined up the target in my gunsight, the view made me think of Pickett's charge across the open ground at Gettysburg.

By the time Larry Hull arrived with the package, I was winchester, or out of ammo. On the valley floor, we counted twenty bodies scattered about. Larry called to me, "Hey, 221, you're a real killer. You bagged the limit today!"

Before he could say anything more, I snapped, "Shut up, Larry. Let's worry about getting the team out."

I wasn't actually mad at Larry Hull. Looking down at the scene below, I suddenly felt tired, emotionally drained, and irritable. He clearly didn't mean anything by his comment. It was me. In ten months of combat flying, I'd fired a lot of rockets and bullets at the bad guys, but this was the first time I'd actually seen dead bodies as a direct consequence of my actions. The sight of those lifeless forms left me with an unsettling panicky feeling. The mood passed after only a few minutes, but the vivid picture of two of the enemy soldiers sprawled on top of each other lasted for days.

While Larry worked over the area with the set of F-4s I had ordered, I ducked into Quang Tri for a quick rearming. When I returned, any doubts about having the stomach for the job evaporated instantly. Shortly after the fighters left, the enemy launched another charge across the valley. With Larry running the extraction, I concentrated on the new threat. I lost count of the number of strafing passes and only stopped when I ran out of bullets. Between the F-4s, the Cobras, and my OV-10, the team confirmed an additional forty enemy troops KBA—killed by air. One of the SOG team members with a flair for the dramatic dubbed the action "The Saint Valentine's Day Massacre—Laos Chapter."

Two days later, we ran an instant replay on the same ridge. This time, the team was all indig, and the weather was terrible.

I had the early-morning go to Quang Tri. For some unexplained reason, I flew straight to the AO instead of swinging by to pick up a Covey rider. Lately, I felt much more comfortable flying alone than with the new crop of SF back-seaters. It was nothing personal—they were great guys. But they weren't Blister or Satan, and the bond just wasn't there. My thinking on the matter had really become twisted: I was the old head; nobody had ever done this as long as I had; the new troops slowed me down; I could handle the hot situations better and faster alone.

When the one-zero came up on Fox Mike in his broken English, I wasn't at all surprised. In fact, I had suspected the night before that the team would be in trouble by morning. Smiling at his choice of words, I listened to the ARVN team leader's whining voice: "Cubby, Cubby. This is Papa Delta. Have very bad situation. Many VC. You bring big bomb right now."

As a general rule, our ARVN teams had a knack for overstating the threat. This time, however, I believed him. Papa Delta was working on top of the same karst ridge from the action two days before. The place had to be crawling with bad guys.

When I arrived overhead, there was nothing visible below except a solid stratus deck of dingy gray clouds. To help, I'd have to fly below the stuff. Luckily I had calculated an accurate bearing and distance from Quang Tri's TACAN during the earlier action, so I had a good instrument fix on a relatively large valley slightly west of my team. My problem was the three-thousand-foot peaks jutting up around the valley. If my altitude calculations were off or if the TACAN signal developed a false lock-on, I could end up splattering myself and aircraft 831 against jagged limestone karst—the irresistible force meeting the immovable object.

On entering the cloud deck, the cockpit became very dark. I strained to see the instruments before me while simultaneously peering out the front windscreen for a glimpse of ground I knew was getting close. The pitot boom mounted on the Bronco's nose represented the limit of my forward visibility. Back inside, I fought to hold a picture on the attitude indicator that would give me a very shallow rate of descent, between two hundred and three hundred feet per minute on the vertical velocity indicator.

Easing below three thousand feet indicated, I was committed. From here on, I needed luck and patience. Descending the next thousand feet seemed to take forever; losing the final eight hundred feet took an eternity. With sweat dripping into my eyes, it took a moment before the visual cues registered when we finally broke out of the clouds.

The scene in front of me was devoid of color. The valley stretched out slightly to my north, draped in dark shadows, like in a black-and-white film. Two hundred feet directly below me, patches of fog clung to the karst and trees. I made a mental note to add another two miles to my TACAN DME reading.

A quick swig of water, and then I pointed us eastward down the familiar little valley. As I approached the team's position on the east end of the ridge, the one-zero kept moaning, "Cubby, bring big bomb right now."

Contemptuously, I thought to myself, what a doofus. He must realize fighters can't work below all this crud. Then, as if he were reading my mind, the indig team leader played me like a Stradivarius. He cooed, "Cubbies always help us. We need big bomb—now!" I was a sucker for flattery.

The karst ridge sloped gradually up from west to east, reaching a height of about eighteen hundred feet on my altimeter. On the north face, the steep cliffs gave way to a flat valley four hundred feet below. The Saint Valentine's Day Massacre had occurred on the center section of the ridge, directly opposite another karst. Located on the east tip of the south ridge, the ARVN team would be easier to support. The northern ridge abruptly ended a mile to the west, leaving me a clean run-in to the target.

After the team marked their position with an orange panel, I went to work. The one-zero reported a company of NVA regulars moving against him in a pincer movement. While one group climbed the karst directly below him, the other one was angling in from the west. Since the climbers were closest, I went after them first.

Flying due south at three hundred feet, I zeroed in on the ridge directly in front of me. At approximately fifteen-hundred-feet slant range, I put the pipper on some heavy brush one hundred feet below my team and opened up with all four machine guns. I held the trigger down until the last possible second, then jinked up and over the ridge. For several seconds I inadvertently slipped into the base of the clouds, hanging only a few hundred feet above the crest. I had to maneuver for several minutes to get back in position for another strafing run.

After my third or fourth pass, the bad guys began returning fire with a vengeance. Small-arms fire chattered away from the western attack force. With each jink up to miss the ridge looming in front of me, a trio of 12.7mm machine guns located south of the team got in on the act, spraying tracers and smoke all over the dark morning sky. The one-zero, in a genuine show of concern, dropped his monotonous chant about big bombs and replaced it with a warning. On each pass he'd yell, "Cubby, you be careful. Many VC shoot at you. Please be careful."

In an effort to extract more precise information, I responded, "Papa Delta, tell me exactly where the fire is coming from."

Without missing a beat, the voice replied, "Everywhere! Everywhere!"

Several minutes later, I had fired off all two thousand rounds of 7.62. I quickly adjusted the mil setting on my gunsight and switched over to rockets, a move that proved to be a costly mistake. Taking aim on a pocket of troops one hundred meters west and just below the team, I fired a pair of marking rockets into the side of the karst. When I completed the 360-degree circuit for a second pass, I was horrified to see the brush on top of the ridge burning fiercely, apparently ignited by my rockets. Even more disturbing, the light westerly wind pushed the flames toward the team. As the fire grew, I couldn't believe the mess I had created. The team had no choice but to start moving to the east. Once they reached the end of the karst, only five hundred meters away, there was no place to go but straight down.

First in pairs, then singly, I fired all my remaining HE and willie pete rockets into the bad guys to the west, hoping to slow if not disrupt their movement. When I was winchester, I threw in a couple of dry runs to keep everyone's heads down—and as a necessary penance for my own stupidity. Then, trying to sound as confident as possible, I told the team the fire would keep the NVA away long enough for me to rearm and return with the rescue helicopters. The one-zero acknowledged calmly and asked me to hurry. Climbing back through the clouds, I felt sick about leaving the team in such a jam. Cobbing the power, I coaxed the Bronco back to Quang Tri as fast as she would fly.

The Barky crew chiefs refueled and rearmed my OV-10 in a blur of churning legs, bending arms, and sweaty bodies. In record time Sergeant First Class Jim Parry and I were back in the air and crossing the fence. It was a relief to have a partner. Although Parry was new to the business, he had the natural instincts of the best, Marty Martin. Jim had a more rugged-looking face and a quieter demeanor than Satan, but he was hard-core Green Beret and a welcome addition to the depleted Covey rider ranks.

En route to the battle, two Cobras and three Slicks joined us. As we flew over the solid cloud deck below, I was really scared wondering about the team's situation. I hoped we'd get to them before the fire or the bad guys did.

At the adjusted TACAN let-down point, I turned my navigation lights on full bright. Leaving the Slicks in the holding pattern, I had the Cobras tuck in as close to my wing tips as possible. Since they weren't trained instrument pilots, my OV-10 was about to become their total frame of reference. Slowly at first, with careful, deliberate stick movements, I eased the strange formation into the weather. Through the colorless mist I could just make out the two helicopters with their pilots watching me intently, mirroring every move of the Bronco. By the end of the first racetrack pattern, the bouncing had stopped and everyone settled down into a smooth, functioning unit.

Three thousand feet and five minutes later, we coasted out of the dreary soup and into the clear. This time we ended up on the north side of the valley. Once everyone had his bearings, I poured on the coals and told the Cobras to follow me.

As we approached the target area, Jim Parry began calling

the team on Fox Mike while I searched for the fire. For the life of me, I couldn't see anything burning. For one brief, heart-stopping second, I thought I was lost. Then a heavily accented voice brought a big smile to my face. In broken English, the one-zero picked up where he had left off. It was a relief to hear his familiar refrain, "Cubby, Cubby. Very bad situation. You bring big bomb right now."

Miraculously the fire had apparently burned itself out in the wet brush, with only a 150-meter stretch of scorched ground to mark its passing. Taking advantage of the burned-off area, the cagy one-zero had his team dug in with weapons pointed in that direction, ready to cut down any fool who might try to cross the open ground.

While we circled, my back-seater digested the tactical situation as explained by Papa Delta. From what Jim could piece together, the determined enemy troops were below the crest, working their way east along the steep sides of the karst. The closest bunch were on a ledge only thirty-five meters from the team. The bad guys were in no position to fire, but they kept climbing.

The first order of business was to mark some targets and put the Cobras to work. Not wanting to take a chance on starting another fire with the willie petes, I shot several HE rockets into the ledge. It felt like old home week as we jinked up and over the ridge, greeted by familiar volleys of fire from the 12.7mm positions. As I banked us hard to the left, Jim Parry spotted one of the machine-gun pits. He didn't exactly suggest we go after it, but we both knew that gun would cut our Hueys to pieces as they hovered to pick up the team. With Jim directing, I snapped us into a turn back to the right. In what amounted to a sneak attack, we maneuvered well to the south before heading north toward the gun. I had us right at the base of the clouds, two hundred feet above the terrain. As a diversion, Cobra Lead began the attack on the ledge.

We were on top of the gun so fast that it surprised me. There was almost no time to aim and fire. I pressed the red pickle button on the control stick twice, sending two high-explosive rockets with ten-pound warheads streaking toward the pit. The startled two-man crew had just begun swinging their weapon in our direction when they disappeared in an explosion of gray smoke and flying brown dirt.

While the Cobras worked over the karst, I pointed the Bronco's nose up for the three-thousand-foot climb through the weather to our orbiting Slicks. Breaking out into the blue sky and bright sunshine, we spotted the Hueys a mile farther east. As I flew toward them, the warm sun streaming into the cockpit seemed to sap the strength right out of me. I dreaded going back down into that repulsive weather, so cleverly hiding the mountain peaks, karst rock formations, and enemy fire. Inexplicably, I thought about the Prairie Fire business cards most of us carried. The front of each card included the particular pilot's name, rank, call sign, and a series of gag boasts: casual war hero, world traveler, philanthropist, hero of the oppressed. On the back of my cards, there was a short verse:

> *Yea, though I fly through the valley*
> *of the shadow of death,*
> *I shall fear no evil,*
> *For I am the meanest son of a*
> *bitch in the valley*

It had been my choice to make that bit of poetry part of my Prairie Fire image. Now it was time to live up to the boast. For the third time in four hours, I throttled back for the let-down. With the third Slick remaining on top in reserve and the other two invisibly linked to my aircraft, we slid into the waiting cloud deck. Throughout the descent I kept wondering if fate had ordained the fight in the valley below to fulfill the prophecy of the verse on the back of my cards.

The Slick pilots hung in there beautifully. With my gear and flaps down, our speeds matched perfectly. We were in passable fingertip formation when we finally glided out of the clouds and into the valley of the shadow of death.

In our absence the Cobras had done a great job of beating up the area. Following a brief conversation with the team and the Cobras, we knew it was time to go for the extraction. Our problem would be lack of air space for maneuvering. During most extractions we had the luxury of operating in all three dimensions. On this one the low cloud ceilings compressed us into two dimensions, with virtually no use of the vertical. Studying the situation, I could see there wasn't going to be room in the small valley for two Cobras, two Hueys, and one OV-10, all maneuvering toward the same spot on top of the karst ridge.

With a certain amount of guilt, I sent the package in for the pickup while Jim and I moved roughly one klick to the north to watch. I should have never given the decision a second thought. As the Slicks started their runs to the makeshift LZ with the Cobras providing covering fire, Jim and I got caught up in our own private little war. From one of the mountains immediately to our west, a pair of 23mm guns opened up on us. Although their fire was flat trajectory at maximum range, the exploding flak appeared more frightening than normal. With the surrounding ridges and the ragged ceiling of clouds only a few hundred feet above us, I felt trapped, hemmed in. No matter which way we jinked, the nasty little white air bursts followed us. In a fit of desperation, I yelled to Jim, "How 'bout singing a verse of 'The Ballad of the Green Beret.'"

Probably thinking I'd lost my mind, Jim shouted back, "What on earth are you talking about?" A new Covey rider, he evidently didn't know the story behind Satan's famous renditions of the song.

Humming the melody softly to myself, I racked us into a vision-tunneling high-G diving turn to the west. As we scooted down the valley away from our team, all I could think about was getting the northern karst between us and the guns. It worked. As we flashed by the northern ridge, the flak stopped. For the first time in what seemed like an eternity, I heard the radio chatter between the team and the choppers. Slick Lead was in a hover about to pull half the eight-man team. Several anxious moments followed before he called, "Lead's off and heading north to your position, Covey."

The thought of the two 23mm guns blasting the unsuspecting choppers sent shivers down my spine. As I screamed a terrified "NO!" into my boom mike, a 37mm drew a bead on us and hosed away, probably the same rascal who had tried it two days earlier. Jim held his breath as I executed a chandelle up into the clouds, the only way I could see to get us going the other way in a hurry. At the top I kicked in some bottom rudder, crossed my fingers, then zoomed back down on a reciprocal heading. If we hit one of the karsts in a steep dive, I reasoned, we'd never feel a thing.

In a stroke of luck, we came out of the clouds at about the same place we entered. Seconds after we reappeared, ten gray air bursts strung out behind us. For the first time, I found the voice to talk to the Slicks. Moving at full speed due east down the floor of the valley, I advised the Hueys, "Whatever you do, don't move to the north. A couple of 23s sitting up there will have your lunch. Set up a tight orbit where I dropped you off, and keep it very low."

Pulling off the LZ with the rest of the team, Slick Two picked up a few B-40 grenade fragments and some AK-47 rounds in the belly, but nobody was hurt and the bird was flyable. Jim and I dived in behind them, firing an entire pod of HE rockets into enemy positions on the karst.

With the big guns to our north and fire still coming our way from the karst, there was no time or room to form the package up for an instrument climb back through the weather. Instead, I gave the Cobras a heading to climb on while I safed up my switches and joined up with the Slicks. Once again with gear and flaps hanging, I led the Hueys into the soup, to the salvation waiting for us on top. When we broke into the clear at five thousand feet, the sun directly overhead had never looked so good.

I never did find the Cobras who apparently had rendezvoused with the spare Slick and were well on the way back to Quang Tri. We could hear them talking, though. I had to chuckle when the Slick asked, "How was it down there?"

One of the Cobras answered, "No sweat. This was an easy one."

The following day, the Prairie Fire action shifted south from the valley of the shadow of death to a new and equally deadly location, the A Shau Valley. Launching out of the MLT at Hue Phu Bai, we inserted two teams, one on each wall of the A Shau. Each RT had an identical mission. The small teams had the impossible task of setting up surveillance and roadblocks against NVA units attempting to move north against Lam Son 719.

The first real trouble began late on the afternoon of February 18. The team on the west wall made contact with a large enemy force. Surrounded and unable to move through the dense jungle underbrush growing on the steep slope of the ridge, the team leader had no choice but to call for an extraction. When the package arrived on the scene, it was clear to everyone that the team could never make it to the nearest LZ. The decision was made to pull them out on a ladder hanging from one of the Slicks. In a truly remarkable display of bravery, Slick Lead went into a stationary hover while the team scurried to climb up the flimsy ladder dangling just a few feet from the ground. The intense ground fire coming from all directions proved to be more than even the agile Cobras could handle. Riddled with bullets, the hovering Huey lurched forward in a drunken fashion, inadvertently snagging the ladder, along with the five clinging team members, in the tops of the trees. Acting like an unbreakable leash on a straining dog, the tangled ladder jerked the chopper up short, then sent it plunging nose first into the dense jungle. At impact, the UH-1 evaporated in a huge orange fireball. We searched the crash site until dark without finding a single survivor.

At dawn the next morning I landed at Hue Phu Bai to pick up one of the new Covey riders. We headed directly to the crash site and began a slow low-altitude search on the outside chance one of our troops might still be alive. As the sun rose above the hills on the east wall of the A Shau, I picked up what looked like a mirror flash four hundred meters south of the crash. On our second pass at treetop height, a lone figure stepped out of the shadows and waved to us. I rocked the wings to let him know we had a tally on him, then we got on the horn to put the wheels of the rescue in motion.

An hour later a helicopter package rendezvoused with us in the middle of the A Shau. Since I couldn't be sure there weren't other survivors wandering around the area, I gave strict orders to the Cobras and the Slick door gunners. The only permissible use of guns was to return fire for fire. There would be no LZ prepping and no suppressing fire.

Under the circumstances all of us were extremely nervous as Slick Lead inched over the spot I had verbally marked, then dropped his ladder. Fighting the heavy rotor wash, our survivor limped out of his hiding place and climbed on the swaying contraption. Working his cyclic to perfection, the pilot carefully lifted his precious cargo up and clear of the trees before transitioning into forward flight. We flew alongside the lucky Green Beret all the way back to Hue Phu Bai.

At midmorning I launched on my third sortie of the day, this time leading a Bright Light team. The closest usable LZ was over three klicks south of the crashed Huey, but it was the best we could do. We managed to get the Bright Light team in without a hitch, although a heavy machine-gun position did take a few pot shots at us.

At noon Larry Hull relieved me. As I headed in to land at Hue Phu Bai, I cautioned him, "Larry, the Bright Light has a hell of long way to go. My guess is they'll need lots of air support as they move. Be on the lookout for a 14.5mm gun somewhere on the ridge just above the team. He could give your choppers problems."

I was refueled and halfway to Da Nang when the call came in from the MLT. The Bright Light team relayed that Woodstock's O-2 had been blasted by the 14.5mm and had spun in several miles north of them. At the moment there were no emergency radio beepers to indicate survivors.

The crash site sat on top of the west rim of the A Shau, just inside Laos. The Bright Light team had been correct. The plane was still intact, so it must have come down in a flat, upright spin. As I circled over the small meadow with its grisly new centerpiece, I felt dazed and, for the first time, disgusted. I simply wanted to fly back to Da Nang, crawl in my bunk, and sleep out the remainder of my tour. I had finally had enough.

Reluctantly, I stood by while the MLT put together a second Bright Light team. When the choppers finally arrived late that afternoon, I led them to the scene and covered them while they inserted the team next to the O-2. On the ground the twelve-man team found the damage to be much more extensive than we could see from above. With a great deal of difficulty, they managed to remove and recover the Covey rider's body. But no matter how hard they tried, they couldn't get Larry's body out. As it began to get dark, we called off the effort and headed home, leaving Woodstock still sitting at the controls of his Oscar Deuce.

At first light on the twentieth, I banked my OV-10 out of the Da Nang traffic pattern. Following the beach north, I spotted a large school of sharks gliding effortlessly through the clear blue water just off the coast of Monkey Mountain, an eighteen-hundred-foot peak covered with sophisticated radar antennas. In an uncharacteristic move I couldn't even explain to myself, I charged up the M-60s and attacked the unoffending creatures for no other reason than blood lust. As the hail of bullets churned the water's surface, the sharks darted off in all directions, apparently frightened but unharmed by the fusillade. For a few terrible seconds, I trembled in wild rage, infuriated that I had missed, that the sharks had escaped. I slammed the stick first right, then left, trying to line up one of the despicable monsters in my gunsight. Overcome with frustration, I finally gave up. As fast as it had possessed me, the fight drained out of me. I slumped back in the seat, gasping for breath.

Perhaps out of intuition, perhaps out of embarrassment, I realized I was in no mood to deal with a Covey rider. Disregarding a recent promise I had made to myself, never to fly without an SF alter ego in the back seat, I pressed into the A Shau Valley solo.

As I flew overhead, all was quiet for the team on the east

wall. On the west wall, it was a different story. The Bright Light team was still bogged down in the heavy brush two klicks short of the helicopter crash site. The one-zero asked for an air strike against an 82mm mortar position to his southwest. For the past two hours, his team had been taking a beating from the persistent tube. The mortar represented more of a nuisance than a threat, but the one-zero's voice sounded like I felt. He wanted to get even.

After plotting out the coordinates, I gave a halfhearted call to Hillsboro, figuring all tactical air would be tied up supporting the ARVN troops fighting for their lives along Highway 9. Much to my surprise, Hillsboro sent a flight of F-4s directly to my location. My spirits picked up considerably.

The sight of the first string of Mark-82s exploding against the west wall had a cathartic effect on me. The jumpiness, the anger seemed to melt. My perspective balanced out when the bad guys fired a few feeble tracers at the fighters. In response, the Phantoms kept pressing in, dropping their loads wherever I directed. The blast patterns looked great, probably because each bomb sported a Daisy Cutter, a three- to four-foot-long fuse extender protruding from the nose. Instead of burrowing into the dirt, the five-hundred-pounders detonated when the Daisy Cutter contacted the ground, lethally blasting the surrounding jungle. With each explosion I could hear the Bright Light team cheering over the radio.

Shortly after the air strike, my attention shifted to inside the cockpit. The fuel quantity indicator registered a little low, considering I had the external transfer switch turned on. If working properly, the transfer pump in the external fuel transfer line should have been pumping 845 pounds of JP-4 per hour from the 230-gallon centerline tank into my main wing tanks. I cycled the switch on and off several times, then watched the gauge for any sign of filling. Nothing. As a last resort, I pumped the stick forward and aft rapidly in order to porpoise the aircraft, hoping the sloshing fuel would begin feeding. That didn't work either. I decided to give it a rest for a few minutes, hoping the half-full centerline tank would fix itself.

Before I had time to trouble-shoot the problem any further, a scream over the radio made the hair on the back of my neck stand straight up. At full volume the voice screeched, "Prairie Fire! Prairie Fire! We're in heavy contact. We need an emergency extract right now!"

I recognized the voice as that of Captain Jim Butler, the one-zero of RT Python. Jim was highly experienced, one of the best team leaders around. We'd worked together before on several hot ones, and I knew that if Butler was that agitated, his situation must really be bad. I rolled into a steep bank and struck out across the A Shau Valley for the east wall. Until that moment all my attention had been focused on the other side of the valley.

The fourteen-man team was located on top of a bald, dusty hill once known as Fire Base Thor. A few of the old sandbag walls were still visible around the summit. Over the past three days, Jim and his crew of two Green Berets and eleven indig had been fighting a running battle against determined NVA probes aimed at the tiny fortress. So far, RT Python had been holding their own. As a sign of their defiance, the team had run an American flag up a long pole for the whole world to see—and the bad guys to aim at. While fending off the round-the-clock attacks, several of the team had been wounded. Jim probably should have called for extraction earlier, but he knew we had our hands full across the valley. Like the pro he was, he gutted it out.

Once I reached his position, Jim broadsided me with a torrent of excited, jumbled words. I couldn't make any sense of them. The pitch of his voice actually scared me. Meaning no disrespect to a soldier I deeply admired, I shouted back at him, "Goddamn it, Jim, get hold of yourself. Stop feeding me this stream of consciousness crap. I can't help you unless you settle down and tell me slowly and clearly exactly what the problem is."

After a few deep breaths, the feisty team leader regained his cool. In measured tones he told me his team was up against a massive attack in force. The lead enemy elements were already on the northwest perimeter, about to spill over the top. He said prophetically, "We can't hold 'em much longer. Get us out of here."

Arming up the HE rocket pods, I spiraled down to the base of the hill. Sure enough, a pocket of enemy troops sat huddled against the outside sandbag fortification. Every few seconds, several more raced out of the brush at the base of the hill and scampered twenty or thirty yards up the slope to join their buddies.

I yelled to the one-zero, "Get your heads down. I'm gonna put it in close along the western perimeter." Diving in from the north at a shallow angle, I let the pipper drift up to the crouching figures before I squeezed off a pair of rockets. Pulling up in a hard rolling turn to the west, I couldn't see the impact. I asked Jim, "How was that?"

Laughing, he shouted, "You're blowing dirt and rocks all over us. It's great. Keep it coming."

I made one more pass before backing off. The enemy troops were climbing the hill faster than the team or my rockets could mow them down. What we needed was some big-time help. Switching to emergency transmit, I bypassed Hillsboro with a call to anyone listening: "This is Covey 221, transmitting in the blind on Guard. I've got troops in contact in the A Shau. Any fighter aircraft with soft ordnance, give me a call."

As if in answer to a prayer, a two ship of A-1s en route from NKP to Da Nang came to the rescue. Within ten minutes I had the Spads dropping napalm canisters on the hiding troops at the base of the hill. Then we worked over the slopes with CBU-25 and strafe. I marveled at how accurately the big prop-driven machines could lay down the ordnance. When we got back to Da Nang, I planned to buy the two Spad pilots all the beer they could drink.

During the short lull, I called the MLT to get a package moving our direction. The young captain in charge, formerly the deputy to Jerry Stratton, who had transferred months earlier, had been monitoring my conversations with RT Python.

so he knew they were in a world of hurt. Unfortunately, he relayed that all the 101st helicopters were committed to one of the big Lam Son battles. Cobra support was out of the question; however, he had managed to scrounge up two Slicks, if I wanted to take a chance on committing them with no covering fire. As I saw it, we had no choice. I told him to launch the fleet.

As the one-zero's shouts alerted me to another pending disaster, I couldn't help thinking about the old cliché, when it rains, it pours. I never appreciated its significance. Now I did.

Butler was beside himself. The bad guys were attacking the opposite end of the fort with infantry and a barrage of B-40 rockets. One of the explosions had blown an indig down the slope of the hill into the advancing troops. The assistant team leader, Staff Sergeant Leslie Chapman, climbed over the barricade and ran down the hill to retrieve his unconscious comrade. Before I could get in position to help, Chapman had killed four NVA soldiers at point-blank range. Then he threw the injured trooper on his back and started up the steep slope.

I reefed the Bronco around for a west to east run-in. At one hundred yards, I aimed at Chapman's heels and pulled the trigger. The left-hand sponson belched out a twin stream of tracers into the bare ground slightly behind the struggling American. As the red dust and smoke swirled around, I let the bullets walk into a row of bushes. Several figures pitched over into contorted heaps. Zooming straight up to stay in tight, I sucked in my breath when several grenade blasts knocked Sergeant Chapman to the ground. By the time I had fired a second long burst, he was on his feet and climbing. At the top of the hill, RT Python blasted the hillside with deadly covering fire. I broke off the run when the dust became so bad that I could no longer see anything. Butler had to tell me when Chapman finally staggered back into the RT's small defensive perimeter.

I had aged at least ten years by the time the two Hueys checked in on my frequency. In addition to the battle raging below, a serious problem in the cockpit had me worried. The fuel-low caution light had been glowing a bright yellow for some time, indicating something less than 220 pounds of gas remaining. With all the low-altitude rocket and strafing passes, I was burning up the juice at a wicked rate. I cursed the centerline tank for picking such a critical time to act up. Fortunately, the runway at Hue Phu Bai was only thirty miles away.

Quickly briefing the orbiting Slicks, I tried to give them an accurate picture of what they were up against. Dug in around the old fire base, an estimated 350 enemy troops would be aiming their weapons at the helicopters. Except for the door gunners, my Bronco was the only other covering fire available. To complicate things even more, each Slick would have to lift out seven team members, a heavy load under ideal conditions. When I finished talking, the Huey pilots didn't show the slightest signs of apprehension or hesitation. Using my own trademark phrase, Slick Lead said simply, "Let's do it."

We decided to make the run from the southwest, the corridor where I'd taken the lightest ground fire. With the team laying down their maximum rate of fire, we started down the chute. I concentrated my smoke rockets in the southern quadrant while the door gunner fired his M-60 along the steep slope. Crossing the hilltop perimeter, the Huey shook violently from the blasts of several B-40 grenade explosions, but the pilot held on and touched down in a blinding cloud of red dust. After an agonizingly long wait, Lead lifted off. To cover his escape, I laid down a wall of strafe from one end of the eastern slope to the other, then I racked my bird into a high-G climbing turn to the west to link up with Slick Two.

In formation, we ran a carbon copy of the original effort. I fired off all my remaining rockets and added a few bursts from the guns as Two slid into the LZ. When he finally lifted off, I roared in from the south, finger on the trigger. A second later the M-60s went dead. My effort as a fighter pilot was over. The helicopter, unfortunately, paid the price. Unopposed, the bad guys riddled Slick Two from stem to stern. Somehow, the courageous crew kept their chopper flying.

Heading eastbound with my little flock, I was ecstatic. We'd done it. I wasn't sure how, but we'd pulled it off. Out of habit, I asked each Slick to confirm a head count on the team. Slick Lead reported seven aboard. I literally felt faint when Two reported six. I asked for a recount and got the same numbers. We were missing a man.

Although Slick Two had the short load, the UH-1 was in no condition to make a second run into the LZ. Without being asked, Slick Lead executed a 180-degree turn and followed me back to the A Shau.

The pucker factor forced a lump in my throat. The needle on my fuel gauge bounced around the bottom gradation, the one-hundred-pound mark. Flying low over the abandoned hilltop, I started to turn around and make a run for Hue Phu Bai with what little fuel I had left. Then I looked down and saw a solitary figure stand up, pop a quick hand salute, then dive back into a foxhole. Our boy was down there alone, still fighting. He deserved something better than a cowardly FAC leaving him to his fate.

As Slick Lead set up for his approach, I dived in on a simulated strafing pass, hoping the ploy would make a few of the bad guys duck. When Lead was ready, I rolled in to support him, only this time I had a surprise for the waiting enemy troops. Taking aim at the base of the hill, I placed all four rocket pod toggle switches on the armament panel in the drop position. At fifty feet, just like in the low-angle event on the scorable range at Hurlburt, I hit the pickle button, sending the four LAU-68 pods tumbling end over end into the red dirt. The odds were against my hitting anything, but the feeble effort made me feel like I was contributing.

While Slick Lead hovered a few inches off the ground, our boy dived in the left troop door. As the Huey struggled into the air, I came in on the deck from the south, saving the best for last. Moving the number three station toggle switch to drop, I ducked under the Huey and pickled off the half-full centerline tank. It had come in handy after all.

We climbed away from the bald hilltop and the A Shau on a straight line for Hue Phu Bai. Although shot full of holes, both Slicks reported they could make it home. Lead did pass along the sad news that the indig soldier rescued by Sergeant Chapman had died.

I had the runway in sight and three thousand feet of altitude before the red fuel feed warning light blinked on, indicating roughly fifty pounds of fuel left to make it in for a safe landing. There was no time to set up for a flame-out pattern, so I entered on a high base leg, slipped off the excess altitude in a steep final turn, threw the gear down, and pranged the Bronco onto the concrete—with a huge sigh of relief. Once clear of the runway, I watched in a drunken stupor as a jeep pulled up with the de-arming crew. Before they could crawl out, both engines flamed out.

On February 22 I broke my promise again by flying solo into the A Shau Valley. In the early morning light, forward visibility was extremely limited because of smoke and haze. In an age-old practice, the local farmers were busy burning off their rice fields and reclaiming the intruding jungle by use of the torch. In the still air, the gray smoke hung in thick layers, easily matching the worst smoggy day in the Los Angeles basin.

With no teams on the ground, I was inexorably drawn to the little meadow on the west wall of the valley. Sitting there peacefully, Larry's O-2 was just visible through the veil of haze. Dropping down lower for one last look, I froze on the control stick when four or five shapes ran out from under the left wing. As I circled a few feet above their heads, the green clad soldiers disappeared into the tall elephant grass.

Outraged at the thought of what the enemy soldiers might be up to, I fired a couple of HE rockets into the tall grass, with no apparent effect. I had never felt so angry and out of control in my life. My hands shook, just as in the shark attack episode a few days earlier. It seemed like years ago.

When I asked for air from Hillsboro, the controller hedged on me, obviously lukewarm about the idea of diverting badly needed fighters to such a strange mission. When he wouldn't commit, I signed off with a rude "Screw you bastards."

The MLT at Hue Phu Bai was more accommodating. The SOG troops still had a special feeling for Woodstock. Without demanding any explanation, they sent me two Cobras. In the thick haze, the rendezvous was tough. It took us twenty minutes to find each other. Once we joined up, I led the gunships to the meadow.

Buzzing over the crash, I was horrified to see that NVA troops were once again milling around the left side of the O-2. At the top of my voice, I screamed into the radio, "Those sadistic little bastards are back!"

When I attempted to give the Cobras a verbal mark, they lost sight of me in the haze. We tried it twice more, with the same result. In frustration I armed up the willie petes and rolled in. My intention was to put a smoke down near the O-2. When the bad guys ran, I'd direct the Cobras using the white smoke for reference.

Either my shot was lousy or my subconscious took over. The willie pete roared out of the tube and streaked down to the target, impacting in the center of the right wing on the Oscar Deuce. In a matter of seconds the fuel blew up, engulfing the airplane in a ball of orange flame. As the plane burned, black smoke swirled straight up, mixing with the already dirty air.

Nobody said a word as we watched the strange funeral pyre below. After five minutes of circling, one of the Cobras broke the strained silence. "We're gonna head on home, Covey." Then in a hushed tone he added, "Sorry about your friend, but it's better this way. Shake it off and come on back with us."

I couldn't trust myself to talk. Clicking the mike button twice, I moved the control stick mechanically through an aileron roll over Woodstock's final resting place, then pointed the Bronco toward Da Nang.

On short final to Runway 18 Left, I had trouble seeing the approach end numbers. Automatically I rubbed at my eyes with the back of my left hand. My glove came away wet.

When I reached up again, I felt a stream of tears rolling down both cheeks, a stream I couldn't control and couldn't stop. A sickening feeling swept over me. The thought of what I had done to Larry Hull crushed me with a guilt at least as consequential as original sin.

After landing, I skipped the customary stops at the personal equipment and the intel shop. I stole the first jeep I found and drove straight to the Covey barracks. Still wearing my survival vest and parachute harness, I bolted past several wide-eyed Coveys and into the first latrine stall in the long row outside the community shower. I threw up for thirty minutes, until there was nothing left inside me.

MARCH

SAR on the Trail

For all practical purposes, the Prairie Fire mission died on the west wall of the A Shau Valley, along with Larry Hull. During the month of March, we couldn't have mounted a team insert if we'd wanted to. The teams were ready; the FACs were ready; the Covey riders were ready. The missing vital element proved to be helicopters.

Like a giant sponge, Lam Son 719 continued to soak up men and equipment. During the first week of March, the ARVN had first call on all 101st helicopters for the final big push toward Tchepone. When they finally achieved the objective at the bombed-out crossroads, the ARVN disengaged and started the deadly return to the border, again via helicopter. Overloaded Hueys and Chinooks shuttled back and forth to hellholes named LZ Lolo, Liz, and Sophia Two. The valiant chopper crews kept at it until they dropped from exhaustion or from enemy ground fire.

By March 24 the last ARVN troops had been lifted out of Laos. All that remained was the withdrawal from the border back to Dong Ha and Quang Tri. With the main part of the battle over, SOG was anxious to saddle up and put its own teams across the fence. It wasn't in the cards. The lack of helicopters was still the limiting factor. During the forty-five days of Lam Son 719, enemy gunners shot down over one hundred U.S. helicopters and damaged another six hundred. As those of us who had been flying there on a steady basis knew, the arena on the ground and in the air over the Ho Chi Minh Trail was one of the most desolate and deadly of the entire war.

Throughout the intense fighting during the first two weeks of March, I never even got airborne. With no helicopters, we had no job. Consequently, the Prairie Fire pilots sat idle. The inactivity became a tough pill to swallow, especially since two weeks earlier we had been logging seven to nine hours of combat time each day.

To keep me gainfully employed, the head Covey asked me to write a detailed narrative on the Covey bomb dump. For two weeks I sat in the intel shop poring over records, after-action reports, and debriefs relating to the missions flown around Ban Bak. I also interviewed all the Covey pilots and navigators who flew those missions. Their firsthand accounts of the sights, smells, and sounds of an aerial battle were captivating. The events they described to me were far more realistic and entertaining than any article in an adventure magazine.

My writing efforts also kept my mind off the moral and ethical questions that had been eating away at me ever since the burning of Woodstock's airplane. The sick feeling was never far away, but the bomb dump project helped me cope. Turning out fifty pages of text, I was immersed in the effort when an offhand comment jolted me into wanting to fly more missions.

Late one night in the Muff Divers' Lounge, I tried to doze off while an animated bull session raged on in the party half of the lounge. Evidently the participants assumed I was asleep, because the conversation became hushed as they began discussing me. One of the Coveys remarked, "Nah, don't sweat getting grounded. That stuff about two hits and they ground you is a bunch of bull. Hell, Tom's been hit at least six times that I know of and had his plane shot out from under him on another occasion. Nobody grounded him."

Somebody else offered the rebuttal: "Well, he's not officially grounded, but why do you think they've got him doing that busy work over at intel? I heard the bosses want to wean him from flying combat for the next month. Otherwise, they think he'll go out and get himself killed."

Not surprisingly, I never went to sleep that night. An odd

mixture of gratitude and anger buzzed through my mind. On
the one hand, I marveled at the totally plausible logic my
commanders had used on me, assuming they were trying to
wean me off the flying schedule. Their concern flattered me.
On the other hand, the implication that I had some kind of
death wish really chapped my ass. Because of the nature of
the job, the Prairie Fire pilots necessarily saw a lot of action
and took some chances. But they were usually calculated
risks, not reckless, intended to save a team or one of our
chopper crews. There was no time for grandstanding. On any
number of occasions, my judgment could be called into question, but I sincerely believed any shortcomings were
positively motivated, no matter how stupid my logic might
have been. As for all the ground-fire hits I'd taken, they were
proportionally about the same as the other Prairie Fire pilots
had chalked up; I had more simply because I'd been doing it
much longer than they had. Perhaps increased exposure was
the culprit. The four combat losses within Covey during the
past ten months had been in Prairie Fire; maybe it was logical
to assume the next one would be too. Still, I didn't believe
any of the arguments and speculation supported anything as
ridiculous as an operative death wish.

The following day I put the finishing touches on my writing project and turned it over to the 20th TASS historian.
Then, leaning back in my chair, I began rehearsing the
speech I planned to deliver to the Covey commander. My
concentration came apart when someone told me the news
about Evan Quiros.

Some sneaky devil aboard the USS *Lynde McCormick* had
filmed Evan's famous air show. To make matters worse, they
sent the film through the chain of command. Eventually,
somebody in Saigon saw the flick and decided to make an
example of one Captain Quiros. Evan was grounded in dis-
grace for the remainder of his tour and ordered to Saigon to
confess his sins before an assembled group of new pilots.

That did it. One grounded Prairie Fire pilot was enough.
When I stomped into the commander's tiny office, the words
of my carefully planned speech had evaporated into alphabet

heaven. Instead, I stammered and stuttered, demanding to be put back on the flying schedule as a regular Trail Covey. The new Covey boss, a lieutenant colonel with a kindly face and short graying hair, stared at me for a few agonizingly long moments before nodding his head. Ken Summers said quietly, "Okay, you got it. Just remember, you've got less than a month to go on your tour. You've got nothing to prove to anybody, so take it easy out there."

I couldn't believe it. I'd walked in the door ready to do battle to get my way. Instead, the boss had not only said yes, he had done it with poise, consideration, and caring. He could have ripped me a new one for being so impertinent. I came away from the encounter thinking how lucky the Coveys were to have had such high-caliber leaders in command, such men as Bob Dennison and Ed Cullivan, men who genuinely cared about the feelings, the motivations, the natural exuberance of a bunch of young combat pilots and navigators.

With the change of leadership inside the Coveys came a sad but predictable changing of the guard. Shortly after my conversation with Colonel Summers, I found myself at the Da Nang terminal saying good-bye to old friends. We'd been through a lot together, in many cases we'd grown up together, and we'd shared experiences that would bond us for life. It was tough to see Evan Quiros, Sonny Haynes, and Carl D'Benedetto get on the Freedom Bird and fly out of my life. They'd been not only friends but the support network that kept me going. Their departure left a void, which I chose not to fill with new friends. It wouldn't have been the same. Instead, I made up my mind to make the remaining time go quickly by flying as many combat missions as possible.

True to his word, Colonel Summers got me back on the schedule. By March 15 I was cruising up and down the Ho Chi Minh Trail, looking for trucks. After the camaraderie and intensity of Prairie Fire, the solo missions over the maze of dirt roads seemed long and lonely. One thing hadn't changed. The gunners along the Trail still had plenty of ammo.

On my first venture out, I worked a flight of Navy A-6

Intruders against two river fords near an area known as Delta 87. The A-6s carried a special seeding ordnance with delayed fusing. In theory, the bomblets spread out over the area and lay dormant until any metal object approached. Small antennas on the bomblet sensed the metal, then detonated the explosive, hopefully catching a juicy truck loaded with supplies. Because of the risk, the trucks were forced to avoid the bombed area and to delay their journeys by as much as thirty-six hours. On this occasion we had a hard time getting the ordnance on the target.

After marking the fords, I cleared the lead A-6 in hot. As soon as he rolled in, a pair of 37mm guns opened up, spewing flak all around the diving jet. The gunners tracked him all the way down the chute, through the pull-off, and through most of the climb away from the target. The gunners gave the wingman the same treatment. They pumped clip after clip into the hazy morning sky, with no indication of a desire to conserve ammo. In my eleven months of flying combat, I'd never seen so many 37mm shells fired in such a short interval.

As I began flying my final combat missions, the never-ending stream of new pilots continued to flow into the unit, each eager to become combat ready. According to my roomie, Larry "Big Bippy" Thomas, one of the best prospects was a young lieutenant named Jack Butcher, Covey 231. Bippy claimed Jack, with his short-clipped dark hair and even darker smoldering eyes, was the fastest study among the new group. Just before going on two weeks of leave, Larry sang the praises of his student and asked me to keep an eye on Lieutenant Jack Butcher. The opportunity presented itself on March 24.

We took off in formation at first light, Butcher tucked in close on my right wing. As part of his training, Jack had to fly some solo observer missions over the Trail, where he practiced his VR techniques or watched experienced Coveys direct air strikes. The specific training for the day involved Jack's watching me run an Igloo White sensor mission. Once across the fence, we headed for Delta 43, a ninety-degree bend in the Xe Kong River near the now infamous village of Ban Bak.

Our target was a small segment of Route 92 running between two high ridges. From the air the steep tree-covered slopes resembled a dark green shag carpet. The red dirt of Route 92 was clearly visible, accentuated by scores of bomb craters along either side of the road scratched out along the narrow valley floor. Somewhere in the green shag, we knew several NVA triple-A positions sat waiting and watching.

The two ship of F-4 Phantoms checked in with me on schedule. My job was to mark a precise stretch of road approximately three hundred meters in length, one smoke on the south end of the box, another on the north end. Using my rockets as their target parameters, the Phantoms would streak in on the deck at high speed, dropping the sensors between the smokes. A pinpoint drop was vital to the folks at Task Force Alpha, so they could accurately time truck movements against known positions of each acoustical sensor. To make the system work, both FAC and fighters had to be right on the money.

With Jack orbiting in a ringside seat over the east ridge, we went to work on the Igloo White drop. Pressing in low and shallow, I laid both willie petes in a nice bracket. Next, Lead rolled in well to the south, hugging the deck as he zeroed in on the swirling white smoke. At release, Lead stroked both afterburners while pulling up and to the east into the blinding light of the morning sun. The wingman flew a carbon copy, and it was over, without a hostile shot being fired. While the fighters navigated to a waiting tanker for a poststrike refueling, I used the Covey discrete FM frequency to debrief Jack on the strike, putting particular emphasis on the requirement for absolute accuracy and on the risk the fighters took during their low-altitude, highly predictable run-in to the target box.

A few minutes later, Hillsboro asked me to check out two sets of map coordinates for possible enemy activity. I selected the one near Delta 87, location of the two 37mm guns with the endless supply of ammo. I asked Jack to investigate a section of a new road, Route 99, running along a flat plateau a few miles northwest of Delta 43. He banked off in that direction, and that was the last time I saw Jack Butcher.

The heavy foliage around Delta 87 yielded nothing. The trucks were down there all right, but I couldn't find their hiding place. After fifteen minutes of searching, I banked the Bronco around and started back up the Trail to see how Jack had made out.

I didn't give it more than a second thought when Jack didn't answer my calls on company FM. My concern grew when he didn't come up on the UHF strike frequency or on Hillsboro's VHF freq. Switching over to Guard, I still couldn't raise him. Since the chances of all his radios failing at the same time defied the odds, I tried a long shot, asking Panama if they had Covey 231 on their radar scope. Somehow, I knew their answer would be negative.

When I arrived over the general area of Jack's last known position, the morning sky was painfully empty. Below, a thin fog deck obscured the plateau containing Route 99. After calculating the terrain height, I rolled into a shallow dive, directly into the fog bank. I knew Jack had to be down there somewhere under that gray veil.

I coasted into the clear about a thousand feet above the ground. Within seconds, chills ran up and down my spine as the high-pitched shrill of an emergency beeper filled my helmet earphones. One quick jink to the north and I saw it, a burning pile of junk marked by thick black smoke, only a hundred meters west of the new road. There was no real question in my mind, but I circled down to the deck to make certain. Sure enough, I could still make out the numbers on the tail section, 693. It was, ironically, the very same OV-10 from my first trial by fire so many months ago, the same aircraft with the 23mm-induced broken wing spar, only recently put back in action.

As I plotted the coordinates of the crash site, a sound on the radio startled me. A garbled, slurred, almost unintelligible voice said, "Covey 221, this is 213. This is 213." I wanted to believe it was Jack's voice. It sounded a little like Jack, but the call sign was wrong. The voice had it reversed. His call sign was 231.

Disregarding the call signs, I answered, "Jack, this is Tom. Talk me into your location, buddy. I'm orbiting over the crash now. Which way?" In response, the wailing, pulsing beeper filled the airwaves with its forlorn sound. I pleaded, "Covey 231, this is 221. If you read me, turn off the beeper and come up voice."

With the emergency signal pounding in my ears, I felt myself turning into a crazy man. Jack was down there somewhere, counting on me to rescue him. This is what I did for a living. How many SF troops had I found in the jungle and plucked out? What was different about this one? Why couldn't I find Jack? My chest felt like it wanted to explode in ten different directions.

I found it helped to talk out loud through the intercom, my own voice partially blocking the beeper. I reasoned with myself, "Okay, get organized. There's a slight breeze from the west. Watch the smoke. Jack's 'chute probably drifted to the east side of the road. Start the search pattern over there."

I ran a quick swing along the east side of the road at treetop level, looking down through the triple canopy for a telltale parachute. The only sign of life came from a flock of white birds, spooked into the air by the sound of the Bronco's whining engines. Every minute or so I called Jack on Guard, pleading with him to answer me. For my troubles, some impatient pilot, miles away and unaware of the situation, chimed in with a rude, "Get the hell off Guard!"

After crisscrossing the area numerous times, I finally saw evidence of human life. While reversing directions with a steep banked left turn, I spotted a slow-moving stream of .51-cal tracers arching up at me from the south. When I headed that way to investigate, I stumbled across a column of fifteen troops running down the center of the road, in the direction of the crash. With the left-hand set of M-60s armed, I rolled in on the running figures from behind, walking a long burst of fire into their midst. The two tail-end charlies collapsed as I zoomed a few feet over the heads of the remaining soldiers.

As I yanked the aircraft through a tight turn to reengage, a loud tearing sound snapped my head around, just in time to see a string of tracers fill the air space around me. For a brief second the flight controls seemed to bind, then broke free. Looking halfway back on the right boom, I saw the problem. Somebody down there was a damn good shot. Some kind of heavier weapon, probably a .51-cal machine gun, had stitched a row of ragged holes across the sides and bottom of the boom, almost ripping it in half, bottom to top.

In the ensuing confusion, my troops managed to blend into the brush alongside the trail. The two bodies still lay where they had fallen. Something else had distracted me. For a few seconds, I couldn't figure out what it was. Then it hit me. There was no sound. The beeper had stopped. The silence was more deafening than anything I could remember.

As I started to search the west side of Route 99, Hillsboro advised, "Covey 221, I've got the help you asked for. Sandy Zero Three and Zero Four will meet you on Golf frequency." Looking down on my mission data card, I found the letter G and dialed in the corresponding UHF frequency. As I waited for the A-1s to check in, I couldn't for the life of me remember talking to Hillsboro about a SAR or A-1s.

Almost immediately the Sandys and I got off to a rocky start. After briefing them on the situation, I added, "Listen, gents, I know he's down here. How 'bout scrambling a Jolly and get him inbound while we continue the search."

Sandy Lead answered, "We can't commit the Jollies without an objective, and right now buddy, you've got no objective."

I shot back, "For Christ's sake, Sandy. I talked to 231 on the radio. He's down there, I know it. In the hour it'll take the choppers to get here, we'll find him and have your objective. Now let's get on with it."

"Negative, Covey. I know how you must feel, but no objective, no Jollies. And that's final."

His words stung me, setting off a torrent of rage fed by acute frustration. In an angry, bitter shout, I replied, "Hey, Lead. If you're gonna sit up there and quote regs to me, just take your wingman and get the goddamn hell out of here. I'll find him without your help.''

The words were no sooner out of my mouth when I spotted a second group of bad guys trotting north along the road. Somewhat sarcastically I added, "I've got troops in the open down here, gents. If you're not gonna run a SAR, would you like to come down here and kick a little ass?''

With no further coaxing from me, Sandy Lead moved west about ten miles to the edge of the fog bank, reversed direction, then headed to me on the deck. As the big A-1H came into sight, I popped a quick smoke onto the road, scattering the troops in all directions. The Sandy flew several low passes, dumping rear-ejecting CBU-25 into their hiding places. When it was over, we counted two more bodies face-down on the side of the road.

Sandy Lead covered me for several more minutes as I trolled the treetops looking for Jack. He knew what I refused to accept. With no voice or beeper for over an hour, the odds of finding Covey 231 were becoming bleaker with each passing minute. The A-1 jock trolled along with me, probably for no other reason than to pacify me. As I watched him work, as I watched him hang it out in the breeze, I sincerely regretted my earlier tirade—but not enough to apologize.

By the time Lead reached bingo fuel, much of the fog had burned off. The two A-1s rejoined, wished me good luck, then took up an RTB for their home base at NKP. Once more I took up the solo search for the missing Covey pilot. I would have given anything for the companionship and sharp eyes of Satan or Blister strapped in my back seat. Unfortunately, both of them had recently moved on to other assignments.

On one of my low circuits, the Bronco bucked again, this time from a big hole shot in the right flap. Reluctantly, I climbed a thousand feet to escape the worst of the small-arms fire. Given any kind of chance, I knew my beat-up OV-10 could get me home. Good old 693 had saved me once; now I counted on a badly wounded 701 to do the same.

In the excitement, the notion of running out of fuel never crossed my mind. I believed I could stay over the target as long as it took to find Jack and rescue him. My first inkling of a gas problem arrived with the new sector FAC sent to relieve me. When my replacement saw me down in the weeds, he asked "Covey 221, this is 252. You've been out over four hours. Gimme a fuel check." My five hundred pounds of remaining fuel seemed to concern Covey 252 more than it did me. As I briefed him on where I'd already searched, he kept repeating in an increasingly antsy tone, "Go home. Get out of here!"

The flight back to Da Nang was lonely and demoralizing. After a year of involvement in hairy rescues, I felt like a rookie for not being able to find Jack Butcher. I agonized over what his fate might be. The word going around was that the bad guys didn't take any prisoners in Laos, especially FACs. Preoccupation with those thoughts almost ended in disaster for me.

Without paying attention to what I was doing, I rolled into a left base to Runway 18 Left and threw the flap lever down. Before I could react, the OV-10 flipped the opposite direction, putting me into almost ninety degrees of right bank. In the mad scramble to feed in corrective left stick and rudder, I remembered the damaged right flap. I slammed the flap lever full up and wallowed back to the left before getting things under control. The alert tower operator added to my misery and embarrassment by asking, "Covey 221, are you experiencing control difficulties?" Replying with a sullen "Negative," I guided the crippled bird in for a relatively smooth landing and cleared the active runway. In spite of my distress at not being able to find Jack Butcher, I managed a weak smile as I watched the astonished faces of the maintenance folks staring in disbelief at my shot-up OV-10.

Much later, we found out Jack Butcher was captured moments after hitting the ground following the ejection from his OV-10. Although badly hurt, Jack was forced by his captors to talk on the radio, despite a broken jaw. After a brief recuperation in a makeshift field hospital, the gutsy Covey escaped into the Laotian jungle for an extended period, only to be recaptured. After some brutal treatment, Jack was sent to Hanoi, where he remained until repatriation in March 1973, almost exactly two years to the day after his shoot-down. Jack Butcher was one of only nine U.S. airmen captured in Laos to make it back home. Hundreds of other pilots, aircrew members, and SOG personnel have never been accounted for.

APRIL II

The Year of Fifty-Three Weeks

Da Nang tower, Covey 221 three-mile initial—for the last time."

An indifferent American voice answered, "Da Nang landing Runway 18 Left. Altimeter three-zero-zero-two, wind one-four-zero at eight. Report a midfield break for departing traffic."

For some sentimental, incomprehensible reason only another pilot on his final combat mission could appreciate, the tower operator's unemotional response to my very last time in his pattern annoyed me. He obviously could have cared less about the end of my combat tour and all of the emotional baggage that went along with it. To the tower operator, April 4, 1971, was just another day at Rocket City. Covey 221 was just another arrogant FAC bent on showing his fanny.

My own feelings, confused and exposed, didn't help matters any. My final visits to Quang Tri and to Hue Phu Bai had been a lot tougher than I thought they'd be. I felt a deep twinge of guilt and a definite tug at the emotions as I said good-bye to such old friends as First Sergeant Ken Budrow, RT leader Jim Butler, and Covey rider Jim Parry. We'd gone through a lot together; I didn't know how to cut the cord and leave. I didn't want to leave. The only saving grace was that all of them would be leaving too. Following Lam Son 719, CCN had officially shut down, replaced by a temporary caretaker organization known as Task Force 1 Advisory Element. The Prairie Fire mission was over.

Shaking off the snub from the Da Nang tower operator, I went through the checklist items in preparation for landing.

I'd gone through the same drill a thousand times before, and it had become second nature, almost an involuntary response. Yet on this final flight, each action seemed to take on a melancholy significance. Condition levers to takeoff and land. Power set at eleven hundred pounds of torque per engine. Airspeed 160 knots indicated.

At midfield I roll the Bronco into sixty degrees of left bank, then feed in the back pressure for a two-G, level, 180-degree turn. On downwind check below 155 knots, then gear lever down, my right thumb constantly flicks the trim button for a large dose of nose-up trim to compensate for the changing airspeed and angle of attack. Opposite the first yellow chevron painted on the overrun, the flaps go down as I bank into a descending final turn at 110 knots. Rolling out on final at three hundred feet, I slow the Bronco to 100 knots and hold that airspeed and angle of attack all the way to touchdown. The slight bump and the squeal of the main tires tell me I'm down, for the last time.

Taxiing toward the revetments, I could see the fire truck and an excited group of fellow Coveys. After I shut down and climbed out of the cockpit, the strange *fini* flight celebration began. In a ritual of unknown origin, named with the French word meaning "finished," the last flight party had become a tradition throughout Southeast Asia. The festivities got under way when the grinning firemen turned the hose on me full blast, soaking me in an instant with a heavy stream of Da Nang's famous brown water. Somebody produced several bottles of Champagne, and everyone drank and shook hands with me, congratulating me on completing my tour. One of the Coveys even pinned a patch on my dripping wet flight suit: "Survivor, Southeast Asia War Games."

Everyone who was gathered on the hot concrete ramp at the north end of Da Nang's east runway seemed genuinely happy for me. In return, I smiled modestly, uncomfortable at being the center of attention, and secretly sad that the best flying job I could ever hope to have was over. For the party's sake, I acted happy right along with the crowd.

I had the feeling some of my buddies were doing a little

acting themselves. Amidst the handshakes, back slaps, and bear hugs, I sensed they understood how I really felt. Their turn would come, and they too would experience the conflicting feelings about wanting to go home while wanting to stay. The only truly honest person at the party turned out to be the crotchety old maintenance line chief. As we shook hands, he said, "Captain, I'm glad you made it, but I can't say I'm sorry to see you go. You've been a one-man demolition derby on my flight line since you got here, breakin' airplanes and gettin' 'em shot up faster than we could fix 'em. You're a regular MA."

Unfamiliar with the term, I asked, "What's an MA, Sarge?"

Winking, he broke into one of his infrequent smiles and said, "Magnet ass."

The following day was dedicated to outprocessing. It came as a rude shock to find my new status carried no weight in the bureaucracy. When I tried to get the noncommissioned officer in charge of the personal equipment shop to sign off on my clearance form, he refused. He looked me right in the eye and said, "You've got two pair of binoculars signed out, and you only turned in one. Either give me the second pair or cough up eighty-five bucks, your choice."

"Now wait a minute," I argued. "You know that one pair got shot out of my cockpit back in October. You were the one who issued me a new set the next day. It was a combat loss, for crying out loud."

Looking bored with the conversation, the sergeant replied, "Call it anything you want, but my books have still got to balance. When you give me the glasses or the money, I'll sign your clearance sheet."

From the determined scowl on his face, I could tell the man wasn't about to budge or respond to logic. Trying to keep my irritation in check, I turned and walked out the door without a word to my tormentor. I spent the remainder of the morning at Covey Ops composing a letter from the head Covey to the personal equipment shop, explaining the circumstances surrounding the loss of the binoculars in question and further directing the NCOIC to keep the letter as documentation of a valid loss of government equipment.

Without saying a word, I strolled back into the personal equipment shop and carefully placed the letter and the clearance form on the counter, purposely keeping my gaze on the Air Force master sergeant's eyes. After a few uncomfortable seconds of ocular sparring, he grudgingly read the letter from Lieutenant Colonel Summers. Without looking up, he scribbled an unintelligible signature on the form and shoved it across the counter to me. He turned on his heel and walked away. I went out the door thinking that if an outsider had witnessed the little fiasco just transacted, he'd have concluded the two of us weren't really in the same Air Force, that we certainly weren't fighting the same war. Looking down at the space on the clearance form, I couldn't help feeling the signature represented a very hollow victory. I had pursued the issue and won. Yet the bested NCOIC, the same man who a week earlier would have moved heaven and earth to outfit one of "his" combat pilots, saw me now as an administrative loose end to tie up. I wasn't a part of it anymore, and it hurt. For his sake and mine, I should have simply paid the man the eighty-five dollars.

On my last night at Da Nang, my final night as a Covey FAC, a thousand stray thoughts competed with my disorganized attempt to pack the trusty old B-4 bag. As I folded up my flight suits and stuffed them into the zippered side pockets, a curious sadness gripped me. The faded green flight suits symbolized the end of the most intense, emotional year of my life. I had the odd sensation of packing away those memories along with the flight suits. I couldn't allow that to happen. I recalled my father describing World War II as the major global event and experience of his generation. Vietnam was mine. For the first time I understood what he had been trying to explain.

My thoughts also brushed up against the dilemma most of my Special Forces friends had already confronted. The push-pull attraction and lure of combat reduced them to the likes of the moth drawn relentlessly to the heat and danger of the flame. Like the moth, the flame of battle in Southeast Asia attracted the SOG troops, and it became the focus of their existence—of my existence. Like them, the prospect of returning to the States to perform mundane, routine training did not appeal to me. Had there still been a Prairie Fire mission, I would have figured out some way to extend my tour.

Shortly after one o'clock on the afternoon of April 9, a mixed bag of soldiers, sailors, marines, and airmen climbed aboard the 707—the Freedom Bird—for the twenty-hour flight to Travis Air Force Base in California. Saying good-bye in the terminal to my Covey friends, including Larry Thomas, Norm Komich, Henry Yeackle, and Rick Ottom, left a big lump in my throat.

As I strapped into a seat by the window, a fellow Covey finishing his tour sat down next to me. Not really expecting an answer I said, "Chuck, this whole thing about a one-year tour is dumb. Just when we get good at it, they send us home, with no transition and no way to decompress. Why do I have the feeling we're leaving with the job only half done?"

Squirming around, trying to fit his long frame into the tightly packed airliner seats, Chuck responded, "Don't think about it. It'll make you nuts."

As the big bird taxied out of the terminal area, the flight attendant came up on the intercom. In a well-rehearsed but sincere speech she told us, "Gentlemen, I can't begin to tell you how proud we are of each and every one of you. It's a real privilege and honor for this crew to fly you back to the world." Following several administrative announcements, the pretty flight attendant's face twisted into a devilish smile. "Military Airlift Command regulations prohibit the serving or consumption of alcoholic beverages aboard its flights; however, once we get airborne, if any of you would like a cup of ice or a setup, just let one of us know." Predictably, the passengers responded with laughs and applause.

A few minutes later, when the Freedom Bird lifted off Da Nang's west runway, the cabin resounded with more applause, cheers, and rebel yells.

As the 707 banked around to the northwest to intercept Airway Amber One, I had a great view of the dark green foliage covering Monkey Mountain, of the yellow sand on China Beach, of the gray concrete twin runways at the air base, of the dark blue waters of Da Nang Bay. Far to the west, veiled in a bluish haze, I could just make out the fence—the Annamitic cord of mountains separating Vietnam and Laos. The whole panorama had been my home for a year of fifty-three weeks. Taking that one last look, my mind flooded with thoughts of home, the Coveys, and SOG. But the most vivid images glowing in my mind's eye were of Prairie Fire. In uncanny detail I could still see the faces of Satan, Blister, Evan Quiros, Mike McGerty, Jim Smith, Larry Hull, and I could recall every mission we'd ever run across the fence. Along with them, Prairie Fire was history, and I had been there at the end. It was time for me to go home.

EPILOGUE

Two Years Later: August 15, 1973

ruising north over the rugged Cambodian landscape, I had the OV-10 trimmed up for hands-off flight. One hundred miles in front of me lay Ubon Air Base, Thailand, destination for my last landing of the war. At 11:00 A.M. that morning, direct U.S. combat involvement in Southeast Asia was officially to end. After controlling one air strike, I was heading back across the fence for the final time. Absentmindedly I listened over the radio as each of the other FACs and fighter pilots checked out with Cricket, the C-130 airborne battlefield command-and-control ship for Cambodia. Making no attempt at originality, I muttered the same farewell as all the other pilots: "So long, Cricket. See you next war."

Somewhere inside the C-130, a controller answered, "Take care, buddy. Thanks for the good work."

After 608 combat missions in the OV-10, it was hard for me to comprehend the idea that it really was over. I had felt the same way more than two years earlier, leaving Da Nang at the end of my first tour. Yet there had been plenty of war to come back to when the dull stateside training missions and post-Vietnam depression drove me up the wall. After the intensity of Prairie Fire, a routine existence as an Air Force pilot wasn't satisfying. I had to get back in the fight. My feelings had nothing to do with being a glutton for punishment. The second tour was an attempt to recapture the excitement and camaraderie of flying for SOG. It had been another chance to do what I did best, fly combat.

With the warm sunshine beating into the all-glass cockpit, it occurred to me that I had seen about as much as a pilot could through the gunsight of an OV-10. I had seen the deactivation of Prairie Fire, with all its secrecy and high drama. I had been in action on January 27, 1973, when the Paris agreement on Vietnam ended the U.S. war in that ravaged country. I had controlled air strikes on the Ho Chi Minh Trail on February 22, the last official day of the war in Laos. Now I was again a witness to history as the United States ended its combat role in the last of the three war-torn countries, Cambodia.

The touchdown on Runway 23 at Ubon was a grease job. A smooth final landing at the end had to be a good omen. Clearing the runway at midfield, I thought about my first landing there three years earlier under tougher circumstances. I thought about the battle-damaged right wing and the broken wing spar. Had it really been over three years?

Taxiing into the revetment area, I found myself caught up in the exuberance infecting the younger pilots, the very same pilots I had taken under my wing months earlier, the same young pilots who had hung on every word of my ample supply of war stories. Like them, I celebrated the moment by running my smoke generator full blast, engulfing the ramp with billowing clouds of white-gray smoke. It really was over. I felt it this time. And in the smoke and laughter and handshakes on that blistering hot ramp at Ubon, I genuinely felt something else. On most of my missions, I had made a difference. With a lot of help and luck, I had managed to mature from rookie FAC to combat-experienced veteran. Based on my experiences after my first tour, I knew nobody at home would applaud or cheer or care. But I knew something more important, something that would lay dormant, tucked away in my mind, for years. Inside, I felt deep satisfaction and pride in serving as a United States Air Force forward air controller. One day, before all of us old aviators from the Vietnam War faded away, I hoped to have the opportunity to tell my story to the world.

GLOSSARY

A-1: A Korean War–vintage prop fighter capable of carrying large ordnance loads. Used extensively for search-and-rescue missions as well as in support of long-range reconnaissance teams.

AK-47: The standard automatic assault weapon used by North Vietnamese and Viet Cong soldiers.

AO: Area of operations, usually a specific sector assigned to a FAC or a ground unit.

ARVN: Army of the Republic of Vietnam.

BAC SI: Vietnamese for doctor. The medic assigned to Special Forces reconnaissance teams.

BARKY: Call sign of FACs assigned to the First Brigade, Fifth Mechanized Infantry Division, Quang Tri.

BDA: Bomb damage assessment, the reported results of air strikes.

BEEPER: A high-pitched, wavering radio tone broadcast on emergency frequencies, usually indicating a downed pilot.

BILK: Call sign of the FACs assigned to support the 101st Airborne Division, Hue Phu Bai.

BRIGHT LIGHT: Code name for a twelve-man Special Forces team dedicated to recovering POWs or downed pilots in Laos or North Vietnam.

BRONCO: Manufacturer's name for the OV-10, a twin-engine light-attack aircraft used by forward air controllers.

CBU: Cluster bomb unit. A special area coverage ordnance dropped by fighter aircraft, used extensively in Southeast Asia.

CCN: Command and Control North. The Da Nang–based regional headquarters for all cross-border operations, a subunit of Military Assistance Command's Studies and Observation Group.

CHARLIE: A slang term for enemy soldiers, probably stemming from "Victor Charlie," the code words used for the letters VC, or Viet Cong.

COBRA: Manufacturer's name for the AH-1G helicopter gunship.

COVEY: Call sign of the special-mission FACs flying sorties into Laos from Da Nang and Pleiku.

DAISY CUTTER: A fuse extender attached to the nose of a bomb.

DME: Distance-measuring equipment. A digital readout in miles from a specific navigation station.

DMZ: Demilitarized zone. The no-man's-land between North and South Vietnam.

DUST-OFF: Call sign of Army UH-1 medical evacuation helicopters.

FAC: Forward air controller. In South Vietnam and Laos, virtually all air strikes were directed by FACs.

FLAK: Air bursts from antiaircraft fire.

FNG: A derogatory nickname for a new guy; a new arrival to South Vietnam.

FOX MIKE: The code words for FM, or frequency modulation, the radio band used by Army units and FACs.

G: The force of gravity. When pulling off targets, pilots routinely encountered G forces four to six times their body weights.

GCA: Ground controlled approach (radar).

GCI: Ground controlled intercept.

GUARD: A designated radio frequency for use in an emergency situation. While talking on other frequencies, pilots also monitored Guard.

HE: High-explosive, normally referring to rockets fired by fighters, FACs, or helicopter gunships.

HILLSBORO: Call sign of the orbiting C-130 airborne battlefield command-and-control aircraft operating over Laos.

HOLD DOWN: A procedure in which one pilot keys or holds down his radio transmit button while a pilot in another aircraft homes in on the radio signal. A common practice among fighter aircraft attempting to rendezvous with a FAC.

HUEY: Nickname for the versatile UH-1 helicopter.

JOLLY: Call sign of Air Force HH-3 or HH-53 rescue helicopters.

KARST: A large irregular limestone rock formation, often covered with jungle vegetation. Found throughout Southeast Asia, particularly in Laos.

KBA: Killed by air. Refers to casualties inflicted by aircraft.

KIA: Killed in action.

KING: Call sign of orbiting HC-130 aircraft responsible for coordinating all search-and-rescue operations for downed pilots.

KLICK: Slang for kilometer, a standard unit of measurement on tactical maps.

LAU-68: Designation for the rocket pods mounted on FAC aircraft.

LZ: Landing zone, usually an open area large enough to accommodate a helicopter.

MARK-82: A general-purpose five-hundred-pound bomb widely used on missions throughout Southeast Asia.

MIKE-MIKE: Slang for millimeter, as in twenty mike-mike cannon.

MISTY: Call sign for fast FACs flying the F-100 Super Saber.

MLT: Mobile launch team. CCN operated two permanent sites, at Quang Tri and at Hue Phu Bai.

NVA: North Vietnamese Army.

ONE-ZERO: Designation for the leader of a SOG reconnaissance team.

OSCAR DEUCE: Affectionate nickname for the O-2 FAC aircraft.

PIPPER: The aiming dot in the center of an aircraft gunsight.

PLAY TIME: The time that fighter aircraft can loiter over the target, normally five to ten minutes.

POW: Prisoner of war.

PRAIRIE FIRE: Code word for cross-border ground reconnaissance missions. When used tactically by team leaders, the term indicated a dire condition requiring immediate extraction.

PSP: Pierced steel planking. Large sections of metal used for constructing temporary runways and ramps.

ROE: Rules of engagement. A lengthy, complicated list of limitations and conditions applied to a ground target before ordnance could be dropped.

RT: Reconnaissance team. Each team had a distinctive name, usually after a snake or a state.

RTB: Return to base.

SANDY: Call sign for A-1 Skyraiders dedicated to search-and-rescue missions.

SAR: Search and rescue.

SF: Special Forces.

SLICK: Affectionate nickname for the UH-1 Huey.

SOG: Studies and Observation Group.

SPAD: Call sign for the A-1 Skyraiders supporting SOG missions.

SQUAWK: An air traffic control term advising the pilot to set a specific sequence of numbers in the aircraft transponder. Once set, radar can interrogate the signal for positive identification.

STEEL TIGER: Code name for the southern panhandle of Laos containing the Ho Chi Minh Trail.

TACAN: Tactical Air Navigation. A military navigation system designed to provide the pilot with bearing and distance from a ground station.

TAC E: Tactical emergency. RTs in Laos declared a TAC E when their mission would be jeopardized without immediate close air support.

TASS: Tactical Air Support Squadron.

THUD: Affectionate nickname for the F-105 Thunder Chief.

TIC: Troops in contact. A situation in which friendly troops engage enemy forces in a firefight.

UHF: Ultra high frequency, the radio band used by most military aircraft. Also used on personal survival radios.

VC: Viet Cong, enemy soldiers.

VR: Visual reconnaissance, performed either on the ground or in the air.

WHIFFERDILL: Any improvised maneuver in an aircraft, usually involving a steep climb or dive.

WILLIE PETE: Slang for white phosphorous, the type of smoke rockets used by FACs to mark targets for fighter aircraft.

WINCHESTER: Pilots' slang for out of ammunition or bombs.

X-RAY: Laotian nationals trained to fly with a FAC to validate sensitive enemy targets in Steel Tiger.